Bodies of Truth

Stanford Studies in Human Rights

Bodies of Truth

Law, Memory, and Emancipation in
Post-Apartheid South Africa

Rita Kesselring

Stanford University Press
Stanford, California

Stanford University Press

Stanford, California

© 2017 by the Board of Trustees of the Leland Stanford Junior University. All rights reserved.

Printed in the United States of America on acid-free, archival-quality paper

Cataloging-in-Publication Data available upon request.

ISBN 978-0-8047-9848-8 (cloth)
ISBN 978-0-8047-9978-2 (paper)
ISBN 978-0-8047-9983-6 (electronic)

Cover image courtesy of author.

Typeset by Newgen in 10/14 Minion Pro

Contents

Foreword   vii

Foreword from the Series Editor   ix

Acknowledgments   xi

List of Abbreviations   xiii

Introduction   1

1   Apartheid Victimhood before the Courts   23

2   Reparation, Representation, and Class Actions   53

3   Embodied Memory and the Social   77

4   The Formation of the Political   117

5   Emancipation from Victimhood   133

6   Ethnographic Experience and Anthropological Knowledge   167

Conclusion: The Embodiment of Experiences
of Violence as Seeds of New Forms of Sociality   187

Notes   209

Bibliography   229

Index   247

Foreword

AT THE TRUTH and Reconciliation Commission, victims spoke about their losses, their hardships, and their horrendous experiences under apartheid rule. They made us—the commissioners, their fellow South Africans, and the global community—listen, cry, and feel with them. The Truth Commission was very important to mark the point where remorse, forgiveness, and reconciliation became finally possible, but we should not forget that victims' suffering did not necessarily stop when the commission's work ended. The lifetime of the commission was too short to listen to everyone, even though each and every person who lived under apartheid has a singular story to tell. Many, during the commission's lifespan, were not yet prepared to put their sufferings into words.

Twenty years on, the publication of this book is, unfortunately, still timely. Unlike many books about apartheid, Rita Kesselring's is not only about the past. It is about the persistence of the past into the present. It illuminates how the present society sometimes perpetuates the chasms of the past. In our urge to build a new South Africa, we have neglected thousands of victims and their plights. They have been patient. They have joined in building a new society. But memories do not simply go away. There are memories we all share, but which burden some of us more heavily than others.

Victims formed groups, engaged with the Truth Commission, pointed out the shortcomings of the commission's work, and offered their help in addressing those shortcomings. Victims went to court against those who refused to contribute, to show remorse, or to help repair. Meeting in court is not how we had hoped to build our society. The law can sometimes do more harm than good. But sometimes, the law wakes us up and reminds us of our duties to discuss as fellow human beings the questions the plaintiffs raise.

I commend the courage of all those who stood up and spoke out, in the courts and elsewhere. This book brings us closer to those who do not seek the limelight. It offers us insight into the people who cannot or do not want to speak out. We must listen to them. Together, we must finish the work that the commission started.

Rita Kesselring, a young Swiss anthropologist, enhances our understanding of the intricacies of victims' lives in today's South Africa. She listened to victims. She shared their frustration with a society that seems to have turned the ability to move on into a touchstone of good victimhood. Let her book be a reminder that a political transition does not automatically bring social equality. Today, twenty years after the commission, we no longer need to discuss whether retribution, amnesty, or reconciliation is the way forward. We need to deliver on the dream and the promise of a new South Africa.

God bless you.
Reverend Mpho Tutu
November 2015

Foreword from the Series Editor

RITA KESSELRING'S *Bodies of Truth: Law, Memory, and Emancipation in Post-Apartheid South Africa* interrogates the limits of law as a mechanism for translating "experiences of suffering, survival, and solidarity" into new forms of sociality that are capable of grounding political and social change. Her study invites the reader to move between a more analytical consideration of struggles in post-apartheid South Africa around modes of justice-making and reconciliation and the more elusive phenomenologies of embodied harm. This is a difficult task, in part because Kesselring's theoretical framework demands as much introspection as application, since one of the major contributions of her book is to show how even the most expansive discourses of injustice cannot fully encompass experiences of suffering and the ultimately bounded fact of what she describes as "pain's isolating nature."

Kesselring's study is the result of almost two years of ethnographic research in South Africa between 2009 and 2013. Her project took her throughout the country, and her writing is infused with a strong sense of intersubjective connection and empathy as she grapples with the task of rendering analytically meaningful the personal journeys among her interlocutors, from what she calls "victimhood" to "victim subjectivity." Even the photographs in the book reflect a keen sensitivity to the nuanced inflections of everyday life in the still-segregated townships on the outskirts of Cape Town: the weary man pausing between bites of porridge; the street-side food merchant in the midst of serving lunch; two ladies playing with a pet tortoise. The images speak to one of Kesselring's central arguments: that there is an immediacy to lived experiences that resists translation into the categories of identity that are recognized by the state, social psychiatry, and the law. At the same time, by following the trajectories of her interlocutors through political activism, legal argument, and social mobilization, Kesselring's study moves away from trends in phenomenology and practice theory that tend to reduce experience to the embodied self.

And there is also an urgency to *Bodies of Truth* well beyond its theoretical and ethnographic contributions. As Kesselring explains, it has been almost twenty years since the South African Truth and Reconciliation Commission (TRC) completed its work, and yet its enduring impact, its effectiveness in serving its broad goals, is still difficult to assess. This has important consequences, since the South African TRC established a global model for responding to fraught periods of transition after autocratic rule and racial violence, one in which "reconciliatory and restorative measures [were] combined with an investigation in past human rights violations." But as her research demonstrates, it is perhaps not possible to evaluate the South African TRC simply in terms of its original objectives, since the meaning of the TRC and its relation to what she calls "embodied memories of violence" continue to evolve, shift, and defy categorization.

Because of this, Kesselring's study forces us to take seriously responses to suffering beyond legal, political, and psychological categories. As she puts it, "a person is not primarily a victim because the law [has] defined him or her as such." Through her ethnography, we see how victims of apartheid come to form new associations, new forms of solidarity, by sharing with others what must remain, in the end, their own "sedimented perceptions of the world." As Kesselring's challenging volume suggests, it is to these small spaces of "non-predicated" sociality—rather than to the grand gestures of law—that victims of injustice in South Africa will ultimately find emancipation from the body's knowledge of harm.

Mark Goodale
Series Editor
Stanford Studies in Human Rights

Acknowledgments

FOR THIS BOOK, I have to thank many people. I owe my largest debt to the victims, who bear the brunt of the legacy of apartheid. For reasons of privacy, I have changed some of their names, but most wanted to appear under their own names. Many people who have been equally important to my attempts to understand victimhood do not figure in the book. To all of them, I express my deepest gratitude for letting me into their lives and tacitly sharing with me what it means to live with memories of harm. I will never be able to give back what they have entrusted to me: their humanity, their time, and their insights. Some of them explicitly asked me to write about their lives twenty years after the formal ending of apartheid. I hope I have not let them down.

The organization that became the entry point for and has remained important as a partner and facilitator of my research is the Khulumani Support Group, a South African apartheid-era victims' advocacy and support group. Without Khulumani, many experiences of victimhood in South Africa would still not be in the public realm, and the majority of victims would not have found victimhood solidarity in a network of people who share similar experiences. And without Khulumani, this book would probably never have come into being. I want to thank some of the individuals who have always been open to sharing their views and letting me partake in their work within or with Khulumani: Marjorie Jobson, Shirley Gunn, Zukiswa Puwana, Tshepo Madlingozi, Charles Abrahams, Sindiswa Nunu, Brian Mphahlele, Rose Dlamini, Amanda Mabilisa, Nomarussia Bonase, and the late Maureen Mazibuko. Beyond Khulumani, many persons became close friends, and intellectual combatants, during the months and years I lived in South Africa, particularly, Jess Auerbach, Philippe Ferrer, Ghalib Galant, Premesh Lalu, Sean McLaughlin, Sonwabile Mnwana, Isolde de Villiers, and Lauraine Vivian.

I particularly want to thank Fiona Ross, Till Förster, and the late Patrick Harries for their unreserved support in reading, listening, and giving advice. Special thanks go to Richard Wilson, who welcomed me at the Human Rights Institute at the University of Connecticut for one year of writing. Susan Farbstein and Tyler Giannini from Harvard Law School kindly shared with me their experiences as legal counsels in cases filed under the US Alien Tort Statute.

Many friends and colleagues provided helpful criticism and feedback on versions and chapters, and I want to acknowledge their invaluable contribution to this book: Alexandra Binnenkade, Phil Bonner, Gregor Dobler, Jan-Bart Gewald, Patti Henderson, Lucy Koechlin, Reinhart Kössler, Sarah Nouwen, Lukas Meier, Sheila Meintjes, Barbara Müller, Katharine Richards, Rita Schäfer, and Evelyne Schmid. Four persons in particular continuously pushed my thinking through their genuine interest in the realities of victimhood. Conversations with them always took me further, and I owe them much: Gregor Dobler, Jan-Bart Gewald, Barbara Müller, and Siranus Sarak.

The companionship of my fellow scholars at the Chair of Social Anthropology, the African History Chair, and the Centre for African Studies, University of Basel, is irreplaceable; the political interest of the members of the Swiss Apartheid Debt and Reparations Campaign kept me focused; and the scholarly support I received from the members of the *Arbeitskreis Forschung zur Vergangenheitspolitik* was also very helpful. I would also like to extend thanks to audiences and colleagues in Basel, Berlin, Bern, Burlington, Cape Town, Edinburgh, Freiburg, Johannesburg, Montreal, Stellenbosch, Storrs, Uppsala, and Tel Aviv.

The research for this book was made possible by a grant from the bilateral Swiss South African Joint Research Programme; a grant from the Swiss National Science Foundation for a writing fellowship at the Human Rights Institute, University of Connecticut; a stipend from the *Freiwillige Akademische Gesellschaft Basel*; and by the Department of Social Anthropology at the University of Cape Town, which hosted me as a visiting researcher. Finally, I want to thank the anonymous reviewers for their valuable comments and suggestions, and the Stanford University Press editors, the series editor, and the editorial assistants for their unfettered support and commitment.

Abbreviations

ANC	African National Congress
ATS	Alien Tort Statute, a statute in the U.S. Constitution (28 U.S.C. §1350)
CODESA	Convention for a Democratic South Africa
COPE	Congress of the People
COSATU	Congress of South African Trade Unions
CSVR	Centre for the Study of Violence and Reconciliation
ICTJ	International Centre for Transitional Justice
NDPP	National Directorate of Public Prosecutions
PAC	Pan Africanist Congress of Azania
PTSD	Post-traumatic stress disorder
RDP	Reconstruction and Development Programme
SANGOCO	South African National NGO Coalition
TRC	Truth and Reconciliation Commission
UDF	United Democratic Front

WHEN SYSTEMIC VIOLENCE has become endemic in a society, its traces will continue to shape the political sphere long after the violence had ended and what we call "normality" has been restored. Experiences of violence do not simply go away; they continue to haunt people and to affect the possibilities of sociality. Transitional justice mechanisms, such as truth commissions, acknowledge that the past is "irreversible," but they attempt to lay it to rest, to heal a nation and to make a new beginning possible; yet very often, the past stubbornly remains, not only irreversible, but "irrevocable" (Bevernage 2012). Experiences of violence linger in people's lives and bodies and shape their being-in-the-world.

This book explores how the past remains present in the South African society twenty years after the political transition to democracy. I focus on the legal, political, and social struggles of apartheid victims today and their attempts to move beyond their injured personhoods. I look at how apartheid victims engage with the past in their everyday lives and under what conditions they can find a new way of being in the world, if they can. I thus address questions that haunt every postconflict society. South Africa's relatively successful transition from autocratic rule to democracy makes it a model case in trying to answer them.

My book offers a sober account of what the South African Truth and Reconciliation Commission (TRC) has achieved and how far South African society has come on the way to social equality after two decades of democratic rule. The majority of apartheid's victims were not involved in the TRC process. Even so, the commission has been enormously consequential for the majority of victims. It produced a strong societal image of who a victim is; and it has contributed to the emergence of one dominant discourse, thus excluding many different experiences of victimhood.

Victimhood is a bodily experience, and it remains so unless victims have a chance to transform it. There are many different means through which victims can try to assume a new status in society. One of them is the law, which has the potential to transform a person's experiences in positive or negative ways. With the help of lawyers and support organizations, South African apartheid victims have brought their social concerns to South African and US courts with considerable frequency. I examine the legal avenues available for redress and review the transitional justice mechanisms that make it possible for people to acquire a new social status in society.

Scholars of law and society have criticized taking recourse in the law for its nonemancipatory effects and potential to entrench victims in subject positions. Many have adopted a Foucauldian approach to globally increasing litigiousness by arguing that everyone who engages with the law is subjected to the legalization of his or her personhood. I suggest turning this argument on its head. Pursuing legal remedies does not produce subjection to a discourse; it is the consequence of people's attempt to emancipate themselves from a discourse— under conditions in which the law is a more promising avenue than politics.

In looking at the everyday lives of apartheid victims today and at the bodily dimension of their experience of victimhood, I relate their attempts to move beyond victimhood by way of the law, by adopting dominant discourses, by engaging broader society as a political collective, and by making new bodily and social experiences through tacit practices and shared sociality. The possibilities for radical social change in a post-transitional setting emerge in the everyday practices of the survivors themselves, but to be successful, they have to be taken up by the state and the broader society.

In the lives of apartheid-era victims today, legal discourse and lived experience are enmeshed. If we try to understand what victimhood entails for survivors, we have to take both sides seriously and search for an interwoven analysis of the law and the body. Legal discourses only become effective in specific realities and forms of lived sociality (Bourdieu 1986). While discourses certainly shape experiences, embodied experiences of harm are not (and cannot be) completely absorbed by legal discourse. As I will show, embodied knowledge, to a certain extent, resists discourses precisely because legal logic does not directly relate to lived experience. It is in this mismatch that the seeds of new forms of sociality can be found.

After the Transition

South Africa's transition to democracy has fascinated scholars and practitioners alike. It marked a major turning point in global politics after a half century of national and international struggle against apartheid. Fifty years after the criminal and retributive Nuremberg trials, the South African TRC represented a new global trend in the way countries approached the transition from autocratic rule by embracing reconciliatory and restorative measures, combined with an investigation into the past human rights violations. The South African TRC gave unprecedented attention to the victims of those crimes, an approach that has been vastly influential and applied in many other postconflict situations. In the very month the majority of South Africans were casting their votes to elect the first post-apartheid government, the Rwandan genocide took place. Rwanda's episodic tragedy stood in sharp contrast to South Africa's experience of largely "routinized" (Connerton 2011) and structural violence, but scholars writing about Rwanda still often consider their work in a "transitional justice" frame that has been crucially shaped by the South African experience (Buckley-Zistel and Stanley 2011; Clark 2010).

During its practical work in the second half of the 1990s, the TRC explicitly avoided dealing with past atrocities in a juridical way. It condemned the apartheid crimes as wrong, but granted amnesty to perpetrators who disclosed the truth about their misdeeds. Victims, in testifying before the TRC, accused the apartheid regime of wrongdoing but did not have the power to bring charges against individual perpetrators. The TRC gave "victim" status to roughly 21,000 persons who had, directly or indirectly, suffered politically motivated and "body-bound" (Ross 2002, 11) gross human rights violations. This left tens of thousands victims of similar crimes individually unacknowledged.

Apartheid matters in South Africa did not end with the TRC, though. From early on, victims had expressed their discontent with the TRC process. The most important voice for victims' concerns has been the Khulumani Support Group, a support and lobbying group. Its interventions in the 2000s made it clear that the TRC had not brought full satisfaction to everyone, and that liberation had not achieved all that people had hoped it would. The Khulumani group and other civil society groups have since addressed the role of apartheid victims and perpetrators before courts of law, initiating civil actions around concerns of liability, indemnity, and pardon. The cases have been filed against the South African state in South African courts and in US courts against companies that had not testified to the TRC about their alleged complicity with the apartheid security forces. In other words, although South Africa is still widely known for choosing a reconciliatory path to deal with past atrocities, apartheid matters took a juridical turn post-TRC. Despite the TRC's explicitly nonretributive approach, South African citizens have pursued questions of victimhood and truth through legal avenues.

Many scholars, however, are suspicious of the law—even more so than of reconciliation and the TRC. Taking recourse in the law, they fear, may harden social relations, further entrench enmity between groups, and cement victims' subject positions. The law cannot solve what has been done to victims and does not offer closure. Instead, it subjects victims to a judicial logic. Politically, legal avenues do not necessarily promise reconciliation. Economically, legal cases more often result in the ruin of plaintiffs and the enrichment of lawyers than in the lifting up of victims. And, socially, we generally have little faith in law's power to change subjectivities for the better.

Despite these reservations, globally the law seems to offer an ever more important alternative to the political path. Evidently, referring a cruel phase of history to the courts to judge offers an alternative to restorative measures. This book grapples with the tension between the juridical and the political paths to facilitating the transition to democracy, social equality, and the recognition of past wrong. I offer a new approach to examining the challenges involved in taking social issues to the courts and, thus, to the analysis of the law.

In post-apartheid South Africa, experiences of victimhood have a clear legal dimension; they are importantly shaped by the victims' subject positions as defined by state institutions and courts of law. But despite its legal and discursive dimension, lived victimhood remains anchored in bodily experiences of suffering, survival, and solidarity. One of the principle tenets of this book is that in today's South Africa we can only understand how victims live their victimhood and how they attempt to render it politically effective if we combine two strands of analysis that are rarely looked at together: analysis of the law and of the body. I argue that the bodily dimension of being explains both the possibility of becoming emancipated from past experiences and the limits of social change. Following the practices of subject formation, the book traces global connections by linking research sites in South Africa and, by following a lawsuit filed abroad, the United States. As an ethnography, it relies on an empirically intimate study of apartheid-era victimhood in today's South Africa to understand larger processes of both legalization and the emergence of the political.

The Force of the Law

For a long time, legal anthropology was interested in "indigenous legal systems" and looked upon them as the expression of a given society's prevalent (though contested) cultural norms (S. F. Moore 2001). A newer strand of literature, however, sees law itself as a dominating force affecting the possible forms of sociability within the society in which it is applied. Law is detached from local sociability and culture but influences them by shaping subjectivities. Law is therefore not merely codification of norms that exist outside of law, but also has constitutive power: it ascribes roles and subject positions within a social order whose existence it facilitates in the first place (Nader 2002). The law is a tool, but it is not a neutral one. When people make use of the law, they have to engage with its logic and are changed by this engagement in ways that are often unforeseeable to them.

Legal anthropologists have examined the adoption of legal and transnational strategies in a pluralistic legal environment, on the one hand, and the applicability of strengthened human rights norms in non-Western contexts, on the other (Goodale 2006; Goodale and Merry 2007; Griffiths, Benda-Beckmann, and Benda-Beckmann 2005; Meckled-García and Çali 2005; Randeria 2003; Wilson and Mitchell 2003). Scholars have looked at people and groups who mobilize around human rights issues in various local settings, and have found discrepancies between the local applications and the codified human rights framework. The increased use of the courts by civil society actors and appeals to universal human rights standards are linked to the growing importance of professional structures for social action, the so-called NGO-ization. Against this background, scholars argue that it has become part of popular political culture to use rights discourses to legitimize claims. Jean Comaroff and John Comaroff (2007, 141) critically refer to a "fetishism of the law" and a "culture of legality" that "seems to be infusing everyday life" (142) and has become a common feature of the postcolony (Comaroff and Comaroff 2006, 27).

The literature on South Africa expresses a general skepticism that the use of the law in post-apartheid South Africa would replace mobilization of a (political) collective, and legal representation dissolve the necessity of a collective (cf. Robins 2009). The alleged shift "from politics to law" contributes to an "absence of action, thinking and revolt" (Van Marle 2008, 35). Furthermore, legal actions "maintain an injured status" and make redress "a problem of law and procedure rather than a problem of politics and justice" (Van Marle 2004, 370).

Partly, this skepticism comes from the valid observation that it is difficult to translate experiences of violence into a legal language (Hastrup 2003; Merry 2008). It is difficult to translate subjective and unspeakable (Das 1996; Scarry 1985) experiences into the logic of legal evidence and knowledge (Fassin and D'Halluin 2005, 2007). More broadly, legal actions are unable to identify the "common good and may even impede certain visions of it which emphasize socio-economic redistribution" (Wilson 2001, 224). The narrow vocabulary of the language of human rights, as Wilson (2001) shows, is negative in the sense that it only tells us what we do *not* want for the future.

Speaking for many, Wendy Brown forcefully argues that the law individualizes collective injury and that it depoliticizes social wrongs (cf. Colvin 2004b, 368–70; Comaroff and Comaroff 2003; Torpey 2003). According to her, everything that is conveyed to the law experiences a reduction that is ultimately traceable in the social realm.

> When social "hurt" is conveyed to the law for resolution, political ground is ceded to moral and juridical ground. Social injury . . . becomes that which is "unacceptable" and "individually culpable" rather than that which symptomizes deep political distress in a culture; injury is thereby rendered intentional and individual, politics is reduced to punishment, and justice is equated with such punishment on the one hand and with protection by the courts on the other. (Brown 1995, 27–28)

For Jean Comaroff and John Comaroff (2003, 466) as well, one consequence of processes of legalization has been the breakup of the collective. As they write, various rights discourses, including human rights, advocate a language of individual rights and thereby promote an "idiom that individuates the citizen" (457).

In short, changes in legal subjectivities—increased claims and increased representational claims—are assumed to effect changes in *lived* subjectivities. This causal link between forms of *action* and forms of *sociality*, however, needs to be critically examined. It has often been assumed theoretically, but rarely have scholars tried to prove empirically that taking recourse in law leads to a legalization of subjectivities and to depoliticization.

The Legal and the Social

Anthropologists and sociologists have shown that every norm needs social backing in order to become effective in shaping sociability (Popitz 2006). Norms may produce their own certainties, but they do not have agency by themselves. To understand the effects of law, we have to look at the social realm, and at how the social realm potentially changes in relation to legal norms. It is not enough to analyze what kind of image of personhood the law projects without taking into consideration whether this image actually produces realities. If we miss the second step, we commit a legalistic fallacy ourselves, by granting more power to the law than it actually has and painting it as too hegemonic.

My perspective on the law and its effects on sociability draws heavily on Bourdieu (1986), who addresses the relation between the law and lived experience. For him, the law holds symbolic power that lies in the fact that it creates what it names (Bourdieu 1986, 383). The law is a form of "active" discourse, "able by its own operation to produce its effects" (839). However, he crucially limits the efficacy of the law: there has to be some social reality in which it can become effective.

> Our thought categories *contribute* to the production of the world, but only within the limits of their correspondence with preexisting structures. Symbolic acts of naming achieve their power of creative utterance to the extent, and only to the extent, that they propose principles of vision and division objectively adapted to the preexisting divisions of which they are the products. (Bourdieu 1986, 839)

While the law may trigger an alternative form for understanding one's injury, of redress, and of sociality more generally, it does so only if there *is* (partially and tacitly) an injury and a discourse of redress, or a lived sociality among victims. A person is not primarily a victim because the law defined him or her as such. Hence, in order to understand the "force of the law" (Bourdieu 1986) on victims, we need to look at the lived reality of those people who refer their concerns to courts. It is in these lived realities, if anywhere, that we can track changes that result from their engagement with the law.

The Body and Being in the World

Victimhood is often anchored in bodily experiences and bodily being in the world. The anthropology of the body has brought us closer to an understanding of what it means to be in an injured body, and how experiences of victimhood are shaped by bodily phenomena.

The beginning of the anthropology of the body is typically identified with Marcel Mauss's (1934) lecture "Les Techniques du Corps" ("The Techniques of the Body").[1] Mauss suggested that things we habitually do with our bodies, such as walk, swim, or eat, even sleep, are largely shaped and determined by sociocultural processes. In order to designate "techniques" of the body, Mauss introduced the Aristotelian term *habitus*, which Pierre Bourdieu elaborated on some thirty years later. For Mauss, *habitus* is the totality of what we have acquired by learning, consciously or not: bodily skills, habits, and the entirety of nondiscursive knowledge.[2] He introduced the powerful notion that the way we use our body influences our identity. Even more, the body is an important instrument of social reproduction. We internalize the social structure by developing habitual techniques of the body, which, in turn, reproduce the social structure. The link between the social and bodily practice was, phenomenologically, established. A little later, phenomenological philosopher Maurice Merleau-Ponty (1962) showed us that we need to understand what it means to be in the world *bodily* if we want to describe human experience. Merleau-Ponty (2002, 159) takes issue with Descartes's emphasis on consciousness as the primary source of knowledge (cogito), saying, "Consciousness is in the first place not a matter of 'I think that' but of 'I can.'"[3] The body is a primary means of establishing our perceptual contact with the world.

Social sciences engaged with the body more resolutely and purposefully in the 1960s and 1970s, when the interest in symbols and their interpretation as a way to understand a particular culture also turned the body and its symbolic function in a culture into an object of examination (Douglas 1973; Geertz 1973; Turner 1974). Unlike the phenomenologists, symbolic anthropologists thus focused on meaning rather than practice. They drew on the ideas of the structuralist Claude Lévi-Strauss, who emphasized form over content and structure over meaning, and, later, on the poststructuralist thinking of Jacques Derrida, who thought about the body in representational terms. In their work they succeeded in deconstructing Western notions of the body.

Derrida's contemporaries, Michel Foucault and Pierre Bourdieu, advanced the structuralist endeavor, and both of their approaches to social theory had a singular if distinct influence on the anthropology of the body. Their writing marks, one could say, the definitive turn to power and the formation (and deformation) of the body as objects of study. As different as Foucault and Bourdieu are, the body occupies a central role in the work of both.

Pierre Bourdieu (1977) builds on Mauss to introduce a much more closely defined concept of habitus, to which he attributes a strong bodily component. The body is both *product* of history and *source* of practice and perceptions. This results in a constant process of production and reproduction of society. Society's structures are incorporated and actualized in bodily behavior and the institutionalized practices linked to it, without necessarily being explicitly articulated. Bourdieu's main interest lies in the dialectic between structure and individual agency. He shows how the agency of individuals plays a major role in the reproduction of social hierarchies and contributes to the continuity of social order through time. His understanding of practice as activated—learned—dispositions allows him to uncover the production and reproduction of social classes without employing a deterministic outlook. Bourdieu's work emphasizes the social production of difference and stresses the role embodied knowledge plays in it (bodily *hexis*). Bodily knowledge, for him, is not merely an anchor for cultural symbols but also a practical ability.

Many later scholars have drawn on this insight. For instance, Jean Comaroff's (1985) work on power and resistance, as well, is informed by this new focus on the "socially informed body" (Bourdieu 1977), albeit while retaining a strong interest in symbolism. More recently, Loïc Wacquant (2004), in *Body and Soul: Notebooks of an Apprentice Boxer*, reflects on the training he undertook to become a boxer. By experiencing the acquisition of knowledge and its progressive habituation, he reflects on himself as a subject of his own research.

If Bourdieu gives us tools to systemically look at power in its social context, Foucault focuses our attention on its "ideological" dimension. In his seminal works on prison and on sexuality, he radically re-examines systems of power and of knowledge. For Foucault, the body is a largely passive recipient of structures of power. The body is experience-distant[4] and holds little agency. Agency in general and the emancipatory possibility of resistance to domination were not major concerns of his until late in his life.[5] Foucault therefore portrays the formation of subjectivities as a largely one-sided process: a subject is constituted by dominant discourses, and structures of social control are "inscribed" onto the body. In consequence of their shared interest in structures, both Bourdieu and Foucault have been criticized for not giving sufficient consideration to the possibility of resistance, individual agency, and social transformation.[6]

Foucauldian thinking brought increased attention to the body at the very time when theories of practice influenced by both Bourdieu and by the phenomenological thinking of such scholars as Alfred Schütz and Thomas Luckmann (2003) became more important in anthropological theory. In the 1990s, the notion of lived social experience finally entered the anthropology of the body. Unni Wikan's (1991) "experience-near anthropology" and Joan and Arthur Kleinman's (1991) "ethnography of experience," for example, are a clear move away from a symbolic gaze on the body.

However, phenomenology has informed only a few ethnographies, which mainly came out in the 1990s. These include Michael Jackson's (1989, 1996, 2002) writings on the Kuranko in Sierra Leone before and after the civil war, and the works of Paul Stoller, Michael Lambek and others on spirit possession. Unlike older writings on possession, these new ethnographies (Boddy 1989; Lambek and Strathern 1998; Wafer 1991) did not see the body as a representational means alone, but as part and parcel of the experience of trance, transition, and possession. Paul Stoller (1995) among the Songhay in Niger and Mali and Michael Lambek (1993, 1998) in Mayotte considered "embodiment" to be a major dimension of being and performing. Thomas Csordas (1990, 1995) used and eventually coined the term "embodiment" to analyze the relation between experience and the body, the latter being the "existential ground of culture." In other words, "embodiment" "refer[s] to the anchoring of certain social values and dispositions in and through the body" (Strathern and Stewart 1998, 237). Like Stoller and Lambek, Csordas works from the premise that the self and culture are grounded in the *lived* experience of being in a body.

The theory of the embodied social is virtually omnipresent in anthropological practice today, but it is rarely a defining feature of ethnographies. In many of the more recent studies, the understanding that systems of power have inscriptive force, which is manifest as *readable text*, still prevails. Paul Connerton (1989, 100–101) places the more recent trend of focusing the textual and representational gaze on the body as being influenced by Foucault, in a tradition of a hermeneutics that privileges inscribing practices: "Inscribing practices have always formed the privileged story, incorporating practices the neglected story, in the history of hermeneutics."

Against this development, we need, in Elizabeth Grosz's (2004, 3) words, to find "alternative modes to those inscriptive and constructivist discourses that currently dominate the humanities and social sciences . . . where the body is of interest only in its reflection through discourse, its constitution in representation, or its mediation by images." The embodiment paradigm is a good starting point from which to clarify the relation between discourse and lived experience, between the individual body and society, and between the researcher's and others' bodily experiences. I will come back to this new paradigm and address its shortcomings.

The book contributes to an understanding of the body that does not individualize or trivialize, biologize or medicalize, or further a gaze that "others" the other's body. Such an understanding has to take everyday bodily experience seriously as an object and as a tool of inquiry, and it has to include their habitual and nonpredicated dimension. Consequently, I base this book on four premises.

First, knowledge is at least partly bodily and in that sense habitual and nonpredicated. Experiences become habitual through practice and reiteration. From this follows, second, that emancipation from sedimented bodily experiences can only happen through new social and bodily experiences. Third, it is the bodily dimension of being that presents the condition for the possibility of change. Any kind of agency is anchored in sedimented perceptions of the world. In consequence—the body is both the condition for and the limit to the formation of a social or political collective. Embodied experiences thus also hold the possibility of resistance to or emancipation from domination. Finally, dominant discourses shape social experiences, which, in turn, shape bodily experiences. This analytical order—social and bodily—is important because it points to the fact that discourses become effective through—and only because of—specific social realities and lived socialities. From these four premises, I tease out the conditions for the possibility of resisting discourses and of emancipating oneself from experiences one was (forcefully) subjected to. I inquire into these premises at the level of lived experience that emerges from everyday practices.

Subjectivities and Subject Positions

I do not suggest that phenomenological approaches to the body, such as Merleau-Ponty's, focusing on the embodied being, and poststructuralist, postmodern Foucauldian approaches to the body as a discursive construction and product necessarily exclude one another. Both leave analytical space for the productive, and hence transformative, dimension of subjectivities. In times when trauma specialists and truth commissions continuously reinforce a narrow, body-bound, and individualized notion of victimhood, we need to be attentive to what kind of critique of the state and state power is being expressed through the body (cf. Werbner 1998). Many have looked at the "visible" body, for instance, at how people present their bodies, to demonstrate "signs of injury" (cf. Brown 1995; Colvin 2004b). I want to shed light on other subtler, hidden, and tacit forms of trying to deal with and overcome experiences of harm.

From different angles, the book tries to understand the ways in which people relate their lived experiences to social and political discourses. I argue that making victimhood socially effective necessitates a shift from *nonpredicated* to *articulated* victimhood. I am interested in the ways in which victims connect their selves to discourses and discursive practices, and how their experiences with these, in turn, shape them. This might involve strategic positioning, but in many instances, the very experiences of victimhood preclude any strategic use.

I describe the path from nonpredicated to articulated victimhood in a threefold typology, using *victimhood, victim subject positions,* and *victim subjectivity* to differentiate the three forms that address the relation between experience and discourse. I speak of *victimhood* as a state that is self-ascribed and a genuinely intimate and personal experience. Victimhood is often not in the predicative realm. People often do not express it in a discursive form. In this book, I focus on apartheid-era victimhood and on persons who experienced some kind of human rights violation during the apartheid period. This focus might seem to imply that the origins of victimhood lie in the past and that victimhood is merely a relic in today's society; and it might seem to ground victimhood in a rights model. I argue against both presuppositions. I show the persistence of victimhood beyond the time of political transformation and its reproduction in today's society. By showing how a partly legal notion of victimhood has been produced in courts and in the working of the truth commission, I chiefly argue that victimhood is discursively formed in an environment that prioritizes a legal notion of victimhood.

But the book does not stop at the discursive dimension of personhood. It seeks to understand the embodiment of experiences (which, as I will show, escapes the law and partly resists legal logic). To do so, it takes a strong interest in what is nonpredicated. (I prefer this term to Husserl's more common "prepredicated" because I do not want to suggest a chronological order. Something predicated can always fade away into the nonpredicated realm, and vice versa.) Of course, victimhood as a state never exists outside a discursively shaped environment (the least from scholarly predication of victimhood). Despite this serious reservation, I adopt victimhood as a heuristic type of being.

In my heuristic typology, victimhood as such is not yet political, even though it is very often formed as a consequence of political circumstances. Injuries are always social. Acts of violence, or continuous and structural forms of violence, happen between two, or more, people even if the perpetrator cannot be identified. For the harmed, the act results in the experience of a shift in his or her social status. The act forces her or him to subsequently live in relation to the person or system that inflicted the act. How she or he views the injury may change, as suggested earlier, depending on the kinds of discursive explanation she or he is exposed to, which, in turn, facilitate new readings of him- or herself.

Once a person takes his or her victimhood into the predicative realm and publicly articulates it, the role of victimhood in the person's subjective experience changes. I call the resulting state *victim subjectivity*. One's personhood is now in a relation to other articulated forms of victimhood.

Those articulated forms of victimhood stand in relation to what I call *victims' subject positions*. Victims' subject positions are discourses—often dominant ones such as the law—which give ideas and ideals of what a victim is or is supposed to be. Hence, *victim subjectivity* is necessarily political, as any articulation of one's subjectivity takes place in a context of discourses. A victim subjectivity thus demands a positioning, consciously or not, vis-à-vis prevailing (and often dominant) ideas of victimhood.

Of course, these different positions are not empirically clear-cut. Aspects of victimhood may occupy different positions of this typology, and neither a subject position nor a subjectivity is necessarily stable. A person's self is "the location of multiple and potentially contradictory subjectivities, each established within discourses and discursive practices" (Merry 2003, 349), and victimhood and victim subjectivities may be in conflicting relations to other ways of experiencing and expressing oneself.

Heuristically, the typology may suggest that shifts from one social state to another are unidirectional formations of the subject. This would be a misunderstanding; people do not initially experience the world in a nonpredicated way. I thus do not suggest that the formation of predication is linear. What has entered the cognitive and political realm may again recede into the nonpredicated realm. Also, in South Africa, the category of a "victim" has a history that predates the period under scrutiny in this book. The TRC started its work in an environment with a political and legal notion of victimhood. Contrary to other countries or time periods in South Africa, this book examines a time and situation where discourses of justice, restitution and victimhood are prevalent. The focus of analysis is thus primarily on the ways in which victims relate their experiences to existing discourses, and on the effects this has on both the discourses and the personhood of the injured subjects.

In this typology of states of societal experience, the inclusion of the body is paramount to understanding the conditions for the possibilities of shifts in subjectivities. As Henrietta Moore (1994, 141) stresses, the body has a crucial role in negotiating different subjectivities: "What holds these multiple subjectivities together are the experience of identity, the physical *grounding of the subject in a body*, and the historical continuity of the subject" (my emphasis).

This means that one's realization that a victims' subject position speaks to one's experiences and status in society has a strong bodily and sensory dimension. In order to understand political victim subjectivities, we need to understand what role embodied memories of violence play in people's everyday actions and how they influence their search for new forms of sociality.

Doing Research and Writing about Violence and Victims

Experiences of violence can continue in practice after the conflict officially ended (Cockburn 2004; Meintjes, Pillay, and Turshen 2001; Scheper-Hughes and Bourgois 2004). In her work on the Chilean dictatorship, Macarena Gómez-Barris (2009) calls this *afterlife*. Afterlife captures the "continuing and persistent symbolic and material effect of the original event of violence on people's daily lives, their social and psychic identities and their ongoing wrestling with the past in the present" (6). In contrast, *aftermath*, according to her, refers to the economic and political legacy of political violence. This book grapples both with the afterlife and the aftermath of apartheid-era violence.

Structural violence is not primarily personal in nature, but the harm and pain it creates is felt and experienced individually (Das 2006; Farmer 1997, 2004; Galtung 1969; Scheper-Hughes 1997). Any account of the effects of systematic violence has to take into consideration these two sides: the structural and the individual, anonymized forms of violence and their effects on individual persons (on embodied political violence, see Feldman 1991; Nordstrom 2004; Taussig 1992).

By exploring violence and its effects on the lived experience of victimhood, my work relates to the most prominent discipline in the South African discourse on victims today—that is, to social psychiatry and its "body-bound" understanding of injury and lived victimhood, primarily expressed through the term "trauma." Trauma, traumatization, and the diagnosis of post-traumatic stress disorder (PTSD) are pervasive discourses in South Africa today (Kaminer and Eagle 2010). Although the characteristics of continuous traumatic stress under apartheid rule have never been fully investigated (Straker and Sanctuaries Counselling Team 1987),[7] there is a fierce debate between scholars who have a psychiatric perspective on trauma and those who mainly argue on social grounds (Summerfield 1995, 1999, 2001; cf. Fassin 2009). A social scientific response to trauma studies can only focus on the social settings in which trauma reveals itself (Das et al. 2001; Reynolds 1995).[8] As I do not directly want to contribute to psychiatric or psychological discussions, I will not use the terms "trauma" and "PTSD" here. I seek to find more empirically and social scientifically informed ways to describe how people experience loss and violence and cope with their embodied experiences of harm (cf. Daniel 1996).

There is a lack of attention to women's experiences under apartheid and their ways of articulating them (Gengenbach 2010; Meintjes, Pillay, and Turshen 2001; Merry 2003; Ross 2002; Wells 1983). Although the majority of the people I write about are women, and although writing about women is a political concern for me, the book does not make an explicit argument about gender. In many ways, claimed victimhood is a male-dominated subject position globally. Victimhood is *given* to women (Govier 2015), but men *claim* victimhood much more successfully. This is particularly the case with political victimhood,[9] a narrow legal category that excludes many experiences of women who have been directly or indirectly affected by civil wars or by entrenched and systematic discrimination and deprivation. In my work I thus not only address particular forms of violence women have experienced under the apartheid regime and their ongoing effects. The book should also contribute to a better understanding of what it means for women to adopt a victims' subject position in an environment that does not necessarily approve of their claims and in which they are not politically effective.

Most of my informants defined themselves as victims. They are members of a victims' support group, which in itself means they have had to put their selves in relation to that specific subject position. I relied on people's self-definition and was not concerned with the actuality or factuality of such descriptions. It is not the goal of social science to pass judgment on an intimate self. It was more important for me to understand why people adopt a subject position and how this interacts with their multiple subjectivities; what it does to their social status in society and to their experiencing selves, how it influences their actions, and how, in turn, this affects society's understanding of and acting upon a particular grouping. The factuality of victimhood is something the law—and truth commissions, for that matter—has to deal with. It is also something a society grapples with. But for me, questions of factuality form an *object for* a study rather than the *objective of* my study.

Most of the informants I have been working with have had some "recognizable" or "tangible" bodily experiences of violence. Such experiences may, but do not have to, result in long-lasting injuries (Reynolds 1995). But nonphysical violence may also alter an individual's sense of self (Menjívar 2011, 9). Examples include verbal insults (Butler 1997), which can, but do not have to, result in long-lasting injury. In my work, I do not conceptually differentiate between physical and nonphysical experiences of harm. My focus on the effects of structural forms of violence suggests a particular understanding of victimhood, though, and generally departs from the legal understanding, which assigns "victim" status based on presentation of evidence of a specific event in which violence was inflicted, a "sign" of injury, and an agent of perpetration.[10]

In my four years of doing the research for this book (between 2009 and 2013), I lived in South Africa for nineteen months. My prime locales were the Cape Flats, on the outskirts of the City of Cape Town, primarily the townships of Philippi, Nyanga, Crossroads, New Crossroads, KTC, and Langa, and I also visited Khayelitsha, Gugulethu, Bellville, and Mfuleni. However, I traveled extensively in the rural parts of Western Cape province, and in the country. I visited Khulumani branches in the provinces of KwaZulu-Natal, Mpumalanga, Free State, Eastern Cape, and Gauteng and often stayed at people's homes for a couple of weeks.

Among the relationships I developed over the course of my research, I distinguish three groups. First, a good dozen people became my key informants. I had regular contact with them over the four years of my research, and saw most of them on a weekly or more frequent basis when I was in South Africa. I shared part of the ordinary lives of these key informants. I gained a good sense of their daily routines and observed each in different social situations. Second, there were about twenty people with whom I spent a day or more or had an intense conversation lasting a couple of hours. We shared experiences that were often immensely insightful, but I did not get to know them in their everyday lives. Circumstances often kept us from meeting more frequently, such as distance or their occupations. Finally, I met many, many more people in short encounters in groups, households, or at public events. I spoke to them briefly or heard them talking in public or referred to in conversations. The knowledge I gained from these encounters contextualizes the lives of people in the first and second groups. They were often not Khulumani members themselves but family members, friends, or colleagues of Khulumani members, and thus part of my key informants' lifeworlds or everyday lives. Also, I interviewed a number of lawyers and other professionals and conducted research in several archives (primarily of organizations).

I sometimes declined when someone encouraged me to briefly interview a friend or an acquaintance of his or hers. Being in the area for a longer period, I had no interest in "quick data," and I wanted to make sure that I would see the person again after I talked to him or her. There was a methodological dimension to this, but mainly, my reasons were ethical. Although I hardly ever directly asked people about their experiences of violence or painful memories, many nonetheless told me about them. Some would start to cry; others would become silent and withdrawn after they had finished. I am not a trained psychologist or a therapist of any sort. I often felt helpless and deeply drawn into the accounts of immense pain. The least I could do, I felt, was to be present over a longer period of time or to help in other ways, such as with writing social grant applications or by driving them to Khulumani meetings, or just being there to show my solidarity and commitment.

I primarily worked in "black" communities; most of my informants were originally from the former Transkei and Ciskei homelands, in what today is Eastern Cape province, and spoke isiXhosa as their mother tongue. English was my informants' second, third, or fourth language. Some, nonetheless, were very eloquent in English, which has been the language of activism and communication across different groups for many decades. I never learned more than basic greetings and some random words and phrases in isiXhosa or other African languages, and I never worked with a research assistant, but there was always someone who would volunteer to translate for me. What I often perceived as a handicap may actually have helped me to become more sensitized to practice, and to the bodily dimension of victimhood that became a major theme in my research.

It was not easy sharing a living space with my informants in the City of Cape Town and its bigger municipal area. Most of my informants live their everyday lives in the townships on the outskirts of Cape Town proper, a city that is still very much segregated in practice. While segregation was a legal norm in South Africa, most cities of the world are economically and socially segregated.

We often do not live where our informants live or do not live among them for a very long time. We thus juggle multiple codes as part of our everyday life during research, and the possibilities of habitualization as part of and during our urban research are limited by the multitude of social spaces in which we move. Although the still-prevalent segregation of Cape Town, for instance, was a challenge on many levels (causing me to spend less time and share fewer direct experiences with my informants; cf. Gupta and Ferguson 1997), I did share with my informants and acquaintances the fact that there *are* nonpredicated or articulated social boundaries. What seems to be an obstacle to following informants across their different socialities is also the condition of the informants themselves: their lives are fragmented and they somehow have to bring different subjectivities into one experiencing personhood. In other words, what counts for the researcher also counts for city dwellers in general: we have to find creative ways to establish and maintain strong intersubjective bonds with people across different forms of sociality and places.

Overview of the Book

The historical and the ethnographic run throughout this book as two entwined threads. The book traces the *Wirkungsgeschichte* of the South African TRC and offers an ethnography of apartheid victims and their social recognition in today's South Africa. The history of the impact of the TRC on the South African society has not yet been written, but almost two decades after the commission held its last hearing, it is time to understand the consequences of the path chosen to mark the transition. We can only fully understand these consequences if we take into account the everyday lives of the victims of apartheid, and ask whether the commission succeeded in facilitating their societal recognition.[11]

I use ethnographic vignettes and interpret them in relation to my theoretical aims. This approach runs the risk of seeming anecdotic. Although this method allows closeness, it does not allow easy control over the degree of representativeness. The vignettes are based on encounters I had with people; they are very much centered around individuals and their attempts to find a social world in which to live as victims. My interpretations of these encounters are, of course, based on a much broader base of experiences I've gained over the years of conducting research for this project; but in the text they remain centered around individuals. Hence, the gap between ethnographic encounters and analysis is more visible than in other ethnographies that conclude on the general more seamlessly.

Chapter 1, "Apartheid Victimhood before the Courts," revisits twenty years of post-apartheid South Africa in relation to apartheid victims' standing in society. The TRC, national and international politics, and legal cases filed in South African and US courts have all crucially shaped where victims find themselves today. Since the TRC completed its investigations, and contrary to its reconciliatory approach, the issue of apartheid victimhood has become more judicial. This institutional formation of a victims' subject position is largely based on initiatives and interventions from civil society in South Africa and abroad. The Khulumani Support Group is probably the most important actor in victims' advocacy. During the group's gradual formation over the last twenty years, both its work and its reception have undergone major shifts. Under the Mbeki administration, when the state lost interest in the concerns of apartheid-era victims, the legal avenue proved more successful than political action. The domestic and US cases, in which the TRC, and specifically its shortcomings, is an important reference, have in turn helped to bring victimhood back to the attention of the state and the broader society.

Each of the four subsequent chapters examines a dimension of victims' attempts to move beyond victimhood using the law as a means of emancipation and explores the link between the bodily dimensions of victimhood and emancipation. I look at the potential of both legal procedure (chapter 2, "Reparation, Representation, and Class Actions") and bodily memory (chapter 3, "Embodied Memory and the Social") to work *against* the formation of a collective and political notion of victimhood. In chapter 4, "The Formation of the Political," and chapter 5, "Emancipation from Victimhood," I explore the potential of the law and bodily memory to serve as a foundation for a new collective of similarly situated human beings and to provide a basis for social change.

Apartheid victimhood has a collective and an individual dimension. Victims share many experiences, but at the same time, they carry their own individual and irreducible victimhood. Legal practice, as scholars caution, overemphasizes the individual dimension of injuries. Consequently, submitting shared social concerns to the courts can jeopardize political solidarity. To examine this claim, chapter 2 highlights the actual workings of courts to show the tension between structural injuries and individual victimhood in class actions. These practices and procedures have consequences for plaintiffs' subjectivities in their everyday lives. I show this by presenting two ethnographic cases. The first uses the testimony of a victim who singles herself out as an individual. Her account swings between the shared experience of suffering, on the one hand,

and her insistence of her own individual experience, on the other, which she tried to prove to me as if we were in a court of law. The second example shows how being singled out as test case for a class of plaintiffs in a class action suit filed in a High Court of South Africa affected an individual who was chosen to stand in for and represent many thousands of potential plaintiffs. These vignettes show that collective legal action may indeed legalize subjectivities, but that we can only understand its effects on subjectivities from the specific political and social conditions the cases have emerged from. The law derives its force from a societal postconflict situation in which being different makes one potentially suspicious to others who collectively share similar experiences.

The subsequent chapters move closer to the everyday lives of victims. Chapter 3 looks again at the individualizing dimension of victimhood. It does so, not through the lens of law, but through the lens of the body. The chapter presents ethnographic data showing how people attempt to communicate their pain: a group of victims fighting memories provoked by a theatrical performance that confirmed their victimhood rather than transformed it; a women struggling with the pressure that exists in today's South Africa to speak publicly about one's pain; a woman's capacity to take on and relieve others' pain by way of casual chats out of her roadside stall; and a woman's account of how experiences of political and criminal violence tend to merge whenever the former has not sufficiently been addressed. The vignettes suggest that there is real risk in speaking publicly about one's experiences, and that silence is a viable option for many. The lack of social recognition victims often experience is partly due to unsuccessful attempts of communication. Society seeks closure and offers victims only a limited number of social roles. Since victims in turn search for recognition by their society, they try to take on the subject positions offered to them—but their experiences are not completely malleable and easily adapted to existing discourses. As a result of the difficulties of articulating one's experienced victimhood in a socially effective discursive form, victims' injured personhood often turns them into suspicious subjects in the eyes of the society.

Chapters 4 and 5 examine the collective dimension of victimhood and the possibility of collective action based on shared victimhood. Chapter 4 looks at the TRC as a governing institution and analyzes how its governance in relation to victimhood has opened up the possibility of political action but has also constrained social actors trying to emancipate themselves. The chapter examines the conditions for the emergence of a political subjectivity—as a basis for social and collective action—in the context of a legalized and politicized bureaucratic notion of apartheid-era victimhood. Whereas shared experiences of victimhood foster sociality among victims, victims need to relate to dominant victims' subject position in order to be politically effective. This requires emancipation from the bodily dimension of victimhood. The chapter presents three different attempts to achieve emancipation: a man who finds solidarity among victims despite his criminal record; an internationally traveled woman who receives strength from her political opposition; and a lawyer who, thanks to his professional authority, momentarily takes his clients beyond their victimhood. The vignettes show that the law (and lawyers) plays a crucial role in making it possible to move beyond one's immediate experiences. Under specific social and political conditions, the law not only individuates but also has the potential to help create a collective.

In contrast to chapter 3, where I show how injuries and bodily memories separate people from each other, chapter 5 highlights the body's potentiality for social change. To allow incorporated memories of harm to heal, the bodily dimension of injury needs to be addressed. Far outside the TRC or other official institutions, people develop responses to routinized forms of suffering. In many ways, this chapter forms the core of the book. It relates unspectacular practices that explore new forms of sociality based on lived experiences that are not directly related to the dominant discourses. I write about women tacitly sharing their pain by informally coming together for a chat or some tea, about two sisters running a crèche and looking after other people's children, and about a commemorative meeting for victims, where they are safe to try out new ways of speaking about and seeing themselves. All these practices are fragile and easily disrupted, but the chapter shows that through new social and bodily experiences, people try to add new layers of habit memories to their subjective and social beings. The tentative forms of sociality that emerge may help them to assume a new social position. Many of these practices rely on the continuous performance of a new subject position, for which at least some minimal form of a public is necessary.

Chapter 6 reflects on anthropological ways of knowledge production in relation to bodily and sensory experiences. The researcher necessarily undergoes processes of habituation in the course of his or her fieldwork. From this follows the question how we can attend to the experiences of other people once they have become part of our own lifeworld. There are ways through which we can recognize knowledge we have acquired bodily. These *moments of dislocation* help us to access knowledge cognitively what was previously in the realm of the habitual or nonpredicated. By way of an intersubjective approach to research, we establish pieces of overlapping perception and thus a nonpredicated access to the experience of the other. A shared perception of the world gives us clues to what is relevant in our informants' lifeworlds.

The conclusion brings the four parallel strands of the individualizing and collectivizing dimensions of the law and of bodily memory together by weighing their respective force in a politicized and legalized environment. The juridification of transitional justice issues through victims' initiatives has to be seen in a post-TRC context in which apartheid-era crimes have constantly been decriminalized. The apartheid litigations and other civil cases are reactions to the state's unresponsiveness in matters of apartheid victimhood. This analysis goes against some of the main assumptions in legal anthropology—namely, that seeking recourse in the law does not result in subjection to a discourse; it is the attempt to emancipate from a discourse under conditions in which the law is more promising than the political avenue. The search for emancipation is rooted in the lived realities of victimhood. The conclusion makes the case that the social sciences need to take bodily memory seriously, to understand both the effects and the limits of discourses but also the possibility of their emergence. Bodily memory is the seed for new forms of sociality.

Chapter 1

Apartheid Victimhood before the Courts

THE SOUTH AFRICAN Truth and Reconciliation Commission (TRC) put the concerns of apartheid victims on the agenda of the state and society. It made victims visible in post-apartheid South Africa. Despite this, victims were not content with its work, as subsequent legal and political developments attest. Why is this so? What kind of politics around victimhood did the TRC trigger? What are the concerns of victims, their demands, and the problems associated with the legal and political routes to finding acknowledgment of their suffering and redress?

The South African state has put in place a number of redress mechanisms for the structural inequalities produced by apartheid, from social grants to the Black Economic Empowerment policies, affirmative action, land reform, and land-redistribution programs. Most of these programs do not directly address the injuries people experienced under apartheid rule; rather, they are forward looking, economically oriented, and operate on a primarily individual basis. The majority of them also require that a potential recipient have a certain standing in society in order to successfully claim the benefits.

The main institution to directly address the injuries of the past and to be empowered to recommend forms of redress to victims was, of course, the TRC. Much has been written about its successes, shortcomings, and failures.[1] The TRC hearings were intended to signal a break with the past by uncovering and condemning the atrocities committed by the apartheid regime. A number of the hearings were broadcast daily on the radio, and South Africans learned much about what had until then been hidden and unknown. The commission called on individual perpetrators of human rights violations to come forward, but it also had a mandate to investigate companies' roles in such violations. The commission's driving forces were theological notions of reconciliation and forgiveness, and it concentrated on the cathartic performance of truth and reconciliation. It was an effort that was globally unparalleled at that time. But the commission was also empowered to grant amnesty to perpetrators who voluntarily came forward and testified about their wrongdoing. If these perpetrators gave full disclosure of their crimes and provided proof that they had been politically motivated, they could be freed from civil and criminal prosecution.

The commission took testimony from about 21,000 victims, about a tenth of whom were invited to testify publicly. They testified about the gross human rights violations they or their relatives had experienced at the hands of the former regime. They spoke about experiences of torture, remembered loved ones who had disappeared, and told of family members who had been killed, of being put in detention without a trial, and of other forms of severe ill-treatment. However, many victims' submissions were not accepted by the statement-takers because they did not fit the TRC's narrow legalistic categories of *gross* human rights violations and *political* victimhood (cf. Cronin 1999, 6).[2] Many other victims were not prepared to speak about their painful experiences (Ross 2002, 163; 2003, 172); others did not even know about the commission and its work. As a result, the majority of victims did not testify at all.

The major and most prominent measure suggested by the TRC was to provide financial reparations to the victims of gross human rights violations and to the communities that were most deeply affected by the violence. Approximately 12,000 victims received a one-time payment ranging from R2,000 to R6,000, paid out between June 1998 and October 2000 (Crawford-Pinnerup 2000).

To carry out its work, the commission attempted to develop a representative definition of victimhood, and in doing so, collectivized the suffering and pain of all survivors performatively (cf. C. M. Cole 2009). It did this, however, by singling out individual victims, who would then speak for all victims and survivors. This idea of a representative, one-size-fits-all victimhood was fictive from the start and bound to fail. Its failures were exacerbated by its individualist approach: by focusing on individual cases, the commission lost sight of structural violence (cf. Feldman 2003; Mamdani 2002). The representation of the majority by the few thus failed in a double sense: it relied on the fiction of healing by proxy, and it remained blind to collectively experienced structural victimhood. Hence, injury ultimately remained individualized, as an act and as a status and, still, for most victims today, as an experience. This has had important consequences in the years after the TRC.

After the TRC

In the eyes of the international community, South Africa had dealt with the past through the TRC; yet in South Africa, apartheid issues did not end when the commission finished its work. Even though the hearings had run for only fifteen months, in 1996 and 1997, it took the commission's Amnesty Committee and the Reparation and Rehabilitation Committee an astonishing six years to table their findings and make their recommendations to the South Africa's president. When the two final volumes of the TRC Final Report were handed over to the president, Thabo Mbeki, in 2003, it was he who decided which of the TRC recommendations to endorse and implement. To the 21,000 listed victims, his announcement came as a shock: instead of the recommended Individual Reparation Grant of R20,000 a year for a period of six years, he granted victims a one-time payment of R30,000 per victim or surviving relative. By September 2008, approximately 16,341 of the 21,000 victims had been assisted, either through payment of interim or final grants.[3]

By the time the Amnesty Committee completed its work, in mid-2001, it had granted amnesty to 1,160 of 7,094 applicants and rejected 5,392 applications (Du Bois-Pedain 2007, 35–39; Sooka 2003). The TRC itself always made clear that if amnesty was refused, or if perpetrators did not submit an application, criminal investigations should continue and suspected perpetrators should be brought to trial (Du Bois-Pedain 2007, 54). The TRC staff had compiled information about three hundred cases that they thought should be prosecuted. The files were turned over to the National Prosecution Authority (NPA) when the TRC closed down. There were rumors that the South African government was considering initiating what would have been a second amnesty process (Du Bois-Pedain 2007, 54–55; Klaaren and Varney 2000). But Mbeki denied this in a speech to Parliament in April 2003. Yet despite his assurances, the state made little attempt to pursue the cases. As Antje Du Bois-Pedain (2007, 55) noted, "[P]ost-TRC prosecutorial policy can be summed up in a laconic 'much talk, little action.'" Apart from a few high-profile cases,[4] only a small number of trials, against lower level officials, were conducted, most of which resulted in acquittals (Sarkin-Hughes 2004, 373–81). In consequence, "the amnesty intended to be individual turned into a group amnesty. For any perpetrator who was not so identified was a perpetrator who enjoyed impunity" (Mamdani 2002, 34).[5]

In 2005, the NPA, in line with the TRC recommendations, created the Missing Persons Task Team, whose mandate is to search for the missing graves, including mass graves, of political prisoners. The NPA has since followed up on some disappearances and facilitated the reburial of the remains. By February 2012, it had identified seventy-two individuals, and returned the bones to their families for burial (Aronson 2011; Fabricius 2012). The head of the Task Team, Madeleine Fullard, estimates that there are still another 200 to 250 missing persons inside South Africa, and about two thousand activists who disappeared in exile in such countries as Zambia, Tanzania, and Angola. A strong quest to exhume bodies came out of the victims' testimony before the TRC. Up until 2003, the commission itself had carried out some fifty exhumations.[6]

Many questions remain. For example, the TRC archive has not yet been opened to the public. The information it contains is not only important for researchers but also for surviving families seeking to find out what happened to their loved ones. (It would, of course, also provide grounds for civil lawsuits against individual perpetrators.) Issues of confidentiality would need to be carefully addressed; but the state has not yet communicated any clear intention.

Furthermore, not until 2005 did the South African government establish the TRC Unit in the Department of Justice, which was supposed to consider the commission's recommendation of the payment of community reparations. The TRC Unit was established, under rather vague terms, to develop and implement programs for communities particularly burdened by the legacy of apartheid-era violence. The unit's precise mandate and organization remain unclear, but its programs will be financed from the President's Fund.

Another major pending TRC-related issue is the President's Fund, which was created by the government under terms of section 42 of the Promotion of National Unity and Reconciliation Act (Act No. 34 of 1995) to fund "all amounts payable to victims by way of reparations in terms of regulations made by the President" (subsection 2) and "all amounts payable by way of reparations towards the rehabilitation of communities" (subsection 2A). Many states, including the Netherlands, Switzerland, and Germany, have contributed to it. The fund is administered by the Office of the Chief Financial Officer in the Department of Justice and Constitutional Development. Since its establishment in the mid-1990s, it has accumulated more than R1billion. The first explicit policy on how the money should be used was formulated only in May 2011. The Department of Justice gazetted draft regulations to govern the provision of basic and higher education and medical benefits for victims and their dependents, and invited responses. The regulations stipulated that only the victims identified and listed by the TRC were eligible. Civil society groups harshly criticized this "closed list" approach and demanded, in the courts, that the process be stopped until "meaningful consultations are carried out with victims and interested parties."[7] In regulations gazetted in November 2013, the Department of Justice and Constitutional Development announced its intention to use half of the fund's money for infrastructure projects in 18 of the 128 communities the TRC had identified as particularly in need of reparations. For Khulumani, which was not involved in the drawing up of the regulations, it fails to address apartheid victims' specific needs and represents an abuse of the department's mandate to manage the fund.

Even though the TRC had no executing powers (apart from its Amnesty Committee, which could grant or refuse amnesty), the state's negligence simply confirmed victims' ambivalent perceptions of the TRC's work. These perceptions have been triggered by the state's failure on two measures that were supposed to facilitate social justice and social equality: the prosecution of perpetrators and the payment of reparations to individual victims and severely affected communities. Measured against the expectations raised by the TRC process, the state has failed on all counts to properly deliver on them.

Khulumani Support Group

Although victimhood became a legal category for which only some qualified, the commission's work did facilitate the emergence of a victim subjectivity that had effects beyond the TRC. Across South Africa, disappointed victims started to organize. The Khulumani Support Group was launched in 1995,[8] and has grown into a national organization, with provincial, regional, and local branches, all operating under the Khulumani umbrella. It is the only membership-based group of apartheid-era victims in South Africa.[9] To date, Khulumani comprises around 104,000 members.[10] During my research period alone, between 2009 and 2013, about 20,000 people applied for membership—a number equivalent to the entire TRC list of victims.

Members are persons who survived some form of violence inflicted by the apartheid security forces or its collaborators, including torture; detention without trial; sexual assault, abuse, or harassment; banning and banishment orders; deliberate withholding of medical attention, food, and water; the destruction of homes, and the mutilation of body parts.[11] Members also include those whose family members were abducted, disappeared, or killed. Only about 10 percent of Khulumani's members were officially recognized as victims by the Truth Commission and received reparations (Madlingozi 2007a, 120). Prospective new members usually contact an executive member at home or after a Khulumani outreach meeting, or apply in person at a provincial, regional, or local office. There, they tell their stories to a data collector, who fills in the Needs Assessment Form for them. The data collector is either an active member in a specific community or an office manager. Applicants have to provide proof of identity; sign an affidavit; bring newspaper clippings of the event their injury relates to if they have them; and, if their victim status is linked to a death in the family, a copy of the death certificate.

Sporadically, the organization makes statistics about its membership public. They are based on Khulumani's Apartheid Reparation Database, a project formally started in 2003 when Khulumani launched the Needs Assessment Form, which both serves as the membership application and captures the profile and the needs of the applicants.

The latest available data are based on 44,931 entries dating back to October 2009.[12] According to the organization, 69 percent of its members are female; 46 percent are single, 40 percent married, 11 percent widowed, and 3 percent divorced. Furthermore, 76 percent of the membership is unemployed; 12 percent are employed; 7 percent are pensioners; and 5 percent are self-employed. Only 4.9 percent of members have one dependent; 10 percent have two dependents; 52.5 percent have three to six dependents; and 32.6 percent have between seven and ten dependents.[13] If one considers that 76 percent of members are unemployed and around 85 percent have three to ten dependents, one sees that the material situation of many members is precarious.[14]

The kinds of violations applicants reported give an idea of what a majority of the membership experienced in the past and still grapples with today. About a third of the applicants reported "extra-judicial killings" of people close to them.[15] Forty percent reported "indiscriminate shootings," which are defined on the form as "random shootings mostly during times of violence by the police, defence force, opposing political groups, and vigilante groups." About 6 percent of the applicants said they went through "prolonged arbitrary detention," a widespread practice, especially during a state of emergency. Furthermore, 22 percent of the applicants reported what falls under Khulumani's category of "torture and inhumane treatment," which includes torture, police brutality, violent assault with a political motive, and total destruction of property. Finally, 0.4 percent reported that they or their late family members experienced rape, which includes any reference to sexual assault.[16]

One of three members experienced a killing in his or her family or has a family member who disappeared. An even larger proportion of the membership experienced shootings, which often left them with disabilities or unable to work. Thousands of members were kept in prison without a trial, many in solitary confinement. A fifth of the membership experienced torture or other forms of police violence, including the destruction of property.

Members assess their most important needs as follows: medical assistance (20.1 percent), housing (27.8 percent), education (24.3 percent) and employment (27.8 percent). In a breakdown of "urgent needs," 7.3 percent indicated mental health support; 5.8 percent, support or treatment of disabilities; and 5.5 percent said they needed home care and suffered from chronic illnesses. Almost a quarter of applicants stated that they urgently needed new housing. Education—skills training, adult basic education, secondary and tertiary education alike—ranks highest as an urgent need (46 percent). With regard to age, there is no recent breakdown. The latest data go back to 2006 and are based on only 9,648 members. Of these, 25 percent of the roughly 10,000 members were aged over sixty years at that time, and 5 percent were under thirty. The majority, 70 percent, were between thirty and sixty years old—a broad category that includes members of different generations who experienced apartheid quite differently.

The Making of a Victims' Support Group

Khulumani started out as a self-help group with a focus on providing psychosocial support to victims. However, it soon began to focus on politics and made more articulated demands for reparations. This shift was partly the result of internal developments within the organization, but broader political and social changes were much more important factors. One major factor was an increasing frustration with the TRC process. Five years after the TRC had completed its hearings, the victims had still not been paid individual reparations, and many of them felt it was time to take a more aggressive stance toward the government. Less tangibly, people started to realize in the early 2000s that economic change in their lives had yet to come (Robins 2005); and from about 2004, public protests throughout the country confronted the state on the nondelivery of services. This, too, contributed to an increasing politicization of

Khulumani members and to what may be best described as a *turn to the state* in Khulumani's work.[17]

The second shift within Khulumani can be called a move from "charismatic leadership" to professionalization.[18] In Khulumani's early years, a few founding members led the formulation and articulation of victims' concerns.[19] Khulumani's origins are closely tied to the TRC, especially to victims' testimony, and its early leaders, victims themselves, came to epitomize the victim who engages with the TRC and demands to be listened to. The victim subjectivity of these early leaders was closely linked to the national project of reconciliation and justice. They were critical voices, even though at the time real transformation still seemed possible. Many important Khulumani members had been fieldworkers who had assisted the TRC in its deeply complex work before becoming more fully involved with Khulumani and its programs.

The political climate radically changed in 2003 following President Mbeki's announcement that the state would act on the TRC's recommendations in only a limited way. Also, the apartheid litigations were filed in 2002. It is in those years that Khulumani started to "professionalize"—that is, to undertake a partial shift from loose and voluntary to more stable, bureaucratic, and internationally oriented governing structures.

Today, half of the staff at the national office still see themselves as victims, the other half do not. As is the common practice globally, private donors mostly provide most of Khulumani's project funding.[20] As a consequence, the national office frequently employs temporary and part-time international interns sent to it by partner organizations from abroad. Apart from the advocacy coordinator, who receives a salary, the information manager, the program leaders, and several fieldworkers work on a voluntary or sporadically paid basis. The person who has been central to the growth of the organization in the past few years is executive director and ex officio national board member Dr. Marjorie Jobson.[21] The everyday governance of the organization is carried out by the board and the management.[22] Khulumani's main decision-making body is the National Steering Committee, composed of delegates from the provinces.

To live up to its constitution and to democratic standards, Khulumani would need a well-functioning system of presentation and representation between all levels. Instead, the director, together with the board or the staff at the national office, takes many decisions without consulting the membership. This small circle of people in governing positions is the result of the emergence of a few key figures within the organization who have not only the skills and the educational background but also the stability in their lives to dedicate much of their time to the organization.

South Africa presents a spectrum of forms of social organizing. On the end of the spectrum, one finds an increasing number of professionalized NGOs. Due to the exigencies of donor funding, a small professional leadership earns good wages while claiming to represent their constituencies. This model is increasingly negatively critiqued by scholars, who fear an NGO-ization of the civil society. At the other end of the spectrum, many forms of popular mobilization (e.g., the recent service delivery and student protests) rely on instant organization around a particular grievance or set of grievances (cf. Alexander 2010).

Khulumani holds the middle ground between both types. It is a membership organization that ultimately depends on the initiatives of individual members in all the villages and towns of South Africa in which the organization has offices. Khulumani has no research mandate, no well-paid positions, and few resources, and, most importantly, the work it does is continuously evolving in line with the needs of its members. The mandate that the executive and the membership had set themselves is a highly complex one. Its internal dynamics are, therefore, also difficult to compare with those of other NGOs. The national leadership straddle two fields: they seek recognition from the international arena of human rights, but continuously have to reflect on their own capacity to recognize Khulumani's membership not only as a constituency but as the only reason the organization remains alive and necessary.

The provincial and regional leaders have gained considerable expertise in how to keep the organization going. They constantly reconstitute and reinvent what Khulumani is and what it stands for in very creative ways, with next to no financial resources. Even more difficult is the position of leaders of the local branches, many of which are always on the verge of collapse. The strain of the everyday life may easily erode a leader's capacity to function effectively; if she or he gets sick or takes a full-time job, it jeopardizes the Khulumani activities in the area as well as that group's links to other branches and to the national office. Local activities simultaneously depend on the capacities of individual leaders and on their recognition by the membership. Trust is essential. A leader can be trusted or mistrusted, sometimes because of his or her role in the past, but also because of his or her ability to balance the needs of the different communities or individual members in a fair, impartial way, and to reliably and effectively communicate information to the membership.

Local Khulumani leaders and members relate to the organization through their lived experiences as victims. For some, membership is an opportunity to assume a leadership role in a community, but for most, the local group is a place where they can find solidarity with other victims. They, however, rely on the national leadership for guidance and acknowledgment, for keeping up the flow of information, and to do the lobbying and advocacy work. The national activities produce a more receptive public and actively shape the discourse around apartheid-era victimhood that, in turn, is important for the success of the local activities.

The national leadership in turn depends on the membership and the provincial and local exponents. To speak as a membership organization, it needs a visible and active membership in the first place. It initiates programs that have to be rolled out in the communities. Beyond that, the administrative and governing leadership of Khulumani draw much of their inspiration from members themselves.

Khulumani's professionalization on the national level was partly driven by the necessity of articulating victims' concerns vis-à-vis the state. Communicating with a government that, outside the TRC, has largely been deaf to those concerns seemed to demand a level of organizational sophistication and professionalism, including a series of documentation projects (one of them the database). The relation between the state and Khulumani has been erratic and changeable. Whereas Khulumani has employed both collaborative and oppositional forms of engagement, several ministries have shown inconsistent and unpredictable support and poor follow through on expressions of interest. Khulumani has repeatedly offered the government its advice and networks to help in planning projects and programs. State institutions generally show little interest, and only engage with Khulumani when they have a specific need for its expertise or constituency, or want access to its database (which Khulumani usually denies).

Khulumani has not managed to establish a working relationship with a ministry that lasts longer than an elective term. The Mbeki administration in particular blocked the organization's efforts to work with the state. At the same time, Khulumani has received a great deal of attention from the international media because of the apartheid litigations, the Zuma administration's tentative withdrawal of the state's opposition to the apartheid litigations in 2009, and some successful interventions in the state's policies and practices around indemnity and pardons for apartheid-era perpetrators. Despite these successes, the state's response to Khulumani's demands and offers remains unpredictable and unsatisfying for Khulumani. The state has not made any advances toward the recognition of an apartheid-era victimhood that goes beyond the TRC list.

Khulumani has forged partnerships with a number of civil society organizations and NGOs to sponsor programs or projects with and for apartheid-era victims. These groups are all more or less stable and close partners of Khulumani and its regional groups.[23] There are sporadic battles of personalities and interests between Khulumani and its partners, but the partners do not pose a threat to Khulumani as an entity. Hence, Khulumani has managed to become the almost uncontested voice for apartheid-era victims; no rival group has a similar reach and standing.

In its own work, Khulumani has a broad conception of victimhood. The organization adopted a multigenerational approach by trying to get youth involved in projects dealing with the legacy of the past. It makes no distinction between military veterans and other victims, even though Khulumani largely speaks for those who have not received military training and official recognition. The state, however, does distinguish "general" victims from military veterans, and actively works with the latter. Khulumani's activities have recently also expanded to include other forms of victimization, such as the plight of foreign nationals who have been targeted in the so-called xenophobic attacks in South Africa. More recently, collaboration with Zimbabwean human rights groups has strengthened around questions of a possible truth commission and with regard to the Zimbabwean refugee population in South Africa.

This new inclusivity is most apparent discursively on the national level and is not always realized in the daily workings of the regional branches. Khulumani has come to stand for apartheid-era victimhood, and it undertakes membership-based and professional activities that rely on this subject position. It is not yet clear how far members' notions of victimhood can be extended in response to theoretical reflections, and how far their solidarity can expand to other groups. The answer will most likely depend on the experience of victimhood members make, and the kinds of victimhood they relate to in their perception of their lived experience. If apartheid-era victimhood increasingly recedes into the background because more structural and current forms of marginalization and exclusion are shaping the daily experiences of Khulumani members, their notion of victimhood is likely to change.

Khulumani as an organization, as it operates today, is chiefly bound to members' experiences of victimhood. The memory of experiences of violence is not only its raison d'être but also its driving force. It seeks both the recognition of victims in society and victims' emancipation from their experiences of violence. For that, creating a responsive public that recognizes experienced victimhood and that allows for shifts of victim subjectivities is crucial.

Victims in Courts

An essential part of Khulumani's fight for the recognition of apartheid-era victimhood has been fought in courts of law (see Kesselring 2012). For most Khulumani members and for the leadership, this was not a choice but a necessary reaction to political developments.

The Truth Commission's mandate was controversial from the beginning (Giannini et al. 2009, 17). A core provision of the TRC Act was challenged in South Africa's highest court, the Constitutional Court. In *Azanian People's Organization (AZAPO) and Others v. The President of the Republic of South Africa and Others*,[24] victims alleged that the possibility that perpetrators would be granted amnesty deprived victims of particular rights as protected in the Interim Constitution of 1993. Victims were concerned that the granting of amnesty waived both civil and criminal liability. The Constitutional Court ruled that the granting of amnesty was constitutional. The decision made clear, however, that the amnesty process was a one-time event in a unique moment in South Africa's history, and that perpetrators who failed to satisfy the amnesty requirements could face civil and criminal charges. It thus argued that victims had not been deprived of the right to seek prosecution. In justifying the possibility of amnesty by the extraordinary circumstances given in the TRC process alone, the court, as well as the commission's practice, made sure that processes of granting amnesty to or pardoning perpetrators became fiercely contested in the 2000s. In fact, the Constitutional Court's decision was successfully interpreted as granting victims the right to participate in such decisions.

On December 1, 2005, the Ministry of Justice promulgated amendments to the prosecution policy concerning prosecutorial discretion. Victims understood the policy amendments as a clear indication that the Mbeki administration wanted to move away from concerns with the past. The amendments added an appendix to the original prosecution policy, which determines the limits of prosecutorial discretion in deciding whether or not to prosecute alleged crimes.[25] The changes only relate to the prosecution of offenses "emanating from conflicts of the past" that were committed on or prior to May 11,

1994. The amendments provide that perpetrators can apply to the National Directorate of Public Prosecutions (NDPP) for "indemnity" from prosecution for politically motivated crimes. For President Mbeki, this was a way for those who did not participate in the TRC process to "cooperate in unearthing the truth" in exchange for prosecutorial leniency.[26]

Although the president and the Ministry of Justice emphasized that the new guidelines would not be a rerun of the TRC amnesty process, the criteria for whether or not to prosecute resembled those applied by the Amnesty Committee—namely, whether the perpetrator had made full disclosure; showed an "attitude towards reconciliation" and "willingness to abide by the Constitution"; and, something the TRC did not require, whether she or he had demonstrated remorse (cf. Chapman and Van der Merwe 2008, 285).

Two years later, in 2007, five victims supported by Khulumani Support Group, the International Centre for Transitional Justice (ICTJ), and the Centre for the Study of Violence and Reconciliation (CSVR) filed a challenge to the policy amendments on the following grounds: they would undermine the integrity of the TRC process, which was predicated on the assumption that those who did not receive amnesty would be prosecuted, and they would undermine the rule of law, the independence of the prosecution authorities, and, by extension, the legal system. Further, they argued that the policy amendments infringed on the human rights of the victims (the individual's right to life, dignity, freedom, and security, and equality). Lastly, the applicants suggested that the policy amendments were in breach of international law.[27]

The Legal Resource Centre represented the applicants. In December 2008, the policy amendments were struck down by the High Court in Pretoria.[28] In its judgment, the court found that the policy amendments did in effect amount to a repeat—a "copy cat"[29]—of the TRC amnesty provisions. This was unlawful because "when there is sufficient evidence to prosecute, the [NDPP] must comply with its obligation."[30] In addition, the court found that the policy amendments contained "a recipe for conflict and absurdity."[31] The NDPP and the minister of justice applied for leave to appeal. In May 2009, their application was dismissed by the High Court in Pretoria. Victims' support and lobby groups thus succeeded in fighting the extension of prosecutorial discretion beyond the temporary limited TRC process.

The amended prosecution guidelines had dealt with the issue of when to grant indemnity from prosecution in exchange for information and disclosure.

The next important case focused on convicted perpetrators and centered on the right to pardon, a special construction that in conventional legal theory represents an unconditional and discretionary sovereign act.

In 2008, President Mbeki created a reference group, made up of members from all the political parties represented in Parliament, to recommend convicted perpetrators as possible candidates for a pardon. He established a "special dispensation" to grant pardons to persons who had been convicted of offenses committed in pursuit of political objectives before 1994.[32] Later, President Mbeki extended the cutoff date for the committal of these crimes to June 16, 1999.

The reference group received and considered about two thousand pardon applications and made its recommendations. It specifically rejected the "full disclosure" requirement. Nor was there any victim participation. Civil society organizations tried to get involved, but the group refused to disclose the contents and motivations of the pardon applications. When the then recently formalized South African Coalition of Transitional Justice requested the right to make representations to the reference group on behalf of victims, the request was denied.[33] Interim president Mothlanthe, who had been elected upon Mbeki's resignation in late 2008, declared that victims or other interested persons would not be involved in the political pardons process.

This induced the coalition to file an urgent application in the North Gauteng High Court for an interdict preventing the president from granting any pardons, arguing that excluding victims and other interested members of the public from the process was unlawful.[34] Archbishop Desmond Tutu filed an affidavit in support of the application. The respondents were the president and the minister of justice. The state argued that the NGOs lacked standing and that the victims had no right to be heard when the president exercised his power to grant pardons.[35]

The applicants won an interim interdict. The High Court found that the NGOs did have standing because they were acting on behalf of victims who could not act in their own names, in the interests of victims, and in the public interest as well. Significantly, the court also ordered the president and the minister of justice to release the names of the prisoners who had been recommended for pardons (there were 149). Before releasing a prisoner on pardon, the president must "have considered all the relevant information relating to the said prisoner. The said information should include the inputs of victims and/or families of the victims of that particular crime and any other relevant information which might come from any interested party."[36] However, Ryan Albutt, one of the applicants and a member of the Afrikaner Weerstandsbeweging (AWB), asked the Constitutional Court to grant leave to appeal against the order of the High Court. The president and the minister of justice, the respondents in the High Court case, supported the application.

In February 2010, the Constitutional Court simultaneously granted leave to appeal and dismissed the appeal. Upon the Constitutional Court's judgment, the Ministry of Justice released the list of prisoners recommended for a pardon and publicized it via the newspapers. For the first time, the public and the coalition had the names of the applicants. Victims, their relatives, and members of the public could file submissions supporting or opposing during a thirty-day period starting on the date of the release of the list. The list contained the name of the applicant, the offense for which the pardon was requested, the date of the offense, the place where it was committed, and the date and court of conviction. The offense was described in a technical way and the place of the offense was anything from a huge township to a city like Johannesburg.

The list of 149 names included the former law and order minister Adriaan Vlok and former apartheid police chief Johannes van der Merwe (who pleaded guilty to the attempted murder of the United Democratic Front leader Frank Chikane).[37] It also included persons who committed murders after 1994 that were not believed to have been politically motivated. Most of the applicants were members of a liberation movement. According to the South African Coalition for Transitional Justice, only thirty objections to pardons were filed. Real participation for victims would have required more knowledge of the context of the committed offenses, particularly of the place and nature of the offense. In addition, distributing the list via newspapers, when illiteracy is widespread in South Africa and newspapers do generally not reach the communities where victims live, further hampered the participation.

On February 27, 2015, President Zuma, who had taken office in 2009, announced his intention to resuscitate the Special Dispensation for Presidential Pardons for apartheid-era perpetrators of political crimes and to pardon another 926 applicants. It was a move that failed to honor the ruling of the Constitutional Court.

These domestic cases are not well known outside South Africa, but they were very influential in defining victims' subject positions and the possibilities and limits of politicized victim subjectivities. Although the cases strengthened victims' rights, they also helped to cement the TRC's notion of victimhood by stressing the extraordinary nature of the commission and its importance for South African society. A different set of legal actions have gained much more international prominence by challenging the TRC's shortcomings. In Alien Tort Statute claims filed in US courts, victims demanded reparations for the injuries they had sustained at the hands of the security forces of the apartheid regime.

Unfinished Business and the Litigating Business

When the first five volumes of the TRC final report were tabled to President Mbeki in 1999, he seized the moment to clarify the state's position on apartheid-era victimhood:

> [S]urely all of us must agree that reparation will be offered to those who fought for freedom by ensuring that monuments are built to pay tribute to these to whom we owe our liberty. . . . We must however also make the point that *no genuine fighter for the liberation of our people ever engaged in struggle for personal gain.* There are many who laid down their lives, many who lost their limbs, many who are today disabled and many who spent their best years in apartheid prisons. None of those expected a reward except freedom itself. We must not insult them and demean the heroic contribution they made to our emancipation by turning them into mercenaries whose sacrifices we can compensate with money. Very many among these have not asked for any money, because their own sense of the dignity of the freedom fighter leads them to say that there is no cash value that should be attached to their desire to serve the people of South Africa and all humanity.[38]

Mbeki's remarks must be understood in the context of national and international lobbying for debt release or relief at the time, which was increasingly being linked with demands for reparations. In 1997, the South African Coalition Against Apartheid Debt made a submission to the TRC in which it requested an investigation into the financing of apartheid by foreign banks. A year later, the International Apartheid Debt and Reparations Campaign was officially launched in Cape Town. It lobbied for the cancellation of apartheid-caused debts and for compensation from businesses that had profited from the apartheid system and its abuses. Although the campaign focuses on South African matters, another, much broader movement grew rapidly—the largely faith-based International Jubilee 2000 Coalition. Founded in the United Kingdom, in 1996, as a movement of individuals, faith-based organizations, NGOs, trade unions, and student bodies from more than forty countries, Jubilee 2000 pushed for unconditional debt relief for heavily indebted poor countries by the new millennium. The debts it targeted derived from loans from the World Bank, the International Monetary Fund, and private banks.

The South African state had voluntarily repaid most of the former regime's debts by 2001, and the government refused to engage in anything related to the cancellation of debt. Jubilee 2000 in South Africa early on complemented the campaigns for debt release with its efforts to gain financial and nonfinancial reparations for victims of apartheid crimes; its Apartheid Debt and Reparations Task Team was funded in 1998. Its campaign included representatives from the South African Council of Churches, the South African National NGO Coalition (SANGOCO),[39] Khulumani Support Group, Congress of African Trade Unions (COSATU), CSVR, Institute for Justice and Reconciliations (IJR), legal specials, researchers, and patrons of Jubilee 2000. The themes were broad social reconstruction and development programs in affected communities, individual compensation to victims of apartheid human rights abuses, and corporate responsibility of international companies that had backed and profited from the crime of apartheid.

There was a shift in focus from debt and reparations to reparations only: what started as a quest for the state's rejection of debts that the predecessor regime had accumulated was now a demand for individual and community reparations for suffered harm and structurally constrained development. South Africans, the campaign argued, should not have to pay for apartheid twice. International companies became a target group; however, they rejected the claims as unjustified and refused to engage in a dialogue.

According to international law, states have an obligation to provide various forms of reparations to victims of human rights violations and violations of international law.[40] The situation is more complex when it comes to the obligations of nonstate actors, who do not have the state's duty to protect its citizens from harm, so that breaches of human rights committed by them are often difficult to prove. Also, the justiciability of corporate human rights breaches is more complicated and much less tested in courts, most of all when it comes to companies' "mere" aiding and abetting of human rights violations committed by the state. Applicants need to prove a causal connection between the companies' actions or omissions and the injuries.

In 2001, the Apartheid Debt and Reparations Campaign instituted legal proceedings against non–South African multinational companies, following the example of the action taken against Switzerland by Jewish plaintiffs over the unclaimed assets of Nazi victims being held in the country. Hence, in 2002, when President Mbeki had still not announced his final decision regarding amnesty and reparations, litigation against multinational companies for their alleged aiding and abetting the apartheid regime's security forces in the perpetration of gross human rights violations was instituted in US courts: *Khulumani et al. v. Barclays National Bank et al.*

The original complaint, led by Michael Hausfeld from the US litigation firm Hausfeld[41] and advised by South African attorney Charles Abrahams, sued twenty-three multinationals and banks in six different countries (Switzerland, Germany, France, the Netherlands, the United Kingdom, and the United States) and involved six different industries (arms and ammunition, oil, transportation, banking, computer technology, and mining). The plaintiff organization Khulumani and eighty-seven individuals alleged specific violations of international human rights law that corporate actions had made possible: extrajudicial killing, torture, detention, and cruel treatment, all of which had taken place between 1960 and 1994.

A few months before the Khulumani litigation was filed with the Eastern District Court of New York, an American personal injury lawyer, Ed Fagan, filed *Lungisile Ntsebeza et al. v. Daimler Chrysler Corporation et al.* against Daimler Chrysler, UBS, Credit Suisse Group, Citicorp, and others in the Southern District Court of New York.[42] In an amended version of the case, Anglo American, de Beers, Sasol and Fluor Corporations, Barclays, Deutsche Bank, Dresdner Bank, Commerzbank, Crédit Lyonnais, Banque Indo Suez, IBM, Novartis, and Sulzer were added to the suit. The South African government, former president Nelson Mandela, and then president Thabo Mbeki, as the legal successors of the apartheid regime, were mentioned as defendants. Fagan's South African legal partners were advocate Dumisa Ntsebeza, head of the TRC's Investigative Unit, and attorney John Ngcebetsha. Because of controversies around Fagan's credentials (he was eventually charged with professional misconduct in a number of cases and disbarred in New York and New Jersey[43]), the American human rights litigator Paul Hoffman, a partner in the firm of Schonbrun, De Simone, Seplow, Harris, and Hoffman, took over the case. The South African companies and the South African state were taken out of the complaint. In December 2002, the US Judicial Panel on Multidistrict Litigation decided that the multiple apartheid cases should be consolidated and heard by the Southern District Court of New York.

The lawsuits are based on the common law principles of liability and on the Alien Tort Statute. The ATS is a curious and hotly contested statute that dates back to 1789, when US president George Washington signed legislation for an antipiracy bill (28 U.S.C. sec. 1350) that read: "The district courts shall have original jurisdiction of any civil action by an alien for a tort only, committed in violation of the law of nations or a treaty of the United States." The statute gives foreign citizens the right to sue in a US federal court over violations of international law, whether they arose in the United States or abroad. The ATS lay practically dormant for almost two hundred years, but since 1980, it has been the basis of some hundred lawsuits. In the mid-1990s, many Holocaust-related litigations gave it visibility, and statute's claims became a rapidly growing instrument in bringing to justice persons who have committed human rights violations. Up to today, there has never been a ruling in favor of the applicants in a case filed under the provisions of the statute; the litigants have always opted to settle the case out of court, not least for fear of being ordered by the court to open their archives (Stephens et al. 2008). The ATS has been discussed at length by numerous scholars and legal experts (Henner 2009; Mattei 2003; Stephens et al. 2008). On the one hand, it is seen as the ultimate expression of US legal imperialism; on the other, it is heralded as the last option that potentially establishes accountability for (complicity in) breaches of international law and international human rights standards.

Despite the initial assurance by the Cabinet of South Africa that government neither supported nor opposed legal action in this matter, on the occasion of the tabling of the two final volumes of the TRC report (April 15, 2003), President Mbeki strongly condemned the legal actions:

> [W]e consider it completely unacceptable that matters that are central to the future of our country should be adjudicated in foreign courts which bear no responsibility for the well-being of our country and the observance of the perspective contained in our constitution of the promotion of national reconciliation.[44]

On the one hand, Mbeki was determined to look to the future of his country instead of one-sidedly looking back, and hence to focus on construction instead of punishment, as he confirmed in an interview during a state visit to Switzerland (Kapp 2003). On the other hand, he must have felt sufficient pressure from Western countries to feel the need to clarify the government's position on apartheid litigations matters (*Pambazuka News* 2003). Apparently, Colin Powell, then US secretary of state, encouraged Justice Minister Maduna, in a phone call, to file a submission to the District Court.[45]

South Africans and individuals and organizations around the world wrote letters in support of the applicants, so-called amicus curiae briefs. For instance, the now retired Archbishop Desmond Tutu, in his capacity as chairperson of the TRC, emphasized that the apartheid litigations were in line with what the TRC had found:

> [T]he obtaining of compensation for victims of apartheid, to supplement the very modest amount per victim to be rewarded as reparation under the TRC process, could promote reconciliation, by addressing the needs of those apartheid victims dissatisfied with the small monetary value of TRC reparations.[46]

Other supporters included solidarity coalitions, such as the Swiss Apartheid Debt and Reparations Campaign, and individuals, such as the economist Joseph Stiglitz, a Nobel Prize winner in 2001 and the former chief economist of the World Bank.

Objection to the apartheid litigations was just as fierce. South Africa's then minister of justice, Penuell Maduna, filed an affidavit calling upon district court judge John E. Sprizzo to dismiss both lawsuits. According to the ministry, the litigations preempted the government's ability to handle domestic matters of reconstruction and reconciliation and discouraged investment in the South African economy.

Many objections were not directed at the court. For instance, the then South African minister of trade and industry, Alec Erwin, told Parliament: "[W]e are opposed to and indeed contemptuous of attempts to use unsound extra-territorial legal precepts in the USA to seek personal financial gain in South Africa."[47] While Erwin acknowledged the right to seek recourse in law, he condemned "the abuse to use the law of another land to undermine our sovereign right to settle our past and build our future as we see fit." He reproached the plaintiffs for "break[ing] that indefinable collectivist identity that was the origin of our strength" and for "exploit[ing] our history."[48] And the late Kader Asmal, then South Africa's minister of education, in an address to the National Assembly, argued that South Africa "does not need the help of ambulance chasers and contingency fee operators, whether in Switzerland, the Netherlands, or the United States of America."[49]

While the plaintiffs were labeled unpatriotic and treacherous, some of the distrust of the apartheid litigations has to be attributed to the involvement of Ed Fagan, who had initiated the Ntsebeza litigation. By the time Paul Hoffman took over, political damage had already been irreversibly done. As Terry Bell, labor activist and journalist, told me:

> Once it has started, you can't stop it, that's the trouble. You have already committed yourself to the courts, which is why the case is such a mess in America. . . . I think you also had the slick American lawyers who—the English expression— talk a hole in your head. They just completely outfoxed the locals.[50]

On the US side, soon after the cases were filed, then US secretary of commerce, Donald Evans, described the litigations as "unhelpful development" (Friedman 2003). In a statement of interest issued by the Department of State, the Bush administration argued that the "continued adjudication of the [apartheid litigations] risks potentially serious adverse consequences for significant interests of the United States" by threatening to be "irritant in U.S.-South African relations" and for international economic relations with other countries whose firms are defendants.[51] Indeed, Switzerland and Germany, together with the United Kingdom and Australia, officially spoke out in favor of the companies with headquarters in their territories, and filed amicus curiae in their support.[52]

In early 2004, the applicability of the ATS in US courts seemed finally confirmed when the US Supreme Court handed down a positive judgment in another case involving the statute: *Sosa v. Alvarez-Machain.* The Court's decision in the case was widely quoted. It upheld the right of foreigners to seek compensation under the statute's provisions. However, the Court urged the federal courts to interpret the statute narrowly to avoid judicial interference in foreign affairs. The judicial power should be exercised "on the understanding that the door is still ajar subject to vigilant doorkeeping, and thus open to a narrow class of international norms today."[53]

Later that year, the first procedural decision in matters of the apartheid litigations was passed down. Judge Sprizzo of the Southern District Court of New York dismissed the litigations on the grounds that aiding and abetting international law violations was not a universally accepted standard of international law.[54] The judgment did, however, grant the right to appeal, and plaintiffs appealed to the Second Circuit Court of Appeals. Yet again, Desmond Tutu, together with former TRC commissioners and committee members filed an amicus brief to the Second Circuit Court of Appeals, urging it that the District Court's decision be reversed.

In October 2007, the Second Circuit Court of Appeals reversed the lower court's dismissal. It centrally held that "a plaintiff may plead a theory of aiding and abetting liability"[55] under the statute and referred the cases back to the lower court, which offered the opportunity to file amended cases.

Only days after the Appeals Court handed down its judgment, Maduna's successor, Justice Minister Brigitte Mabandla, reiterated the South African government's position as one of an "essentially of a political nature." "We submit," she wrote, "that another country's court should not determine how ongoing political processes in South Africa should be resolved."

The amended complaints were lodged in October 2008, and the trial was supposed to be reopened in February 2009. Before that, though, the defendant companies had petitioned the US Supreme Court for an order of certiorari, asking the highest authority to hear their appeal of the October 2007 Appeals Court decision. It was a difficult moment for the plaintiffs and their supporters. The Supreme Court has the power to dismiss cases. And in this case, a dismissal could potentially jeopardize the application of the Alien Torte statute in all other pending and future cases. The outcome was different: the Court could not pass judgment for a lack of quorum of six. Four of the nine justices had to recuse themselves because they owned stock in some of the corporate defendants. The Supreme Court had no option but to uphold the decision of the Second Circuit Court of Appeals, and it referred the cases back to the District Court, where they had first been filed.

The plaintiffs' legal teams seized the opportunity to strengthen their complaints and change some crucial characteristics of the case. The Khulumani complaint underwent three substantial changes: it requested a jury trial, reduced the number of defendants from twenty-three to eight, and reformulated it as a class action suit. The latter resulted in a reduction of the number of named plaintiffs from eighty-seven to thirteen individuals.[56] Typically, class plaintiffs sue on behalf of themselves and all other individuals who are similarly situated. This meant that every South African who or whose relative had experienced torture; prolonged unlawful detention; cruel, inhuman, and degrading treatment; or extrajudicial killing was a potential plaintiff. Khulumani Support Group remained a plaintiff. The eight defendants were Barclays National Bank, Daimler AG, Ford Motor Company, Fujitsu, General Motors Corporation, IBM, Rheinmetall Group AG, and UBS.

After the detour through the US Supreme Court, the case was yet again before the Southern District Court in New York, which heard the amended complaints in February 2009. Since the first hearing, Judge Sprizzo had passed away (B. Weber 2008) and been replaced by Judge Shira Scheindlin, who had been nominated by President Clinton and was generally seen as progressive. After procedural questions had dominated for seven years, Justice Scheindlin finally issued the first substantive ruling on April 8, 2009.[57] In favor of the plaintiffs, she allowed the claims to proceed. She opened her decision with a quote from Desmond Tutu: "The truth about apartheid—about its causes and effects . . . about who was responsible for its maintenance—continue[s] to emerge. This litigation is one element of that emergence."[58]

Judge Scheindlin ordered two major changes. First, she excluded those defendants about whom it was difficult to prove that what they had done was more than "merely doing business" (i.e., banks), which reduced the defendants to Daimler, Ford, General Motors, IBM, Fujitsu, and Rheinmetall Group.[59] And second, she argued that the Khulumani organization had no standing as a plaintiff.

The plaintiffs' attorneys filed the second amended complaints based on her order. The defendant companies, however, filed yet another appeal to dismiss with the Second Circuit Court of Appeals, which heard the cases on January 15, 2010.

In September 2009, a few months after Judge Scheindlin had issued her opinion giving the go-ahead to the apartheid litigations, previously deadlocked positions fundamentally shifted. The South African government reversed its opposition. The new minister of justice, Jeff Radebe, communicated to Southern District Court that it was "now of the view that this Court is an appropriate forum to hear the remaining claims of aiding and abetting in violation of international law."[60] He also offered government's assistance to mediate a settlement.

While the decision on the apartheid litigations was pending, a case against Royal Dutch Petroleum (*Kiobel and Others v. Royal Dutch Petroleum Company and Others*) took the lead in ATS matters.[61] It came as a shock to the international human rights movement when the Second Circuit Court of Appeals, a panel of three, ruled on September 17, 2010, that companies could not be held liable for violations of international human rights law.[62] The Nigerian plaintiffs filed petition of certiorari with the US Supreme Court. Given that the application of the statute became the core issue, the Court halted all the other cases filed under the provisions of the statute. This was the first time that the

Supreme Court was expected to substantially address the question of corporate liability under the statute.[63]

The Supreme Court, however, dominated by conservative judges, went on to question the ATS as a whole by rehearing the case in the next term. It called on the parties to submit supplemental briefs on whether the statute allows federal courts to hear lawsuits alleging violations of international law that occur outside the United States that do not involve US citizens. The Court's conservative judges seemed ready to set a precedent on extraterritoriality. On April 17, 2013, the Court affirmed the lower court's dismissal of the case. It restricted the application of the ATS in cases alleging violations outside the United States. It referred to extraterritoriality in all its dimensions: whether the alleged tort occurred on American soil, whether the defendant was an American national, and whether the defendant's conduct substantially and adversely affected an important American national interest.[64] In April 2013, the US Supreme Court ruled in *Kiobel v. Royal Dutch Petroleum* against the extraterritorial application of the statute. As a result of the Court's ruling, Judge Scheindlin in the Southern District Court of New York granted the plaintiffs in the apartheid litigations the motion to hold corporations liable under the statute but excluded non-US companies (leaving IBM and Ford). The US lawyers filed an updated complaint, which Scheindlin dismissed on August 28, 2014, on the grounds that the plaintiffs had not shown sufficient connection with the United States.

On January 30, 2015, following the recent decision by the US Court of Appeals for the Second Circuit in *Mastafa v. Chevron Corp.*, the South African plaintiffs submitted a brief to the court appealing the dismissal of the apartheid case. On July 27, 2015, the court affirmed Scheindlin's order of August 28, 2014, on the grounds that "[k]nowledge of or complicity in the perpetration of a crime under the law of nations (customary international law)—absent evidence that a defendant purposefully facilitated the commission of that crime—is insufficient to establish a claim of aiding and abetting liability under the ATS."[65] The plaintiffs' legal teams are considering petitioning the US Supreme Court for an order of certiorari.

In sum, in *Sosa v. Alvarez-Machain*, in 2004, the US Supreme Court upheld the constitutionality of the ATS. In *Kiobel v. Royal Dutch Petroleum*, in 2010, the Second Circuit Court of Appeals held that only individuals—not companies—could be sued under the statute. This, together with the Supreme Court's decision in *Citizens United v. Federal Election Commission*, in 2010, in which the definition of corporate personhood was expanded, gives the impression that companies mainly have rights, and very few responsibilities (cf. Baxi 2012; Weiss 2012).

"How Will Society Facilitate Their Healing?"

The TRC was consequential for the standing of apartheid-era victims in its aftermath and up to today. Because of its strong emphasis on victimhood, which it deemed necessary for successful nation-building, the TRC facilitated the formalization (albeit incomplete) of victimhood in post-apartheid South Africa. To victims, however, the limitations of the commission's work and the state's weak follow-up weigh heavier than the state's assurance that the past was dealt with by the TRC. As a consequence of its work, the commission enabled alternative interpretations of victimhood and made it possible for victims to claim inclusion in processes following from the TRC.

For many victims, the apartheid litigations were a test case of the South African government's political stance. Nelson Mandela's policies had already been criticized by many as too friendly to business and not focused enough on redistribution. During Thabo Mbeki's administration, this trend was radicalized. Neoliberal politics were often, however, still clad in redistributive rhetoric. The litigations against international companies pressed the government to take a visible position on the matter. The Mbeki administration expressed its unambiguous support for the business community, growth, and competitiveness by siding with the defendants in the litigations, the corporations. For many victims, this marked a turning point, eroding the government's credibility and their belief that the administration's intention to better the lives of the millions of South Africans still struggling under the legacy of apartheid was genuine. The government's opposition to the litigations invited criticism by civil society organizations and parts of their constituency. Criticism previously held in check by patience and goodwill toward the postconflict regime was henceforth uttered more aggressively.

For the Khulumani Support Group, the increasing attention on the apartheid litigation by the international human rights community meant that it had to professionalize its structures to a degree that allowed speedy communication with the media and other interested parties. The group's number of national leaders remained small, and this has not been contested by the provincial executives. However, the shift in the management from charismatic leaders to people with administrative skills in communication and program building is clear. The unique position Khulumani occupies as a membership organization has given it a certain independence; at the same time, it has subjected the leadership to severe criticism for the lack of accountability in its decision-making processes.

Most importantly, what kept Khulumani going were the local initiatives of individual members and groups. The local leadership had to deal with accusations of exclusion from "normal" members; they had to communicate to members the highly technical developments in the US courts; and they had to roll out programs for the many communities with literally no funding, and balance the hopes and the realities of embodied harm in their fellow members' and their own lives.

In July 1994, while the draft bill for the establishment of a truth commission was still being debated, Mamphela Ramphele presented a paper on the commission at a conference. She asked:

> There are countless ordinary South Africans whose human rights have been violated as a direct consequence of apartheid or conquest—abused youth and children, abused wives who abuse those children, abused workers who abuse their wives, their children and their fellow workers. There are also abused activists who in turn abuse members of their community. How will society facilitate their healing? (Ramphele 1995, 35–36)

It is to the victims and their experiences that I turn in the rest of this book. In this politicized and partly legalized environment, how do victims cope; what paths do they pursue to move away from their victimhood, and what difficulties do they face? The chapters that follow include stories of real people intended to bring the reader as close as possible to the lived experience of victims and victimhood. Chapter 2 is in some ways still a technical discussion of the effects of the law and institutions of law. While it looks at how courts in both South Africa and the United States grapple with structural injury, the chapter's main focus is on the social effects of such practice on the plaintiffs. Chapters 3 to 5 continue and deepen the ethnographic exploration into victims' everyday lives.

Figure 1. Monthly meeting of Khulumani, Community House, Salt River, Western Cape, April 2010

Figure 2. March organized by the Right2Know campaign, Cape Town, Western Cape, October 2010

Figure 3. Khulumani meeting in Ashton, Western Cape, November 2009

Figure 4. Charles Abrahams at the Western Cape High Court after the bread cases hearing, Cape Town, Western Cape, November 2010

Figure 5. Brian Mphahlele and Sindiswa Nunu, Khulumani office, Salt River, Western Cape, September 2009

Figure 6. Ethel Khali in front of her house, Philippi, Western Cape, May 2009

Chapter 2

Reparation, Representation, and Class Actions

CLAIMING REDRESS FOR structural human rights violations is often more difficult than proving the harm done on an individual basis by individual perpetrators. The large number of people affected and the differences between them in the degree of harm suffered make structural violations difficult to prove and more difficult to redress. How do apartheid victims deal with this tension between individuality and collectivity?[1] How does the balance they find in their own lives, and in political activism, change once they use legal avenues to achieve their aims? And how do courts deal with the dogma of individualizing injury when collective complaints such as class actions are brought before them?

These questions form the core of this chapter. I want to begin with one of many accounts I heard of experiences that left people injured. We should never forget that problems of redress start here, in the experiences of violence, not in the courtrooms.

As a major part of my research, I spent time with women in Philippi Township, a suburb on the fringes of Cape Town. I describe here a somewhat unusual encounter with Beauty Notle Kotta in 2009. It was unusual in the sense that she had literally commanded me to come and visit her in her house. She had come to know about me through fellow members of the Khulumani Support Group and requested that I, together with two other members of the Khulumani, come and see her, too. These two other members can broadly tell the same life story, certainly in relation to dates and places but also to experiences.

Ms. Kotta is in her sixties and the head of a six-person household consisting of herself, her son, and her daughter, who is the mother of three children.[2]

They live in very poor conditions in a standard two-room RDP house, built in the 1990s with subsidies from the South African government as part of the Reconstruction and Development Programme. Ms. Kotta's family comes from Komga, in the former homeland Transkei, a two-day bus ride from Cape Town. Although she lives at the margin of a city, and in the densely populated township of Philippi, Komga remains her home; it is where the family meets, the deceased are buried, and where she hopes to return to live as soon as she can afford it. She had heard about Khulumani from people whom she knew from the struggle in Nyanga Bush.

Nyanga Bush, which is just across the road from today's Philippi Township, where Ms. Kotta lives now, was an informal squatter settlement that the police frequently raided and eventually destroyed in 1986. Nyanga Bush was part of Crossroads, the large, low-lying area outside Cape Town that was home to many settlements and satellite camps (such as Nyanga Bush), which in the early 1980s became a central locale of organized resistance to the state (J. Cole 1987). In these squatter communities, "nonwhites" settled and continuously fought for services and tenure security; against the destruction of houses and makeshift shelters, forced removals, and generally against state authorities wanting to stop what they considered an illegal influx of people into urban areas. In this context, many violent and deadly encounters between the police, local authorities, the youth, the United Democratic Front (UDF), and the *witdoeke* took place (for this complex history, see J. Cole 1987, 2012). Witdoeke were vigilantes who wore bits of white cloth (hence the name "witdoeke") to identify themselves, and who collaborated with the security forces in often opaque ways.

In May 1986, one particular raid by the witdoeke—carried out hand in hand with the police—commonly known as "the fires of 1986," resulted in the destruction of the satellite communities (Portland Cement, Nyanga Bush, and Nyanga Extension) and in the death of Ms. Kotta's elder son.

On the day of my visit, we sat down, and I played a bit with her granddaughter, who was learning to walk. Not much time had passed, though, before Ms. Kotta started telling me about the fires of 1986. She spoke with raw memories of the injuries sustained, but she also made claims. (I have transcribed her words exactly as she spoke them, and I hope the reader will, as I do, feel the grief and the power behind her unorthodox use of English.) Ms. Kotta first spoke about the destruction of the Nyanga Bush:

Not right. That time, they [were] burning out. You believe, you can see the head of people throw away there. The bodies here. The head is there. Sometimes you see the leg. Sometimes you see the . . . True, man! Was very bad. Frightened. If you go, you see, this is a person. They didn't bury [him/her]. The head of people, the head of people, the legs, the body. Other people, the one they saw, we saw, was burning out. You can't see who is this. Burning out! Black!! You see the legs there. You don't know who is this. Yoh. Yoh. . . . It was not nice, very bad . . . We're running, we're running.

She also spoke about how she tried to save some belongings,

that Monica [her daughter], . . . I was brought on my back [I carried my child on my back]. She was five years of age. . . . I went there to try, I must get my things inside. I saw at that time, it was afternoon like this . . . I go little bit, I must get some things. Because I've got nothing. Ehwe. . . . When I went there, it was late, it was late like sometime seven o'clock. . . . In the evening. I try to take my things. They come, these men, I think—like next door. I am here, my house is here. The men got witdoek and all people they fighting. I couldn't . . . I run. I run with my child. I was put on my back. I don't know who is the other children in the fight there, the boys. You see. You see. The government said we must move there [to Khayelitsha]. . . . We didn't buried, put away there. We have no time. If you go there, the people they can kill you. They kill you. They don't mind. . . . Otherwise you going to death. We running, we running. Yoh.

And then she turned to her son's death:

Was burning there. And the Boer was take the dog, close, can't get out. Was burning there. They didn't buried. And too, my son, too, my son. I had two son. But I have one son now. I had two son.

Before I left her house that day, she looked for an old piece of paper and showed it to me. "You see, I have two witnesses, you see. I have their ID numbers. They know what happened, they were there."

Ms. Kotta was not present when her son passed away in 1986. He burned to death in the Nyanga Bush settlement, when the residents were forcibly removed as part of the "clean-up" of the Crossroads Complex and KTC, a mushrooming informal settlement that was considered a national security threat by the State Security Council. The 12-year-old boy did not survive the attacks by the police, who worked hand in hand with their "helpers" from the communities, the vigilante groups witdoeke. Ms. Kotta's younger son Laurence fled to the Zolani Centre in Nyanga, where hundreds of others who had been dispossessed and displaced overnight had gone, hoping to find shelter with another estimated 20,000 to 30,000 refugees. Today, Laurence lives with his mother in Philippi. In Philippi, many people built provisional shelters in what was then bush and forest. During my visit in 2009, Laurence seemed restless and did not join us. "My son was frightened." Ms. Kotta explained. "Not right in there [in his mind] since he saw . . . he saw . . . He got a picture [of the fires of 1986], you know."[3]

Ms. Kotta bore witness that day in a raw, rapid-fire, and breathless manner. Her words vacillated between euphemism and the "unheard." She repeated herself often, stuttered, and seemed to fall back on exclamations that "it was so bad." She had bravely presented the events before in public, for example in a healing workshop sponsored by a human rights group.[4] However, this had not diminished the embodied knowledge of the event that she carries with her every day, and each time she speaks about it, she is as unprotected as ever.

Many parts of her testimony expressed shared suffering. In the settlement raids and in the fights between witdoeke, security forces, and the community members, women and children were often not singled out as targets of violence, but became targets nonetheless (J. Cole 1987). The destruction of lives, belongings, and housing was often part of a broader government strategy to frighten communities and demonstrate its power. She spoke of the "us" dimension ("events as they happened to 'us'"; Jackson 2004, 71). However, Ms. Kotta singled herself out when she described how her son died or how she tried to save some of her belongings. These are experiences she has to cope with herself that do not necessarily socialize. By the same token, these painful experiences are those for which she can claim specific violations carried out against her person.

Her testimony to me bore traces of the prior coaching she had received about how to communicate her experiences. She produced evidence she might not include in an everyday account: the piece of paper with ID numbers of two persons who she said were eyewitnesses to her son's death. It was both a kind of a written record and a referral to the words of others, which should serve as objective external testimony to the violations. She produced this evidence in a non-legal setting, in a situation she believed was conducive to expressing her grief and making her claims heard. I came to represent to her a person who wanted evidence.

Evidence, of course, is one of the major elements of legal claim-making. Being able to produce evidence of injury should be enough to prove a claim of victim status in the realm of the law. Of course, Ms. Kotta's prime interest was not in conforming to a legalized discourse; she wanted to relate her experiences in a way that would be legible to a relative outsider. She used her understanding of legal logic in order to make her victimhood legible to me. To do so, she had to differentiate between the us-dimension of generalized suffering, on the one hand, and the *specific* experiences that she can claim as wrongs committed against her directly, on the other. To be legible as a victim, she had to differentiate her own experiences from those of the others.

Individuation

Drawing on this encounter, I want to explore the notion of *individuation*. Individuation (from the Latin *individuare*) is a process that changes a person's relation to others by singling her or him out as different. I use the term *individuation* in this social sense, and refer to a process that distinguishes a person from others of the same kind.[5]

This process is a possible effect of a discursive formation onto forms of sociality. I explore individuation in relation to a very dominant discourse in apartheid victims' lives—the law—and offer an analysis of how legal thinking affects those who appeal to the law. To use Bourdieu's (1986) term, I trace the "force of the law" on the subjectivities of those who stand before courts.

Out of technical, procedural, and legalistic notions, the law needs to personalize injury—that is, to pin down general injury to one single person's injury. Even in class actions, the law needs representatives for the proposed classes (of injuries), which the courts treat as if they were individual cases.[6] In its search for a touchstone to test the relevant questions, the law needs to single out actions and to differentiate the suffered harm even if the aim is to adjudicate structural (i.e., not personal) violations.

This personalization of injury runs counter to the intentions of many plaintiffs who bring class actions or join a class of plaintiffs. Generally—and especially in the human rights cases this book focuses on—class actions offer the opportunity to make structural violations actionable. Not each specific injury to every harmed person has to be alleged in a separate case; the class comprises those harmed in similar ways by the same agents. Class actions hence point to a context where plaintiffs want to highlight their similarities and present their injuries in a united manner. The whole notion of a class rests on the assumption of *shared* structural injustices. Class actions are thus the prime example of efforts to address general harm in general terms.

We see this tension between structural and individual harm in Ms. Kotta's testimony. In order to understand the efficacy of that testimony, we need to explore the context in which it took place. Every utterance around apartheid-era victimhood necessarily takes place in an environment infused with dominant victims' subject positions. It is an environment, as I described in the previous chapters, in which victims are not free to define and live their victimhood because the subject position has been politicized and partly legalized.

Making One's Victimhood Legible

In post-apartheid South Africa, witnessing (giving testimony) has always been fraught with political and structural subtext. When victims spoke before the commission, they were part of a religious-reconciliatory and nation-building endeavor set in place by the first post-apartheid government of President Mandela (Wilson 2001); but from the victims' own perspective, testifying was both an act of political and legal accusation against the agents of the apartheid regime and a positioning in the new South Africa. As much as the TRC has rightly been accused of depoliticizing apartheid and its legacy in the interest of reconciliation, giving testimony was never an apolitical act (cf. Ross 2002).

But we not only need to understand the context a person testifies in but also the positionality of the witness within that specific context. A person who testifies to the effects of structural injuries after suffering violations is a "witness." In Latin, the modern notion of "the witness" comprises two designated roles.[7] A *superstes* is a person who has experience a specific event herself, a survivor. She guarantees the credibility of the testimony with the authenticity of her experiences. A *testis* is a third party who stands between two parties in an argument or a judicial process and reports on an event that she only observed but was not involved in. A testis establishes credibility through facts and the coherence of a testimony, contrary to a superstes who establishes credibility primarily through her personhood.[8]

The commission gave victims the opportunity to present their personal subjectivity by testifying. They thus spoke as *superstites*. At the same time, many victims spoke for their late or disappeared family members, and thus simultaneously bore witness as superstites, aggrieved by a persons' death, and as *testes*. They became testifiers to what had happened under the apartheid regime in a more general sense. Some of their (and the perpetrators') testimonies now constitute the seven-volume final report of the TRC, completed in 2003, which remains the most expansive publicly available accounting of the crimes committed during the apartheid era.[9] In short, knowledge of life under the apartheid regime was produced through the accounts of victims. "Expert witnesses," such as historians, remained strikingly absent from the hearings and during the process of writing up the report (cf. Posel and Simpson 2003).

Apartheid-era victims thus assumed a double subjectivity: as testes and as superstites.[10] In both roles, their accounts became a part of the official discourse on victimhood. This production of a double-witness subject position through the workings of the TRC is important to understanding the position from which victims speak in the aftermath of the commission's work.

Victims such as Ms. Kotta speak from their irrevocable position as superstites. For them, giving testimony requires considerable effort and comes with uncertainty about whether or not they will be heard. Victims themselves can only attempt to speak from their embodied knowledge and try out their political victim subjectivity in some rare settings. This often remains a contingent undertaking, and their own personhood and experienced injury always play in it.

Victims live in an ambivalent and fluctuant environment. Success follows failure; a sudden surge of publicity on TV or in the newspapers follows several months of little coverage of their concerns. Most members necessarily rely on the executive organs of Khulumani to communicate their concerns to a broader public, nationally and internationally. As a result of this, victims are irrevocably trapped between their experienced victimhood and the necessity of regularly articulating their victimhood. One manner of articulation is offered by the legal view on their victimhood. This is the realm in which Khulumani has been engaging with its various court cases (see chapter 1) and which the TRC had advocated by virtue of assigning victim status to some survivors and not to others.

It is in this light that I read Ms. Kotta's testimony: she referred to legal logics of victimhood and, by necessity, had to distinguish *her* victimhood from that of others' and to objectify her personal suffering by taking the position of a testis. The moment of shared memories of suffering produced new sociability between her and her listeners; simultaneously, the need to articulate her victimhood as testis resulted in individuation. This legal logic played out in a highly mediated political and societal environment that resulted in a legalization of her personhood.

The poststructuralists focused on the position of the superstes and reflected on the question whether testimony to the Holocaust is even possible (Felman and Laub 1992). They drew our attention to what it means for victims to bear witness to a public and sensitized scholars on their own positions and obligations as witnesses of such processes. On the other hand, critical work on the practices of governments and on civil society's strategies to render unheard voices public has focused on the production and representation of victims' voices in a globalized context (Keck and Sikkink 1998; cf. Niezen 2010). This latter subject position has many similarities with the third-party testis because her voice is rendered professional and detached in order for her to testify to broader atrocities or grievances.

Witnessing is both an effort to overcome silences *and* claim-making. I see both forms of witnessing as interrelated, even though one or the other becomes more prominent in specific moments. To understand their relation, the shift in subjectivities from a state of intimate and personal embodied experiences to the public articulation thereof is particularly revealing, but it can only be analyzed if we conceptualize witnessing as a *process*, not as a position. Givoni (2011, 20) suggests that we "re-examine witnessing as an ethical laboratory in which selves are made and re-made in reflective, contested, free but not completely haphazard ways." In other words, witness subjectivity, like any other form of subjectivity, is adopted and learned in contingent circumstances and ways. One becomes a witness in an environment of dominant political and legal ideas about who qualifies as a credible witness and who does not.

The law individuates, but it is not easy to see how it accomplishes that. It certainly does not do so directly; one cannot ascribe agency to the law. The law's individuation is produced in situations of contact in which victims relate to a legal logic in order to make their claims readable. These situations of contact are not neutral, and legal and political discourses influence the expectations people have about what listeners expect from them. Ms. Kotta's referral to evidentiary-based testimony was produced in a specific political environment that has turned the law into an important point of reference for proving one's victimhood. In other words, legalization of subjectivities should be viewed *as a practice*; shifts in subjectivities result from an everyday engagement with the legal process.

Having looked at how victims who are plaintiffs in the class actions relate their experiences to the logic of the law in an everyday setting, I now turn to examining how the courts that hear class action cases relate to victims' experiences. I thus employ a *vue croisée* by looking at courts' and victims' respective attempts to take on each other's perspective on the law. The ways the respective parties attempt to relate to the other's view of the law tells us something about processes of rapprochement, about the irreconcilability of standpoints, and also about power hierarchies (Conley and O'Barr 1990; Merry 1990).

Victims' Personhood in US Courts

If persons who have fallen victim to crime, as tens of thousands have, feel the need to articulate their individual victimhood by way of producing evidence and singling themselves out, how do courts then deal with the individual injury resulting from general forms of violence? In what follows, I look at a single hearing in a consolidated case, the South African Apartheid Litigation. The Apartheid Litigation consists of two cases that were lumped together in 2008 and that were, at that point, reformulated into class actions: *Khulumani et al. v. Barclays National Bank et al.* and *Lungisile Ntsebeza et al. v. Daimler Chrysler Corporation et al.* Both cases allege companies' complicity in apartheid era crimes by aiding and abetting the security forces of the apartheid regime; the plaintiffs are apartheid victims (see chapter 1). Looking at a single hearing, I point out the moment when attorneys and the judge attempt to transcend the notion of the legal plaintiff in favor of an idea of the plaintiff (who is, by definition, a witness) in her or his personhood. This effort of the judicial mind is a shift to a superstes—that is, a shift of attention from legal subjectivity to a person with specific experiences. It is a rapprochement between the lifeworld of the plaintiff and the experiential and existential side of injury and claim-making.

The South African Apartheid Litigation comprises civil lawsuits about the liability of corporations that did business in South Africa during apartheid for perpetrating gross human rights violations. Nonetheless, those who claim victim status for the alleged violations are prominently present; their individual experiences of subjection to violations are part of the argument and the evidence. Unlike in parts of the international criminal justice system, where victims are limited to witness status, and are not granted plaintiff status,[11] these civil cases rely on plaintiffs' testimony for the compilation of the complaints and on their victim status for the institution of the lawsuits. As we will see, the plaintiffs are a source for argumentation, even with respect to procedural questions, for the attorneys on both sides.

On February 26, 2009, Judge Shira Scheindlin heard the South African Apartheid Litigation that was before the Southern District Court of New York.[12] She heard oral arguments from the attorneys of both the defendants and the plaintiffs. The purpose of the hearing was to consider the defendants' motion to dismiss the claims. This motion was a reaction to the amended claims filed by the plaintiffs on October 24, 2008.[13] The major change in the amended complaints was that they had been re-formulated as class action suits. At the time of the hearing, the classes had not been certified by the judge. The proposed class consisted of groups of individuals that had suffered a common injury (extrajudicial killing, torture, detention, and cruel treatment).[14]

In the two-hour hearing, the term *plaintiffs* included the plaintiffs and the plaintiffs' attorneys. There was no distinction between the actual individuals alleging violations and the persons acting on their behalf in court. This (usual) way of semantically consolidating the plaintiffs and the plaintiffs' attorneys may explain why the plaintiffs themselves for the most part did not enter into the hearing as persons. The consolidation only collapsed toward the end of the hearing, when the defendants had the chance to reply. Francis P. Barron, an attorney for the defendant companies, asked for permission to raise a topic of concern: the consideration of adjudicating the litigations for practical reasons, given the "huge and amorphous nature of this case" and "the distance of those events [injuries committed by the apartheid regime] from our shores, 8,000 miles."[15] He pressed the Court to consider

> the impossibility of doing reasonable discovery, the volume of materials that this Court would have to review, and keep in mind that each of the plaintiffs, of which there are many, and each of the punitive members of the class would have his own individual story, or her own individual story, taking place at different times in different places in South Africa with different witnesses, different facts.[16]

In US civil law, discovery is a pre-trial phase in which each side requests documents and various other forms of evidence from the other side. In the cases discussed here, this means the plaintiffs' attorneys would, for the first time, have access to the defendant companies' archives. It would also mean that the defendants' attorneys could request any kind of evidence from the plaintiffs' side.

Mr. Barron cited the high number of potential plaintiffs in arguing that the claims be dismissed. He referred to the complexity of individual lives and violations all packed into one class action suit. In doing so, he unveiled the individuality of the plaintiffs, however limited. Willingly or not, Mr. Barron introduced a perspective that had been totally absent up to this stage of the hearing. When his turn came, Mr. Hoffman, plaintiffs' attorney in the second apartheid litigation, drew on the plaintiffs' visibility as it had been partly established by the other party: "The thing is even if the court didn't certify the class, there are people with real claims in front of the Court that have come forward and deserve to have their rights adjudicated."[17]

Mr. Hoffman pointed out the fact that dismissing the case would not resolve the problems or put an end to the claims. He attempted to bring the plaintiffs into the court and into the judge's reality by visualizing their personhoods, bringing them—rhetorically—across the Atlantic and from the Southern to the Northern Hemispheres, and putting them right in front of the court. Hence, for the plaintiffs' attorneys, the plaintiffs' individuality within their numbers served as a plea for recognition and attention.

There is a second instance in which the plaintiffs were granted recognition as persons. Another of the defendants' attorneys, David Greenwald, cited a principle of limitation, the time bar: "Just to state the obvious, this case concerns events that occurred 15, 20, 30 years ago." He presented a chart (which the judge later commended as "the very beautiful—very beautiful chart he has here") and argued that the cases had not been brought within ten years after the end of apartheid and had therefore been filed too late:[18]

> There is a distinct difference between when Mandela was elected and when apartheid ended. Indeed, it was so distinct that in 1991, the first President Bush lifted the sanctions that President Reagan had imposed under the CAAA [Comprehensive Anti-Apartheid Act].[19]

Because the cases had first been filed in 2002, the defendants argued that they had not been filed within ten years after what was, according to their reading of history, the end of apartheid. This claim provoked the judge to ponder the plaintiffs' lived realities in the early 1990s. In her response, she talked about the lifeworlds of the plaintiffs:

> The fact that our [US] government became comfortable enough to lift restrictions doesn't tell me what it was like to be a black person living in South Africa

in 1991 who was contemplating suing some South African companies or sub-
sidiaries of national companies that do business in South Africa claiming that
they were collaborating in the apartheid system when the control was still in the
hands of the very white politicians who had enforced the system. So there is a
disconnect here between our government lifting a restriction on certain things
and what it would have been like to be a plaintiff.[20]

The judge refused to assume that there was correlation between a foreign
policy move by the US administration in 1991 and the lived reality of black
South Africans between the time of Nelson Mandela's release from prison in
1990 and the first democratic elections in 1994. Mr. Greenwald allowed that
Judge Scheindlin could think what she wanted, despite her "highly questionable historical assumption," and then played his second trump card. He insisted
that his team's argument that even if plaintiffs qualified for "equitable tolling"
in general, according to precedent cases, they still had to explain the passage
of eight years between the end of apartheid and the filing of the lawsuits. In
other words, the judge summarized for him, "what did they do for eight years?"
The question at stake was thus: even if plaintiffs filed their complaints within
the ten-year limitations period (i.e., 1994–2004), there was only so much time
plaintiffs should need to file a suit. According to Mr. Greenwald, "It would be
inequitable to apply [equitable tolling] in every case";[21] the judge has discretion
not to apply the full toll, especially at the motion-to-dismiss stage. This left the
judge pensive:

> Can I begin to explore when is the timing for when they could have brought
> the action, whether it's '90 or '94, would that not take some discovery. Because
> I really don't know what it was to be a claimant in South Africa during those
> four years.[22]

Later in the hearing, Mr. Hausfeld, the attorney in the Khulumani case, was
asked to take a stand on the judge's question, "why is '94 the trigger date?" He
replied that that year was the "first practical time when South Africa had its own
government not associated with apartheid." In the early 1990s, the country was
still under control of the white South African government. The judge pushed to
the "eight years of doing nothing" question. Mr. Hausfeld's answer was a vague
reference to the situation in South Africa, which at the time was experiencing
"innumerable issues and challenges." The judge was quick to tell him what his
argument should be: "Maybe the better answer is the TRC process," adding "[s]o

now I'm the judge and the lawyer?" Mr. Hausfeld emphasized that the TRC process had only ended in 2003, when the final report was issued.[23]

Both legal parties were careful not to place too much emphasis on the aspect of lived experience, despite the judge's desire to understand what it was like to live as a victim in South Africa in the early 1990s. She left the hearing having gained little (new) knowledge of the slowly growing global awareness of corporate accountability in the mid- and late-1990s. She had heard little about what it meant and means politically for a South African to stand up as a "victim" of human rights violation in the context of the Mbeki administration. The hearing tells us little about the slow formation of a victims' support group organization across the country and the formation of a victims' subject position in the time the TRC was operating and after.

In summary, the notion of the victim is strikingly absent from the hearing. If they are present at all, the plaintiffs figure in the arguments for the lawyers of both sides: as proof of the unmanageability of (or as an unfortunate obstacle to overcome in) the class action suit, or as being justified (or not) in not submitting the case for several years after 1990 or 1994, respectively, depending on the viewpoint. Even if to institute the complaints and in the subsequent hearings, the applicants have to prove that they experienced an injury on an individualized basis and individuality is an argument for the unmanageability of big class actions, class actions do not further the visibility of the individual plaintiffs. An astute judge may make a difference by inquiring into the plaintiffs' lifeworlds; but the procedure generally does not allow for this kind of inquiry, nor are attorneys particularly prepared to provide such information.[24]

In what follows, I introduce another class action through which I was able to directly trace the effects of such legal personification—resulting in *social individuation*.

Class Action in South Africa: "A Strange Animal"

Roughly two years after the hearing in the US District Court, in 2010, similar debates took place in the Western Cape High Court in Cape Town. The issues in this hearing were whether companies had a responsibility to prevent the infringement of socioeconomic rights and the certification of a class in a common law system. There are similarities between the apartheid litigations in the United States and this South African domestic case: both allege structural violations of human or constitutional rights; in both, claimants chose to pursue a class action lawsuit. The Khulumani Support Group is involved in both, and now Charles Abrahams, from the law firm Abrahams Kiewitz Attorneys, legal adviser to the attorneys in the US litigation, acts as the attorney for the South African claimants.

The cases allege the infringement of basic socioeconomic rights by three South African bread companies (Pioneer Foods, Tiger Consumer Brands, and Premier Foods). The plaintiffs are consumers (first case) and distributers (second case) of bread. This is only the second class action to be filed in South Africa, and the first ever of this kind (seeking actual damages for open classes of victims). The discussions in court reveal the court's deep suspicion and the defendants' vehement rejection of an instrument that is mainly promoted in the federal judiciaries. The hearing also reveals how a South African court grappled with the question of corporate liability for the infringement of constitutional rights. Unlike in the Apartheid Litigation hearing, the certification of the class of consumers was also at stake in this hearing. It is this context that allows me to further problematize the tension between personalization of harm as demanded by the law and allegations of structural violations as brought forth by applicants in a class action.

The cases followed the South African Competition Commission's findings in 2006 that the three giant companies had participated in a cartel that was fixing the price of bread. The Commission had handed down administrative penalties, but consumers and the companies' distributors had not been compensated. Against this background, the Abrahams Kiewitz Attorneys law firm, together with the plaintiffs, decided to file two distinct cases. The plaintiffs of the first class action, the *Consumers Case* (*Children's Resource Centre Trust and Others v. Pioneer Foods Ltd and Others*), are civil society organizations (Children's Resources Centre, Black Sash, Congress of South African Trade Unions [COSATU] in Western Cape, and the National Consumer Forum) and the individual bread consumers (Tasneem Bassier, Brian Mphahlele, Trevor Benjamin, Nomthandazo Mvana, and Farreed Albertus). It seeks compensation on behalf of similarly situated consumers in the Western Cape province. The plaintiffs of the second case, *Mukaddam v. Pioneer Foods Ltd. and Others*, are distributors.

The cases were first heard in the Western Cape High Court in November 2010 on an urgent basis due to prescription. The applicants were seeking permission for the class representatives to stand for the classes. Given the lack of precedent cases, they were also asking the court whether the classes had to be certified before or after the actual institution of the cases. Acting Judge van Zyl heard the cases on November 23 and 25. I was present on both days.

The courtroom was visually segmented. The applicants, their lawyers, interns, and supporters were non-whites; whereas the respondents, including their interns, were exclusively white and male. The disparities in who represented which community and interest group were thus very apparent. The judge, as well, was white and male. The visuality of such a transitional set-up, which testified to the legacy of segmentation in the professions involved, was amplified by the issue at stake: the infringement on the basic right to sufficient nutrition; a connection I will return to later.

The judge opened the first day of the hearing with a question that was symptomatic of both the societal representation in the courtroom and the intricacies of the class notion the court was trying to come to terms with. "I am a consumer," he said. "I live in the Western Cape. Can I hear this matter?" The judge raised the issue that troubled him most: how could he certify a class of consumers he thought was too loosely demarcated, if at all, and of which he would unwillingly form a part. He raised it as a conflict of interest question. The judge and the respondents spent a good hour on the topic of the "absurdity" of anyone being a plaintiff in the case that was about eating bread and living in the Western Cape. But, though unarticulated at first, it was clear to everyone that the *Consumers Case* had a strong poverty component. Only slowly did it become clear that the applicants were not merely alleging that the companies overcharged consumers, but also that this was an infringement of basic rights defined South Africa's bill of rights. The so-called positive obligation of the state to provide access to the socioeconomic rights guaranteed in the Constitution, such as the right of access to housing, had been established by the Constitutional Court in such prominent decisions in the *Grootboom* and the *Treatment Action Campaign* cases.[25] In the bread cases, the negative obligation not to prevent or to impair existing access to adequate nutrition was at stake. "There is a negative content to socioeconomic rights," attorney Renata Williams, the advocate for the applicants, insisted, referring to sections 27.1b and 28.1c[26] of the Constitution and arguing that these negative obligations applied not only to the state but also to private persons, such as companies.

In his response, attorney for the first respondent, McNally, vehemently challenged this assertion: "Socioeconomic rights are asking the state, not private companies." This caused a few of the supporters and the applicant plaintiffs present to shout out, breaking what was dead silence throughout most of the hearing. McNally was referring to the progressive realization standard the Constitutional Court had established (i.e., that rights have to be realized over time and that the progress toward full realization is dependent on the availability of resources), as opposed to a measured guarantee (say, a liter of water a day per person) in light of the transitional process.

> If this [progressive realization as opposed to measured guarantee] is so for the state, how can you possibly elevate this to the duty of a private company? . . . We only have a vertical application, citizen-state, but no horizontal application. . . .
>
> You can't come to the court and allege the infringement of these rights by a private company. . . . The duty [to guarantee the noninfringement of these rights] is and always remains with the state.

At one stage of the hearing, the judge put numbers to the allegations, asking, "If I pay 50 cents too much [for a loaf of bread], does this infringe my rights?" The attorney for the first respondent replied: "The fact that the bread was maybe 50 cents too high does not suggest at all that the rights were infringed . . . It is not enough to say that people might have to live below the bread-line." The applicants brought forth their estimate that 50 percent of the population had been affected. "This needs to be proven!" McNally contended. "Numerosity," he fulminated, "it can only be in America that they came up with this term!" Indeed, it is necessary to show that the affected parties are too numerous for single suits to be effective.[27]

On the second day of the hearing, the defendants played out the argument of the "foreignness" of a class action more aggressively. The judge also communicated his lack of familiarity with class actions. A class action "is almost a foreign animal—to me it certainly is. . . . There are no rules to guide us." To establish the legal grounds for a class action, the applicants cited general application of class actions in such jurisdictions as Canada and the United States, in conjunction with section 38c of the South African Constitution.[28] The respondents said that foreign law could not be used to weigh the use of class action in South Africa.

The judge asked the respondents why they thought he could not consult foreign law to interpret section 38c of the South African Constitution. The third respondent argued: "Common law says that there is no such animal as class action" and advised the court to "be very careful not to import foreign federal law. . . . That's my submission: be wary!"

Another attorney for the defendants said: "It is not a proper case. . . . What is the class? You don't get an answer. . . . The class is amorphous and divergent. . . . The class is not sharing common interest in the litigation."

The judge also asked the applicants about representation: "What actions have the applicants undertaken to inform the people it represents?" Ms. Williams obviously could not claim to have informed all the thousands or millions of potential plaintiffs. "The poorest of the poor are the biggest consumers of bread," she said. She refused to narrow the class at this stage. It would be "prejudicial" to those excluded. "The constitution does not differentiate between rich and poor," Ms. Williams held, to which the judge commented: "This is an extremely unruly horse." Ms. Williams insisted that the class was neither limitless nor open-ended: "[I]it is certain individuals." The judge wondered: "Do you have to decide on each individual whether he or she forms part of the class?" Ms. Williams replied that an objective test was being applied and it would be "objectively determined who is poor and who is indigent. . . . Everyone having their section 28 right infringed." It is, she said, "poor and marginalized people of our society who usually don't have access to litigation . . . who only want to claim what the Constitution entitles them to claim."

Here the hearing veered slightly toward absurdity: the issue at stake was indeed a *class* issue. Everyone eats bread, but not everyone may be capable of imagining that higher bread prices can affect one's overall spending capacities. At one stage during the hearing, the judge phrased the class issue at stake in an unreflective manner: "If I look at the people in the court, I don't think that we [were infringed on our basic right to sufficient nutrition]." At this, Marcus Solomon, from the applicant Children's Resource Centre, who was sitting next to me, whispered aptly: "Not *these* people . . .!" It was thus not only "the class" as a legal entity that was causing such turmoil and needed clarification, but also "class" as an imaginary: what does it mean to live in such a poverty that the price of bread (a staple in the diet for many South Africans) affected what else you could afford to buy?

The *Consumers Case* addresses structural issues, such as poverty, dependency on a cheap and unhealthy staple diet, and exclusive access to the justice system. It alleges an impersonal, structural violation that affected consumers of bread on a massive scale. The ensuing injury, however, was personal and affected each and every individual who experienced difficulties because of the higher price of this staple of their diet. Some were more affected than others. Who suffered enough to qualify for redress? The law demands that those who were affected the most have to be singled out—even in class actions, where violations are structural and where it is often difficult to prove variations of harm.

What do such processes mean for the plaintiffs themselves? I spoke to the one Khulumani member who was chosen by the legal team to represent the class in the *Consumers Case*: Brian Mphahlele, who is a provincial board member of Khulumani Western Cape. When I met with him a week before the hearing, I wanted to understand what his new applicant status meant to him. He was in a bad mood and, as so many times before, was thinking about quitting Khulumani. He felt sapped by all the demands coming from the hundreds and thousands of members, and unacknowledged for his work for them and the organization. He also saw the bread case and his representative function in it in a grim light.

> BM: I can get killed for nothing! . . . I don't mean stabbed; I mean by other
>   means.
> RK: Like witchcraft?
> BM: That's it!

There was some pride, too. "They hand-picked me," he had said earlier. But he was clearly predominantly worried about what people would be projecting onto him. According to him, they would either think that he got a lot of money for being selected, or that he would be the first to receive some money if there was a settlement and would take it all for himself. He feared that people would believe the rumors of payouts and try to get what they think is their share by force. This is not necessarily an unsubstantiated fear: the provincial Khulumani office in Salt River, Cape Town, was occupied by members once before, when false rumors of payouts circulated in the communities. To date, I know of no real threats to anyone's life. More generally, there are many stories about people being killed by envious community members for "eating money" (undue enrichment) or due to sudden fortune. As Mr. Mphahlele confirmed, witchcraft is often mentioned as the means by which revenge or jealousy is executed.

An Injury to One Is an Injury to All?

For plaintiffs, the idea of a class relies on solidarity and similarity. As all people experienced the same injustices, all should be represented. A class is a class of individuals, so every person can be represented as a victim in his or her subjectivity. But it is also a class, so structural issues can be addressed without personalizing them. A normal court case (no class) dealing with structural human rights violations would unfairly single out individual injustices; this would sever the ties to other victims. In a class of victims, however, the ties between the representative and the class remain intact, and everyone shares the experience of the superstes singled out. But this personalization simultaneously threatens similarity and solidarity. Some people become more equal than others.

In a society like South Africa's, which is defined by shared structural suffering, to be singled out can only mean to have distanced oneself from the others through unfair means. The logic of the law creates a *suspicious subject position*: the victim who uses his experience to become different from other victims. Witchcraft accusations, or witchcraft fears, are the logical means to keep him from breaking rank (cf. Comaroff and Comaroff 1999; Geschiere 1997; Niehaus 2005).

The legal necessity of representation forces the representative into an impossible position: the unequal representative of a class of equals. As the representative's experience is used to testify to the experience of all others, his role becomes that of a person speaking on behalf of similar others. In the eyes of other victims, this threatens to destroy the very similarity on which his trustworthiness relied. The representative of a class becomes a testis instead of a superstes. In taking this step, he can become untrustworthy and untruthful, as he no longer only speaks for himself, but for others whose experiences are not his own. In a political environment in which claim-making is used by individuals to change their social, economic, or political status, representing a class means to become different, and class actions tend to bring about what they wanted to avoid: individuation.

But what is too individualizing for the victims when the courts look at claims based on solidarity and similarity remains too collective for the law.

In class actions, particularly discrimination cases, the defendant's lawyers often ask for "the right to present rebuttal evidence regarding its reasons for employment decisions with respect to every member of the class" (Lahav 2010, 119). Of course, it is too time-consuming to hold individual hearings for a million potential class members. Such an argument, it is hoped, demonstrates the unmanageability of the case and quickens its dismissal.

As a compromise for both defendants and plaintiffs, Lahav (2010, 123), a legal scholar, suggests that we consider the *variation* among class members; courts should hold a series of "informational bellwether hearings" by selecting a random sample of plaintiffs and holding hearings in each sample case. This statistical adjudication would reveal whether the defendant company would be capable of introducing credible rebuttal evidence in relation to each of the individuals. The court could then extrapolate the results of the sample hearings to the entire class (123–26). Crucially, for Lahav, this would also solve what she sees as a general fairness problem for the plaintiffs in a class action: some injuries are more severe than others but, typically, all the plaintiffs receive the same pro rata amount. Working with samplings, however, the strongest cases would receive the highest awards, and "similarly situated plaintiffs will in fact be treated equally" (124). Determining the variations among class members should thus be advantageous not only for the courts, helping them to get a grasp on the class, but also for the plaintiffs, who are generally discriminated against as a result of lumping their situations together by way of consolidation.[29]

Lahav's argument seems convincing; however, I suspect that this "fairness" only exists in a very technical sense. Lahav presumes that personalized justice is, per se, fairer. For her, the consolidation of plaintiffs into a class is an unfortunate procedural move, which, at least, allows us to address injustice on a grand scale. Sampling is a way of *managing* the class;[30] its prime focus is on the outcome of a case, on the amount of damage, payback, or relief the individual class member receives.[31] Sampling (which heavily draws on quantitative social sciences methodology, e.g., Mertz 2008) replicates a system of personalization that legal actions tend to create in general.

I argue that we should not consider "fairness" exclusively in terms of the monetary outcome of a case (leaving aside the fact that the majority of human rights class actions are either dismissed or settled out of court). Class actions are often pending in courts for a decade or longer, and are often accompanied by civil society activities, such as self-help or advocacy groups and fierce contestations by their own or other foreign governments. This thoroughly shapes plaintiffs' and representatives' subjectivities, as I have shown in the examples of Ms. Kotta and Mr. Mphahlele. The procedural personification of harm the law demands may result in social individuation among the plaintiffs. For plaintiffs, being "managed" in the courts affects their standing in their communities and in broader society.[32] They undergo or are forced to undergo shifts in subjectivities.

Having thus criticized a legal solution to fairness, I also have to give credit to Lahav's suggestion to consider variations of injury among a class of plaintiffs. In this chapter, I focused on the years during which cases are pending in courts. Things change, of course, once the courts decide on damages to be paid out (which is, as mentioned before, rather rare in such cases). For plaintiffs, this may bring about a new dynamic as it poses the challenge of individualized reparations; differences in seriousness of injuries sustained most likely matter and become issues of contestation. The same applies to victims' trust funds, which have recently been the outcome of some human rights cases.[33] Here, communities (however defined) become the entity for distribution of resources, and internal mechanisms for allocation have to be found.

Both the law and the victims have notions that are nonnegotiable. For the law, it is the doctrinal focus on individuality in the causal triangle *agency, action,* and *harmed*. Its agents stolidly apply this focus in civil class actions, filed with different causalities and concerns in mind from, for instance, those in criminal cases. With regard to class actions, the attorneys and justices fear the dilution of the law's focus on individuality of liability and victimhood, its preoccupation with establishing justiciability and evidence of violations.

For the plaintiffs, their nonnegotiable notions are their experiences of harm and their embodied knowledge of injustice. Although the two perspectives are not reconcilable, they depend on each other and affect each other. Plaintiffs make a hard effort to learn to relate to the dominant discourse of law, while remaining irrevocably tied to their embodied experiences. Class actions are often pending in courts for a decade or longer, and are often accompanied by civil society activities such as self-help or advocacy groups and fierce contestations by their own or other foreign governments. This thoroughly shapes plaintiffs' and representatives' subjectivities, as I have shown in the examples of Ms. Kotta and Mr. Mphahlele. The law, in contrast, is relatively inert against changes of perspectives or priorities (for instance, individual to classes, corporate legal person to a fully liable person) and can always rely on procedure and tradition. It is, ultimately, the plaintiffs who want their concerns to be considered by the courts. The proceedings are given. This is why, to a certain extent, legalization happens when plaintiffs attempt to bridge the gap between the law and their experiences.

In that way, experiences in apartheid South Africa are replicated by the legal system. Meierhenrich (2008) argues that the law created a continuity of common language and discourse in the history of South Africa beyond 1994. My study suggests that it also created a continuity of inequalities (Baxi 2000).

I have described these processes of individuation and representations for victims as *civil plaintiffs*, but we see the same relationship at work elsewhere, too. Years before the apartheid litigations and the bread cases were filed, the TRC looked at structural violence by singling out those who were most affected. Further back in the liberation struggle, individual suffering was the key to proving the system's wrongs, but the individual did not count in the rhetoric and practice of liberation. I think that the idea of a class relying on solidarity and similarity draws directly on the way solidarity was framed during the liberation struggle.

The discussion spearheaded by former president Mbeki, which denounces those who seek redress for their apartheid injuries, is telling. It shows how the discourse of "personal injury for the collective cause" continues into post-apartheid and post-TRC South Africa. The debate following the tabling of the two final volumes of the TRC to Parliament (April 15, 2003) epitomizes this discourse. In that context, the apartheid litigations, which had just been filed in the US courts, were condemned by Mbeki, several MPs, and ministers. Any demand for redress was portrayed as selfish and unpatriotic. According to Alec Erwin, South African minister of trade and industry, it represents betrayal because it goes against a "collectivist identity that was the origin of our strength."[34] This reading of the liberation struggle to bring down apartheid "as a collective" suggests that the individual sacrificed her life for the cause selflessly and by choice. This is, of course, particularly in the case of women, a very problematic reading that ignores much more complex local modes of mobilization and resistance (see Ross 2002; Rubio-Marín 2006; Wells 1983, 1993), but it also attempts to silence criticism of the current state.

I believe that both the TRC and the liberation struggle have created *suspicious suspect positions* in ways and forms we have not paid sufficient attention to by singling out the worst affected, or by looking for a touchstone to make violence visible and legible. Partly, this is due to the ultimate tension between structural injustices and adequate forms of redress: violation is inflicted structurally (i.e., not personally), but the effects on the injured person are personal.

A person does not occupy a suspicious subject position as an inherent feature of her personhood; the position is ascribed to her, often temporally only. The position is relational, contextual and discursive. In the example above, it is the law and the procedures around class actions suits that push a person into such a position, but the position itself is shaped and conditioned by its societal context. Precisely because it is based on specific societal conditions and not emerging mechanically from a mere discourse, we see it at work in realms more or less unrelated to the law, too.

Having looked at the individualizing potential of the law, I now turn to the body and show how bodily experiences of past harm and their persistent embodiment equally potentially exclude and individuate. I thus move away from

the more legal and technical discussion and focus on the body and social practice. How do victims, in everyday life, attempt to express and communicate
their pain—in a context that does not make it easy for them. While there are
strong discourses to draw on for such articulation, these forms can just as easily
fail them because they are an abstraction of and removed from lived experience
and guarded injured personhood.

Chapter 3

Embodied Memory and the Social

PAIN, ACCORDING TO Elaine Scarry, has no referential content—contrary to most other interior states of consciousness, which refer to an object in the external world. We feel *for* somebody, we are afraid *of* something. In *The Body in Pain*, Scarry (1985, 5) calls this the human being's capacity to move beyond the boundaries of one's own body into an external world we all share. Physical pain, on the other hand, does not have an object. It is not *for* or *of* something. As a result, it resists objectification in language.

The recognition that "pain has no language" should not sidetrack us from looking carefully at what happens when those who suffer reach out to others seeking to express and receive recognition of their suffering and pain. People in pain attempt to render it public and social, either momentarily or to contribute to a larger social consciousness. In everyday interactions, pain has an origin, an addressee, a cause, and may even have meaning. Most of the objects given to pain are attempts to understand a reason for it and to give it meaning: "I am in pain *because* . . ." Others communicate the experience: "I tell *you* about my pain." The fact that such objects are given to pain *and* are being communicated in words and practices creates the conditions for the possibility of socialized pain.

In this chapter, I inquire into the intersubjectivity of pain and try to understand how pain and the social relate to each other. Of course, pain is always social, as the harm was inflicted within a social relation. What I explore here is the possibility of changing this experience and moving into forms of sociality that are positive and different from those that gave rise to the painful memories. Accordingly, I use the term *pain* broadly and include chronic pain, recurring pain, acute pain, recalled pain, and painful memories or emotions, such as anguish and grief, of a physical and a mental nature, and resulting from physical injury and mental injury.

Expressing pain, on the one hand, is a necessary condition for the possibility of transforming private experiences of pain into acknowledged social facts. On the other hand, talking about their pain may rob victims of their carefully guarded personal and raw experiences and still fail to transform them. Society (including scholars), I will show, also needs to be equipped to listen to victims and recognize them in their injured personhood (cf. Niezen 2010). We must, therefore, understand the political and societal contexts in which injured persons attempt to give a form to their experiences. I begin this chapter with a situation that illustrates and complicates this tension between the potential benefits and the danger of sharing one's pain in the public realm.

This Is Not a Story

In 2009, the Magnet Theatre in Cape Town was touring local high schools with a production about the killing of young protesters at an antigovernment demonstration by police and security forces, in October 1985, in an incident that became known as the Trojan Horse Massacre. The actors and producers of the piece were part of the Full Time Training and Job Creation Programme the theater has run since 2008, in which each year ten young people are chosen from various townships around Cape Town to be trained as actors. Magnet Theatre's goal is to bridge the gap between community drama groups, on the one hand, and professional theater and tertiary education institutions, such as the University of Cape Town and its Drama School, on the other. The *Trojan Horse Story* production was commissioned by the Human Rights Media Centre (HRMC), a Cape Town–based NGO that promotes human rights through various media and oral history projects. The thirty-minute play is based on the center's publication *If Trees Could Speak: The Trojan Horse Story* (Gunn 2007). It tells the story of the killings, which took place in the townships of Athlone and Crossroads. On October 15, members of the security police, railway police, and the defense force hid in wooden crates at the back of a railway delivery truck that drove up to a group of protestors and waited for someone to throw a stone and give the police a reason to shoot into the crowd. In Athlone, three youths[1] were killed and several adults and children were injured in the ambush. On the next day, a similar ambush was carried out in Crossroads, where two youths[2] were killed and several others injured. The incident at Athlone was filmed by a journalist and widely broadcast in the international media.[3] In the days that followed, many United Democratic Front (UDF) and student organization leaders were arrested. On October 25, the state of emergency was extended to include Cape Town, from the original thirty-six districts throughout the country in which it had been called in July 1985. In many ways, 1985 signaled the beginning of the end of apartheid governance in South Africa. Through the enforcement of the initially partial and later national state of emergence, the apartheid government tried to regain control over media coverage and funerals, movement of citizens, and general organizational capacity of the increasingly militant resistance groups. When the murdered youths were buried in Athlone, the police disrupted the funeral (Gunn 2007, 35). Two years later, at an inquest into the shooting, the magistrate ruled that the actions of the police had been unreasonable, and the thirteen policemen were found responsible for the youths' deaths. However, the attorney general of the Cape, Judge Williamson, refused to prosecute. The Athlone families, in turn and as a legal precedent, initiated a private prosecution; it, too, was unsuccessful, and the policemen were acquitted in December 1989. The TRC held special hearings to look into the incidents, the "Trojan Horse hearings," in Cape Town on May 20–21 and on June 2, 1997. None of the accused security force members bothered to apply for amnesty (Gunn 2007, 72).[4] Years later, the City of Cape Town advertised a memorial in Athlone, for which the HRMC won the tender for design and construction and which was unveiled in 2005 (Marschall 2010). The center also raised funds to pay for tombstones for the five murdered victims and for a memorial for the Crossroads victims as well, which was unveiled on Human Rights Day 2009.

The Magnet Theatre's production thus grew out of a considerable amount of post-1994 memory work that built on local memories of both the events and the unsuccessful prosecution of the policemen in the late 1980s. After the run of school performances, the piece was performed on October 31, 2009, at the Khulumani Western Cape general meeting at the Salt River Community House in Cape Town; it was its last performance. About a hundred Khulumani members attended, most of them from Crossroads and other predominantly black communities in the Cape Flats. It is likely that the surviving families and community members of Crossroads had only experienced some attention to their suffering in relation to the shootings when the HRMC started its memory work.

The performance drew on a real event in the past to keep the memory of it alive and to effect a change in each of the spectators so that she or he could act on the basis of new (experienced) knowledge about the past. It was mainly addressed to people who had not experienced the killings themselves. On this specific occasion, however, each member of the audience related a personal experience to the incident, or similar incidents, and brought her or his memories to it.

Eight young people who had grown up in the Cape Flats performed the play. The young actors performed the roles of the surviving parents, community members, and the youths who were killed. The play is immensely powerful and was disturbing to watch, even for me. The set was simple and dark. The costumes were minimal: clothes and drums. The actors chanted the words of the play. Spoken words were few, which made the chanting particularly powerful. One could see that the performers themselves were affected by the piece, that they identified with their roles and the plot. They were too young to have experienced the events firsthand, but they had surely experienced the aftermath of the massacre or similar events. Several members of the audience collapsed during the performance, screaming in anguish and pain; or they hunched down, whining, trying to contain and control their emotions; or they threw their bodies backward emitting excruciating groans. Others in the audience tried to comfort them and took them outside into the yard of the community house; more people in the audience started breaking down. The sound of the drums, I learned later, reminded one of the women of her baby, who had died when the woman's family was deported to what was then the Transkei homeland.[5] She remembered how she had interred the child en route and was unable to give her child a proper burial. Despite the interruptions, however, the performance continued.

The strong reactions were to be expected; similar reactions had been seen at other events.[6] No psychiatrist or psychologist was present at the performance.[7] And, as is usual, audience members had the opportunity to speak after the performance; beyond that, there seemed to be no concept of engaging with the emotions. A rather disappointing "debriefing" took place after the piece ended. Shirley Gunn, who is the director of the HRMC and sits on the national board of the Khulumani Support Group, first gave an account of how the play had been received in the schools. Her long speech had the effect of stilling the first and most immediate reactions to the play. She then asked the audience whether they had any questions for her or the eight performers, who sat huddled together at the edge of the stage, having dried their tears and sweat, ready to engage with the audience, many of whom could have been their grandparents. But it seemed that the audience was not in the mood to ask questions: most remained silent. A few, nonetheless, did communicate their gratitude and appreciation to the actors. It was important, they said, that the story be kept alive. "This is not a story for the members," one said, "this is what we experienced." The discussion soon ended and the audience dispersed, returning to their respective townships to go about their Saturday afternoon business.

For me, this event was not only a theatrical performance but also an act of (intended or unintended) commemoration. Commemorations, according to Connerton (1989, 72), consist of "re-enactments of the past," which depend for much of their rhetorical persuasiveness on "prescribed bodily behaviours." The performance I witnessed was turned by the audience into a commemoration for the dead who had, in many cases, not been laid to rest. Few in the audience had probably been directly affected by the Trojan Horse killings. Most, however, had experienced similarly horrendous events. What most cases of apartheid loss share is the fact that there is no closure. Most members know little about the exact circumstances surrounding the loss of a family member, and in very few cases was there a proper ritual to help begin the healing process, or a radical change in their lives that would allow for healing. The play thus tore open wounds that had barely had the chance to heal. The play was an invocation of the past in all its intensity. For the spectators, the past came alive through the play. It was experience *and* reality alike; and it was simultaneously the cause *and* the experience of their pain. The rawness of the reactions of some in the audience suggests that it was an unreconciled commemoration: the spectators' own experiences had not taken the shape of something to look at and to remember, and those being commemorated (directly or indirectly) were not sufficiently distant to be remembered and honored.

The performance thus cut right to the conundrum of commemoration: on the one hand, its necessity as the condition for the possibility of transforming pain and experiences, and, on the other hand, the ways in which it robs victims of their carefully guarded personal and raw experiences.

The (Non)transformation of Pain

One can argue that such commemorations are necessary. In his social drama theory, Victor Turner (1969) characterizes a ritual as carrying the potential for transforming its participants. A ritual is effective because of the experiences the participants make in it. An event without this intention or power to transform is a ceremony. Ceremonies do not intend transformation and are affirmative, as they confirm a current social configuration.

Looking at the Trojan Horse performance as a ritual or ceremony may fall short of Turner's social drama theory in many ways, but it is helpful for understanding the intricacies of performing a theatrical piece depicting political violence and loss to an audience who have been victims of exactly that. The question Turner raises—that is, whether an event intends and succeeds in transforming participants—helps us to realize the potential of these events to offer alternative forms of subjectivity or to transform individual pain into shared, socialized pain.

The immediate effect of the performance was vivid, and the pain and anguish some members of the audience felt were unprocessed and real. The experience for those who had the most intense emotional reactions was unpleasant and disruptive. The piece had been written and performed for high school students as a lesson about history, to raise their awareness of what their parents had gone through.[8] It was also meant to trigger discussions between generations. HMRC's *If Trees Could Speak* (Gunn 2007) is admirably pedagogical and informative about the law as a means of struggle and about the limits of law under a repressive regime that ruled by legal exclusion and daily discrimination. The book is also a recognition that the story of the massacre is one among many that are in danger of being forgotten, an acknowledgment of the courage of the communities and families, and an account of the brutality of the apartheid state. The performance draws on all that using different means. However, its goals must be rethought when it is presented to the victims themselves. Showing the piece at the Salt River Community House was a quest for healing and mobilization. Neither effort, unfortunately, was properly initiated or facilitated. However, both healing and mobilization assume the potential for transformation rather than the affirmation of a social constellation.

Psychotherapy and most variants of psychology start from the premise of the power of speaking about suffered harm and its contribution to healing and, ultimately, closure. It is assumed that putting one's pain into the public realm transforms what is personal, singular, and alienating into a social experience, which, in turn, is the beginning of a healing process.[9] The TRC's work, for instance, relied on victims who not only were capable and prepared to speak but who also thought the experience of speaking would be transformative.

Speaking was seen as the condition that made healing possible. Also, as noted in chapter 1, being part of a group that claims damages for experienced harm conditions the capability to communicate one's suffering. This dominant discourse is opposed to the notion, coming mostly from social science and the humanities, that denies those who suffer the ability to reach out to others. Elaine Scarry (1985) argues in *The Body in Pain*—speaking for many[10]—that pain radically destroys the capacity to communicate. Drew Leder (1990, 74) finds that pain "is marked by an interiority that another cannot share," and Kirsten Hastrup (1994, 238n2) believes that "pain strikes one alone. . . . In this, pain contrasts with pleasure, which is most often shared."

Pain is a difficult subject to write about, and the effort to do so is often accompanied by a great deal of (self-)criticism, skepticism, and unfulfilled promises. These problems are often the result of disciplinary constraints scholars are facing, which, as Veena Das (1995, 175) suggests, can result in further intricacies and even violence against those we are writing about: "The conceptual structures of our disciplines . . . lead to a professional transformation of suffering" which, in turn, "robs the victim of her voice and distances us from the immediacy of her experience." She includes social science, jurisprudence, and medicine in her astute analysis of the achievements and challenges of an anthropology of pain.

In accounts of pain, the voices of experts are often louder than the voices of those who are suffering. In various instances, state institutions (courts, truth commissions, aid schemes, social services, and election campaigns) or NGOs (development agencies, public-interest law firms) need the voice of the victims to give legitimacy or authority to their projects or concerns. The same goes for social scientists who work with empirical data resulting from their interactions with people suffering from pain. Although these relations of dependency and power are not unique to the study of pain—we find similar imbalances in all research that claims to "represent" or to "speak for" the marginal—it is more acute when pain is the object of a study—an experience which is most intimately bound to personhood and is the "most radically private of experiences" (Scarry 1985, 6). No matter how we look at pain, professionals always transform narratives of pain. This is true for psychiatrists, who read suffering in the aftermath of war, disaster, or times of massive abuse as PTSD or personality disorder; and it is true for medical anthropologists, even though Joan Kleinman and Arthur Kleinman (1991, 1994) interpret the same condition as moral commentary and political performance.

In anthropology, scholars' inability to adequately address the pain experienced by the people they lived with provoked a partial withdrawal from the subject (and a collection of anthropological literature on this very subject matter). But it also provided impetus on another front: Hopes have been projected onto the study of the anthropology of pain that it would finally release us from the ever-entrapping dualism of mind and body. Pain, it was argued, cuts to the heart of the Cartesian dichotomy between mind and body and challenges it profoundly. Chronic pain, in particular, defies such dichotomies as real-unreal, mind-body, subjective-objective, and physiological-psychological (Good et al. 1992). Anthropologists have criticized standard biomedical practices that view pain as an individual experience, contending that the experience of (chronic) pain is fundamentally *intersubjective*. It affects the victim's family and social life, and lets other people shape the experiential world of the suffering person (Good et al. 1992, 9). Medical anthropologists have also criticized biomedical studies on pain which attempt to challenge biological reductionism by contesting the grounding of pain in the objective condition of the body. Instead, psychologists advocate the application of psychological principles. In my view, however, both approaches perpetuate the mind-body dualism. Whether one privileges somatic processes or the subjective mind, both leave the Cartesian dichotomy unquestioned and anthropologists unsatisfied.

If we look again at the performance, we can assume for a moment that if healing was intended, the approach relied on the notion that confrontation equals transformation. As noted earlier, psychotherapy and psychology work on the premise of the power of invocation and its contribution to healing and, ultimately, closure. However, for some victims, healing is a slow process of encapsulating their painful thoughts and emotions inside a cocoon in their minds. At best, their pain is carefully and anxiously hidden away. It is a necessary escape from their memories. This is in contrast to one of the major goals of memory work and commemoration, which is to fight against this process of forgetting and thus to prevent a piece of history from escaping public memory. To keep public memory alive, the embodied memory of the superstes ("experiencing witness"; see chapter 2) has to transform into the testimony given by the testis (neutral witness). This transformation can fail, and attempting it can have unintended consequences for victims.

The performance at the Salt River Community House, in unfortunate ways, confronted men and women with their personal memories and prevented their attempts to forget. They could resort to cries and groans or other pre-language means of expression, or they could leave the room. But invocation irrevocably happened. What is more, the performance took place at a monthly general meeting, which members should attend to retain membership status and receive information. A typical monthly meeting includes a time for remembering, during which members deliberate on their concerns and grieve and support each other. Members emphasize the storytelling aspect of the meetings when they reflect on what Khulumani is about and what their membership means to them.[11] This is a heritage of the first few years of the organization's existence and of the times when the Ex-Political Prisoners and Torture Survivor Support Group was still hosted by the Trauma Centre. The performance as one means to have members speak was thus not an exception; neither was the lack of preparation for what was to come, of proper framing, or of encouragement to leave before the play started.

Genuine commemoration must destroy coping mechanisms that provisionally lock away pain in a most private and intimate place. Pain becomes as real as it was the first time. But here, no transformation of individual pain was effected: the performance offered no alternative to looking at one's own pain, either through objectification or through shifts in subject positions. It simply confirmed the victims' subjectivity as widows, husbands, mothers, comrades, and as children who are suffering great loss and pain and who are, some more, some less, vulnerable to anything calling the dead and the lost too loudly. Despite all good intentions, the setting confirmed victims in their victim subjectivity. It did not offer alternative views on their lives or a new position from which to look at their experiences.

It is, of course, difficult to draw a boundary between the necessity of practices of mourning and the risk of retraumatization. To genuinely understand the effects of the performance, one would have to take a longer-term perspective and see whether some form of transformation takes place later. Here, I attempt to show whether the theatrical performance in itself and the way it was presented to the audience offered an alternative interpretation of one's personhood from which people could create social experiences to take them beyond their victimhood.[12] I argue that the performance did have strong transformative powers, but that all it achieved was the tearing open of old wounds.

These subjectivities are not compatible with the subject position of activists. The play's intent to mobilize was directed to entirely the wrong audience. Khulumani members may be activists, but first and foremost they are people who have experienced loss, violence, and torture and who have not been able to overcome their experiences. *They* are not the audience that needs to be conscientized or confronted with a trauma they have already experienced and lived in real time. The play was not shown to those who should be confronted with the concurrent immediacy of the crimes they committed, but to people who have not stopped suffering from their consequences.

"We Must Speak"

"We must speak," a Khulumani member told me as a truth in which she believed affirmatively when I described to her the Salt River Community House performance (at which she was not present) and the strong but minimally verbal response by members afterward. For all the years I have known her, she and I had a tacit agreement that I would not ask her about the past. She tolerated me and probably enjoyed my presence, but it took many meetings, stretching over weeks, until I could sense her relaxing, realizing that I would not ask her questions she would have felt obliged to answer. Her assertion that we "must speak" therefore contradicted my experiences with her. It sounded like a normative obligation she put on herself but failed to comply with.

She was not exceptional in asserting this "truth." The TRC instilled in many people the expectation that to speak was *the* way to healing, and various NGOs embraced it as the guarantee of success. The commission's work relied on the assumption that victims are capable of speaking and ready to speak. Someone who wanted to qualify as a victim had to speak, sometimes only to a statement taker or sometimes also to a public audience. Even though the TRC's performative and investigative work cannot be reduced to this aspect alone, speech remained the basis of its evidence.

Here, I want to return to my conversation with Beauty Notle Kotta (chapter 2), a Khulumani member from Philippi. She told me how her then twelve-year-old son was killed during the fights between the Crossroads community, the police force members, and the witdoeke and how her second son continues to be deeply traumatized because he witnessed the fighting, was sprayed with teargas, and escaped from the killing and burning of bodies in the fires of 1986. She spoke to me in stops and starts, often pushing herself to continue, despite my attempts to calm her:

> He got a *assegai* [spear]. They cut the people, they cut. And they fought our children. Must go to fight. You see? And my son was dead there. . . . And Crossroad, and witdoeke. You see? Not nice talking about things. It's very sore. That's why

sometimes I don't like to talk . . . because we must speak, we must speak! Because now, I have one son. And my son was frightened. Not right in there since he saw . . . he saw. He got picture, you know. The man got a gun. . . . But he got a picture, yebo. Doesn't alright, but he was right. But now, wasn't right properly.

Ms. Kotta's notion that "we must speak" is not necessarily an immediate legacy of the TRC but, more likely, was brokered by the nongovernmental institutions and their replication of the TRC standard. Ms. Kotta, as she emphasized, participated in the HRMC's art and memory project "Breaking the Silence: A Luta Continua," which encouraged victims to draw body maps of their physical and mental injuries sustained and to speak about their experiences (Pouligny 2007). Like Ms. Kotta, tens of thousands of people lost their homes and belongings in fires deliberately set by security force members in the winter months of 1986 (J. Cole 2012). The fires destroyed the squatter settlements of KTC, Crossroads, Nyanga Bush, and Nyanga Extension.

Symptomatically, at the TRC's Trojan Horse hearing, Pumla Gobodo-Madikizela, a TRC psychologist who served on the Human Rights Committee of the TRC, commented on the commission's difficulty in finding witnesses or activists who were ready to testify:

I think that the facts and the difficulties that there are in general in talking about trauma makes it extremely challenging for survivors and families of the victims to talk about their pain and I think that we should accept that this is a normal thing that happens with talking about trauma. It is part of the experience, the psychological experience of talking about trauma, there is an avoidance of talking about trauma, the repression, the denial but at the same time *there is a need to talk about it,* and I think that, *when people talk about their pain it puts them on the road to healing of their pain* and we should acknowledge that and I think this is part of the reason that we opened up the commission to public testimony and I would like to mention that in fact, there are many people who have proved the fact that this [is] ambivalence. Some people who have come today initially didn't want to come but at the same time they decided that after all they want to come. So that's ambivalence all the time.[13]

Although Ms. Gobodo-Madikizela acknowledges the ambivalence people feel about talking about their horrendous experiences, she asserts that talking is the "road to healing of their pain" and suggests that testifying before the Truth Commission has a therapeutic impact. And the commission did just that: it recognized the pain of those testifying as much as it could by the means of equalizing experiences and promoting "reconciliation."[14] It failed, however, to prove that giving testimony before the TRC had psychological benefits (Kagee 2006; Kaminer et al. 2001).

Where does the idea that speaking helps victims to overcome traumatic experiences come from in South Africa?[15] Its origins are in the so-called "testimony approach" to trauma and therapy or "narrative therapy" (Kaminer and Eagle 2010), whose ancestry goes back to Freudian psychotherapy. "Narrative therapy" has been employed in various contexts within South Africa but is not widely documented globally as a trauma treatment model. It has mainly been used with the African and Asian refugee populations, with the idea that it is compatible with traditional oral storytelling practices. Stories that emphasize resilience and survival, it is thought, should increase the patient's sense of personal agency or potency; at the same time, the stories often become part of a formal record of the traumatic event, used for lobbying, documentation, and the establishment of a public record. For instance, the extension of narrative aspects of this kind of therapy has been used by refugee groups in South Africa to expose atrocities committed in their home countries. Kaminer and Eagle (2010, 91–92) suggest that the TRC methodology of having victims and perpetrators testify publicly assumed the therapeutic benefits of this approach. They do not see, however, a therapeutic relationship between the TRC commissioners and the testifier and are thus not surprised by its failure.[16]

The commission's work succeeded in instilling, in activists and victims alike, the belief, and the necessity, that all healing begins with talking. The model of giving testimony about one's experiences to an audience has been employed in various nongovernmental forums. Encouraging victims to talk and then acknowledging their testimony helped to create a particular victim's subject position: "good victims" are those who speak out about their painful experiences, who do not remain dumb, who manage to overcome their ambivalence and skepticism about going public with their pain. Those who do not or cannot comply are potentially suspect in the eyes of society.

The Trojan Horse performance in itself—as a result of it being staged in front of that particular audience—turned intimate experiences into public discourse. It did not enable the spectators to find a language in which to respond to what they saw performed as their own experiences, nor did the meeting succeed in catching these intimate experiences made public. The performance evoked immense grief and anguish in many in the audience and laid bare their pain. The emotions were as raw as they had been the first time, and remained so. Neither the performers nor the director could offer a therapeutic relationship. Pain was brought from the intimate realm into the public realm, from being hidden to being raw and open, but it was not transformed into something else. The TRC could socially acknowledge pain if people were prepared to express it in words. The reactions to the performance showed that many survivors still live with pain they cannot put into words, but which can be brought into the open when new experiences trigger memories.

I am not suggesting that such incidents do not have any potentiality to establish new social relations. Anxiety and anguish may effect sociality—between those who collapsed and those who patted them on the back or offered them a glass of water, between those who wept and those who handed them a tissue, between those who expressed their gratitude to the actors and those who were glad that someone took the lead to say so, between those who silently suffered and those who recognized their grief, between the youths who offered their skills and interpretation and the audience who acknowledged the intergenerational engagement. But I doubt whether a performance where the people whose suffering is directly addressed in the play are the spectators and not the actors can be understood in Turner's line of thinking: resulting in transformation in sociality. The position of spectators was too constrained to allow them to positively engage with the possibility of looking at oneself differently. Members' lives were displayed in front of their eyes, and the same story with the same end was repeated.

Maybe this comes close to what the TRC was for many of those who did not testify: it related their experiences, but they did not participate. They could not go through the ritual of speaking to an audience, breaking down, or walking away with their heads held high, obtaining new information that had been kept secret. They did not have the possibility of assuming a new status toward themselves and in their communities because of what the hearings had revealed.

Members did not call the dead. The performance called the dead, and they came in their rawest form. They did not offer resolution.

Pain Has an Object

Various scholars assume that it is only when pain is invested with meaning that a process of suffering and a possible socialization of pain can assume its course (Gobodo-Madikizela and Van der Merwe 2007; Ramphele 1997). The account by Nontsasa Eunice Mgweba suggests otherwise: pain can be socialized without first giving it meaning. Ms. Mgweba's pain resulted from close social relations, and she literally took on the pain of someone else. But this should not lead us to conclude that the condition of sociality of pain invests the pain with meaning.

Ms. Mgweba runs a little stall at Station Road in Philippi. It is a shack, and she cannot use it when it is raining because it leaks in all the corners and through the corrugated sheet metal roof. She sells single sweets, roasted nuts, and chicken feet, which are boiled in bouillon and offered as a late afternoon snack to the people passing by. Her daughter, Happiness Bongeka Mgweba (born in 1972), helps out. She prepares the chicken feet and helps with the selling. She also looks after a small garden in the backyard of their RDP house. Like so many houses in the area, Ms. Mgweba's started to fall apart before it was finished properly: "When it is raining, I must put the dishes [to catch the rainwater coming through the roof]," Ms. Mgweba sighed. Happiness does not work. She is always with her mother because she cannot be left alone since the fires of 1986 in Nyanga. It was "burning there," her mother recounts. "She screamed," and "she had a shock." "We lose our clothes, the house, and then lose our . . . sickness [health]. Because it is stressing everyone, it is confusing everyone. Now since these years, it has not been right for us." Happiness experiences sudden attacks of screaming, anguish, fear, and panic. "But she wasn't born like that," Ms. Mgweba emphasized, "since we get that stress for the fire, it is too much stress. That fire make us horrible." Since then, Happiness has performed poorly at school and instantly froze when confronted with someone or something she does not like. "But [she] is a clever lady," her mother said. Although Happiness had liked to read and to write, the teacher advised her mother to take her out of school in the mid-1990s. Not only the daughter has suffered the effects from witnessing the fighting among the security police, the witdoeke, and the townships residents and the shooting and the teargas and the killing in Crossroads, her mother also attributes her poor health to the years of running from the police and the witdoeke, fires, deportations (Desmond 1970; Platzky, Walker, and Surplus People Project 1985), and arrests and harassment by the police. Not only did Ms. Mgweba lose everything in the fire, she also witnessed the horror that her older sister, with whom she lived, went through. Her sister was pregnant in June 1986. Ms. Mgweba recalled, "I am very stressed about that thing. Because the people they got the axe. They wanted to chop us with the axe. It is not good because the people got the witdoeke and everything. It was not nice. [My sister] was stressing so much."

She described how her sister's anxiety for her unborn child affected her: "And I take all that from my pregnant sister come to me. Because I see what's going on. What about my sister? She is pregnant and then they doing like that. . . . All that had get me sickness. It's sickness and me, I am sickness. . . . My sister now has got the sugar diabetes but also she got a very stressful heart. Because she was pregnant." In a separate incident, when her sister was taken into custody for not carrying a pass, Ms. Mgweba tried to bail her out: "And the other day, my sister, they take [her in] the van straight to the police station in Langa . . . all [were] dumped there. Me, I am going there to take out my sister. And then the police come and the teargas. Eyih! They spray us. Oh, oh, oh! I was so white from the spray and the eyes also. . . . It was [a] very horrible time." Her sister was also deported to the Transkei homeland a few times: "My sister was very strong. Twice, three times, to Transkei. She got a baby on that time. [They] take [her] with the baby in the van. . . . When I see my sister, I take it on me. Although me, I wasn't in [the van] on that day. But I was very stressed. Because we stayed together."

Ms. Mgweba has high blood pressure. She raises her son's daughter (born in 1996), who was deserted by her mother when she was four months old. Her son had worked as a cleaner in Cape Town and in Bonteheuwel alongside his mother for some years. Even though he was currently unemployed, he could not look after his child, according to Ms. Mgweba.[17]

I spent an afternoon with Ms. Mgweba in her stall. Another Khulumani member sat with us. She was mostly quiet, but sometimes she complemented, underlined, or translated what Ms. Mgweba told me. As far as she was concerned, what Ms. Mgweba was telling me was nothing new. Although the two women shared many of the same experiences, she told me her own "story," as she called it, to show that such experiences were widespread. She explained how she suffers from chronic pain in her shoulder from an injury she had sustained running away from the police; how her son advised her not to undergo an operation for it now because she was too old; how as a child, her son had hidden a gun when policemen arrived to search her shack. Sometimes their accounts were directed to me; often however, they became less explanatory and the women seemed to primarily be echoing sensations from inside.

Customers came and went. One came with the news that two counselors from COPE, the party that had split from the ANC in 2008, had been jailed; another complained about a woman who had accused him of raping her and took him to court. Happiness sold snacks, joked with the customers, carefully divided up the bulk stock in small plastic bags and posed for the pictures I took of her with customers and her mother. Her mother commented, "She is right now. But tomorrow it can change. She [might] not know you. Happiness is [suddenly in] other moods."

On that afternoon, Ms. Mgweba gave an account of how much she and her family had been affected by the unrest and policing of the townships in the 1980s. She expressed her frustrations about her current living conditions, her children's unemployment, the fact that she looks after her grandchild without receiving a child support grant from government due to the complicated bureaucracy, and the limitations of her job given that she cannot buy sufficient bulk quantities. Her family is often forced to eat the food meant to be sold to customers. "That's why we demand the reparations," she concluded, "because that time was very bad. Still now, we are suffering. And you see now where I am staying. And you see her [Happiness]. And we can't work because all of us are sick. And me, I am sick for my high blood [pressure]. That's why I stay like that. And my child also. And who looks after [the grandchild]? It's me who looks after her. Because he [her father] is sick and me I am not right. . . . All that thing is stress."

Ms. Mgweba told me how she took on her sister's sorrow, literally. She took on the burden physically, and it had affected her health. She *felt* her sister's pain and let it affect her to the detriment of her own health, in addition to her own burden of seeing her daughter withdraw more and more after her horrific experiences. She suggests that sorrow can be passed on, unwillingly or not. She attributes this transfer to the corporal nature of stress. The effects of stress show in the mind and in the body, and reinforce each other. Her daughter is a case in point: she has, one can assume, been traumatized by witnessing the fire, the killing, and the general violence of the police. Her trauma finds expression in such forms as fits and poor concentration and sudden withdrawal from the social world. This, her mother finds, makes her socially uncontrollable and in need of constant company. Happiness's experiences, her former teacher and her mother agree, desocialize her. Her mother is afraid that Happiness will not find a husband, but she praises her daughter for taking loving care of her niece.

Ms. Mgweba gave testimony to the long-term effects of decades of leading a marginalized life in economically precarious and politically unstable conditions. She did not greatly distinguish between mental and physical reactions to the resulting stress. She implied that though the political environment today may be more predictable, precarious living conditions and the lack of educational or income opportunities continued. Ms. Mgweba, like many survivors, has not managed to "capitalize" on her situation in the form of social grants. She is not yet sixty years old and so is not eligible to receive an old-age pension. And she is reluctant to go through the bureaucratic process of applying for a child support grant because it could mean a confrontation with her grandchild's mother. She did not tell me whether Happiness receives a disability grant. No husband and potential breadwinner figured in her account.

In contrast, however, the stall is a social place through and through. Distant relatives, friends, and customers stop by to chat, nibble on crisps or chicken feet, and exchange the latest news about local politics, and they are certain to find a sympathetic listener if they want to share their personal miseries. One lady, also a Khulumani member, stopped by for a quick chat, saying as she left, "I am hungry, I am sick." "The stress," Ms. Mgweba replied. The woman nodded. "The stress," she confirmed, and went on her way. Such small interactions allowed the women a mutual recognition of each other's difficulties; an interaction that recognizes personhood in the other, and her pain.

In *Pain as Human Experience: An Anthropological Perspective*, a comparatively early work on the anthropology of chronic pain and the human condition of pain, Mary-Jo DelVecchio Good and colleagues (Good et al. 1992, 7) note the following: "Something is at stake, frequently desperately so, in the lives of pain patients. Pain can be a massive threat to the legitimacy of the everyday world." If chronic pain defies the dichotomies of real-unreal, mind-body, subjective-objective, physiological-psychological, it puzzles doctors, who have to reconstitute as a medical problem what for the patient is perception, experience, and coping *in one* (8). Anthropologists and others have started to take somatization seriously, that is, as "an idiom of physically painful signs of symptoms," alongside discourses of emotions and inner feelings. Good and colleagues thus advocate listening to those who suffer from chronic pain: "The sufferers of chronic pain, in particular, have elaborated these two parallel and interacting languages in their talk about symptoms and their search for relief," and this may help to transcend the "dichotomy of thought and sensation which is inscribed in everyday language, medical jargon, and treatment setting" (12).

If it is difficult (or impossible) to give an object to acute pain, it is worse for chronic pain. Ms. Mgweba's account suggests that the crux of chronic pain is that it becomes part of the everyday—without ever losing its capacity to disrupt the everyday fully and again and again—and thus renders life unpredictable and unstable. Chronic pain results in a loss of stability and reliability, except for the reliable return of pain.

Pain can assume a life of its own. For the sufferer, it may acquire agency or the status of an object disjointed from the experiencing self. Ms. Mgweba does not separate her pain as an object, as distinct from her experiencing self: "It's sickness and me; I am sickness." Pain is not merely a part of her (objectivized, distinct) body, and neither is it something she has to endure passively. She has been fighting for her health and sanity—over and over again, it seems from her account. But when she speaks about her daughter, pain does assume agency. Pain *does* something *with* or *to* Happiness, with or to her mind and body alike. "It" suddenly takes over and inflicts fits on her. "It" changes Happiness's mood and takes away her gentle side.

As for her own pain, Ms. Mgweba has acquired the capacity to *partly* rationalize it. Pain has a cause: the agents of the apartheid regime inflicted it upon her, her family, and her community. Pain has an origin: her sister's suffering and stress and the continuing impossibility of finding the normality of an ideal everyday life. She recognizes a tormented mind and physical injury equally as origins of suffering. She cannot cure herself, as pain has become part of her "self" and part of *who she is*. For her, suffering from chronic pain is a state she endures. Her pain could be alleviated, though, by better living conditions or relief from responsibility, for instance.

Even if Ms. Mgweba attributes cause, origin, and the impossibility of cure to her pain, she does not give it meaning. Ms. Mgweba does not revert to a religious notion of suffering or to a narrative of liberation and sacrifice. Pain is utterly meaningless and ultimately destructive. Mamphela Ramphele (1997, 114) suggests that pain may assume meaning by being acknowledged: "Personal pain is a degrading and dehumanizing experience unless meaning is vested in it. The investment of personal pain with meaning transforms it into suffering, which then becomes a social process." Ms. Mgweba's account suggests that pain also goes the opposite way: it may originate in close social relations that can result in a state of suffering. Contrary to Ramphele's reasoning, the sociability of pain does not necessarily invest pain with meaning. Ms. Mgweba does not invest pain with meaning when she confirms (and comforts) her customers in the notion that stress leads to sickness. She recognizes its cause and effect. Similarly, Ms. Mgweba struggles with the desocializing effects of her daughter's fits and she has a clear idea of how her condition came about. Pain, as such, challenges the practicability of life and makes it contingent. Pain hindered her from fully providing for her children when they were young; and it prevents her daughter from living a life independent from her mother, from being an agent in her own life and from providing for her mother in her old age.

In her subjectivity, Ms. Mgweba lives what she seemed to suggest to me: she acknowledges the pain of others by trying to make it social. She has been compelled to be the one who cares for others. Although her own painful experiences and those of others have fundamentally shaped and weakened her, she has been the stabilizing tent pole in her family. She relates to others in a most empathetic and *felt* way. Ms. Mgweba's subjectivity is intimately bound to others' suffering and to her strength relative to them.[18] She thus "invests" pain in sociality but not meaning.

The Denial of Mourning

One way in which people can find sociality after experiences of violence is by mourning together. Under apartheid rule, however, acts of mourning were frequently impossible for political reasons or were even actively disrupted by the security forces. To deny victims the ability to mourn an experience of pain and loss robs them of the possibility of closure. Sanders (2007, 10) even characterizes the system of apartheid as "a formation that denied the right to mourn." While listening to victims' testimony before the TRC, Sanders was struck how many asked the commission to help them with funeral rites for their dead. This pattern emerged when the commissioners began asking the testifiers what the commission could to do to help them find closure. Sanders argues that the commissioners and, ultimately, the commission acted as a "proxy" for the perpetrators (namely, those who never came forward to accept responsibility and accountability for their actions). Besides funeral rites, many testifiers asked for help in searching for bones and body parts of the disappeared and with exhumation from mass graves and the subsequent proper burial thereof. These requests were mainly made by women (in the ordinary hearings) and thus gave witness to how profoundly the system of apartheid continued to affect the lives of those left behind (Ramphele 1997).

The prevention of mourning also takes away the possibility of finding *social recognition* for the rupture between the living and the dead and thus secures the impossibility of closing the rupture. Mourning rituals are collective processes. In South Africa in the 1980s, funerals had become political forums for the liberation movements (cf. Mda 2002). "The staging of mass political funerals assumed enormous significance as opportunities to put the evil and brutality of the state in full public view. The more coffins one could line up, the stronger the message that could be communicated in this regard" (Ramphele 1997, 106). Ramphele (1997, 107) describes how crucial funerals were for the mobilization of the liberation movements, especially in the mid-1980s. Inevitably, she says, the wishes of the family and the desires of the politicians clashed. People were dragged to mass funerals against their will. The funeral was "political theater," staged to remind the mourners and liberation fighters of the "invincibility of the struggle," and, at the same time, suggesting the "dispensability of individuals" and the "inevitability of the ultimate price that has to be paid for freedom." Often, people had to run for their lives before the final rites for the deceased had been completed. The "comrade" who was buried had not died of natural causes. Violence was met with more violence.

It is here that the story of Lungile Hlaise (name changed) begins. Ms. Hlaise has been implicated ever since she was shot at a funeral in the 1980s. She had always understood this injury as the price of freedom. But her feelings slowly change as her injuries cause her more intense pain, and as the thread of violence does not seem to stop even in post-apartheid South Africa.

Toward the end of a three-day meeting of the National Steering Committee of Khulumani Support Group, in Bloemfontein, Free State, in 2009, Ms. Hlaise, a woman in her early forties, who had been one of my roommates for these three nights, approached me as we were packing to leave and cleaning the room. We had not spoken to each other before. Now, obviously in both a painful and pensive state, Ms. Hlaise told me stories of her present life and of her life under the apartheid regime. She spoke in an intense and urgent manner, and did not stop talking for half an hour. In the late 1980s, she had been attending the funeral of a "comrade," and was shot by the police when they ordered the crowd to disperse. The injury completely damaged one of her eyes, and she has pain in her back. She told me she thought she had forgiven (but does not specify *whom* she thought she had forgiven). However, the pain has gotten worse now as she gets older. This, she said, re-evokes feelings of "anger" and "bitterness." On top of this, she was raped in the year 2000 and ever since this incident does not menstruate anymore. The rapist, she said, was a Ghanaian lecturer at the university in her locality. It was easy for her to trace him, and she filed a complaint against him. One day, she was called to court, not knowing that it was the day her case was being heard. She was unprepared and could not formulate her case properly. Her rapist was not convicted. He had bribed the court, Ms. Hlaise said. Her daughter was raped in 2007. At the time, her daughter was constantly in and out of the hospital because she had a baby boy who was asthmatic and epileptic. One night, Ms. Hlaise relieved her daughter at the hospital, and when her daughter left the building, she was attacked by a man who pressed a towel over her nose, making her "drunk." She was found the next morning, lying somewhere hidden and still "drunk." Fortunately, her daughter had received some counseling. Ms. Hlaise told me that her parents are "weak," too; both are asthmatic and have high blood pressure. Only her son was healthy, she said. "The police . . . the rape . . . ," she halted, lost in thought. And she repeated that her pain was a constant reminder of what had happened; the older she gets, the stronger the pain.

Ms. Hlaise is a recent member of Khulumani. She came to the steering committee meeting as part of a provincial delegation, although at the time she was not part of the provincial executive. Before the meeting, she knew—as she describes it—"what everybody thinks to know about Khulumani and what everybody hears about Khulumani first": Khulumani would hand out money. She was glad she had come to the meeting. "But it is not done yet." As she became more knowledgeable about the work Khulumani does, she wanted to open a branch in her region. However, now that the three days of the conference were over, now that we were packing to leave, she was thinking about home. She thought about how dependent her family was on her, though she was "weak," too. Before we parted, she said that pain was seen as something "private," that nobody talked about it and that sharing was rare. People hid their pain until they could not take it anymore. Until they went crazy. And then people say that "this one" was being "witchcrafted." "No, this is not witchcraft," Ms. Hlaise was convinced.

Violence was a dominant theme in Ms. Hlaise's account. She talked of both state violence (the shootings at the funeral) and criminal violence (rape). They are different: state violence was legitimated by the apartheid state (maybe under a state of emergency) and executed by its security police forces. It was an act of violence between the official state and a member of the society. It was a legal relationship but also a social relationship, legally enforced. It denied the people the freedom to assemble and criminalized those who gathered in groups.[19] During apartheid, there was no way to receive damages for injuries sustained from acts of state violence (except, of course, much later, through the TRC reparations payments). The second form of violence, rape, is an act of violence *between* members of a society under the post-apartheid government which protects the bodily integrity of the people and believes in enforcing the prosecution of criminal offence violating it. Ms. Hlaise brought a charge against her attacker.[20] In neither of the two incidents did Ms. Hlaise succeed in having the injury acknowledged by an authority. Both times, Ms. Hlaise felt let down by the respective legal system. In the incident of the disrupted funeral during the apartheid era, there was, of course, no reason to even try to claim damages. In both incidents of violence, to her, the justice system proved to be biased in favor of the offender, ideologically or financially corrupt.

Although state and criminal violence have different origins and inflict different kinds of pain on the victim, the difference is not self-evident in an environment of continual daily violence, officials free to act as they choose with impunity, and nonresponsiveness of the courts.

Ms. Hlaise recounts her renewed realization of the experiences of injustice and of the injuries she sustained by revisiting physical pain. Actual pain and the constraints on her bodily performance resulting from the violence bring back her "anger" and "bitterness." Ms. Hlaise felt robbed of closure. On the one hand, she felt angry because there had not been a social other acknowledging the injustice done. Neither the authorities nor the perpetrator would hear her complaints. Neither did she feel that her community responded collectively to experiences of violence. Instead of sharing their pain, they turn on themselves and retreat into silence. As a consequence, people accuse each other of being bewitched, which may result in a victim's social expulsion from a community.

If experiences of the past are not properly acknowledged by (social or state) institutions, they revisit a person in the present in unexpected ways. The official lack of acknowledgment is consequential. It is one of the major factors preventing *social recognition* of her injured subjectivity. Ms. Hlaise's account shows that even today, apartheid-era victims find it difficult to mourn their past or their more recent experiences.

In today's South Africa, as their injuries often remain unacknowledged, apartheid-era victims find it difficult to mourn. In other words, *political* obstacles to coping with loss and pain have been replaced by *social* factors. Mourning is a way to have one's pain socially recognized, and potentially transformed. People who are denied the possibility of mourning are robbed of one way to integrate painful experiences into their lives.

On the one hand, it is her recurring physical pain that challenges Ms. Hlaise's notion of forgiveness. When physical pain was absent, a certain degree of forgetting and forgiving was possible for her. When physical pain is pressing her daily, though, her notion of forgiveness becomes more challenging. Ms. Hlaise said she *thought* she had forgiven. Her ongoing suffering from past injuries is perpetuated by more recent experiences of violence that do not necessarily have anything to do with apartheid-era violence. She was raped. Her daughter was raped. Ms. Hlaise lost her reproductive capability. In her family, she is the breadwinner for her sick parents, her daughter, and her asthmatic grandson. She has high blood pressure. Ms. Hlaise's account speaks of the burden her generation carries: she is supposed to comfort her sick parents *and* care for both of her grownup children (both of whom are uneducated and often unemployed) and *their* children. All these experiences may not be systematically linked to her experiences as a victim under apartheid, but they nevertheless transform her earlier memories and make closure impossible. New experiences can change how old ones are remembered in the body.

But it is not only the bodily dimension of injury that challenges or prevents social recognition, forgiveness, and closure. Ms. Hlaise also witnesses the social exclusion resulting from society's suspicion of unacknowledged injuries. Society does not recognize her and others' victimhood as a lived experience.

These kinds of personal experiences, she holds, can only be transformed if they are shared. She does not mean this in a therapeutic way but sees speaking as a route to social acknowledgment. Successful sharing would prevent social exclusion (as witchcraft victim). According to Ms. Hlaise, reference to occult forces ignores and negates the real causes of confusion, illness, and other social ruptures (Ashforth 1998, 2005).

Participating in the three-day National Steering Committee meeting seemed to have conscientized Ms. Hlaise. New forms of relating to her own pain and burden and of relating to others were offered. Unlike the people in her community, the provincial representatives spoke about their experiences openly and put forth claims. She witnessed a new form of victim subjectivity that emphasized action and recognition rather than silence and exclusion. This is not necessarily a politicization of victim subjectivity (but it may become so; see Freire 2007). It is first and foremost the identification of wrongs committed as *wrong*, and the recognition of the possibility of sharing pain.

In sum, to speak about one's experiences of violence publicly is one means of achieving social recognition. Sharing works against the social exclusion that was fostered during the apartheid era and that still prevails in today's South Africa. Since in the eyes of victims, apartheid-era victimhood has still not been properly acknowledged, the sacrifice that liberation had supposedly required becomes a bitter experience.

Whereas Ms. Hlaise's story points to the intricacies of bodily injuries, and their effects on the possibilities of the social, it also shows that nonacknowledgment of the injuries impedes society's ability to socially recognize injured personhood. One way to break the silence and the cycle of exclusion is to share one's experiences with others. It is only through sharing within a community that societal recognition can start to emerge. Mourning is one way to start to form a collective precisely because it acknowledges experienced wrong.

The Medicalization of One's Self

Brian Mphahlele, whom we met in chapter 2, adopts a medical discourse to speak about himself in certain situations. His relation to the medical and psychiatric world is utterly ambivalent, but he knows that it is in these terms that victimhood is widely understood, and that it may also help him as he tries to articulate what otherwise would be left unsaid. The medical subject position is one of many identities he lives in his complex life; he is also the former rebellious youth who was incarcerated in Section C (maximum security division) for "never obeying," a human rights activist, plaintiff, well-traveled explorer, loyal member of the Pan Africanist Congress, failed lawyer, victim-turned-survivor, man-about-town, and loner.

It is important to Mr. Mphahlele that his condition be communicable in relation to dominant discourses concerning health, human rights, and justice. He harbors professional and intimate personal views about himself. Like many victims of crimes, he relies on doctors' assessments of his condition. But Mr. Mphahlele has had far more access to psychiatric treatment than many victims of human rights violations. As a torture survivor, he was one of the first members of the support group Ex-Political Prisoners and Torture Survivors (later Khulumani Western Cape); he received counseling from the Trauma Centre in Cape Town from 1997 to 2003 and sporadically still does today. He was also treated at the psychiatric unit of the Groote Schuur Hospital, where he still receives counseling and medication. The Trauma Centre assessed him as a person suffering from PTSD as a result of torture and sensory deprivation (due to his physical isolation in solitary confinement). The symptoms are inability to sleep, loss of both short-term and long-term memory; intense, uncontrollable anger toward the police and soldiers; depression; and a pervasive distrust of people. The torture he received also left his face permanently disfigured.[21]

Unlike many other victims, Mr. Mphahlele is versed in the discourse of psychiatry. He is fascinated by the profession and, ultimately, by its power to judge people's psyches, sanity, and position in society. Furthermore, he uses his psychiatric vocabulary to communicate his condition to others and to find his place in the world that keeps him going, the medical world. His feelings are ambivalent, though, ranging from admiration to dependency to detestation.

He has been active in the Executive of Khulumani Western Cape and is one of the most engaged members in the province. His work as a painter is seasonal, and he spends most of his spare time at the office in Salt River or running errands for the organization in the townships or the city. When researchers or journalists look for "good cases," Mr. Mphahlele is often the first to offer himself. He is articulate and his contributions are powerful. Often, he stands out for his irreconcilability and short temper. At one general meeting of Khulumani Western Cape, for example, a film scriptwriter who had done work on forgiveness in other postconflict countries wanted to hear members' thoughts on the notion of forgiveness in South Africa. Mr. Mphahlele got up and said, "Look at us! We have nothing. I tracked them [the perpetrators] down when I was released from prison. I am on medication. I suffered internal head injuries. So what is the point of forgiving or reconciling?" Medical terminology was part of his intervention and gave weight to his emotions and his political stance on the matter of forgiveness. In contrast, other members described what had happened to them by recounting, in the finest detail, their experiences—of never having met their mothers, of seeing their houses burned down, or of having searched for their missing children for thirty years. Several members broke down. Mr. Mphahlele did not break down because he could, in that moment, medicalize his own pain and anger.

One day, in May 2009, we took a stroll through the stalls on Greenmarket Square in the center of Cape Town, stopping at the stall of a book vendor to browse. Mr. Mphahlele found a biography of the Argentine revolutionary Che Guevara. He particularly liked Che because "he was a medical doctor." This was at a time when he was feeling fine, and he told me in a reflective moment, "I no longer have those suicidal thoughts. Maybe it's the medication and also Khulumani people who make me strong," adding, "I compare a lot. Others are much worse off." These feelings would often last for a short period of time; but eventually his ambivalence returned and he would begin to resent his dependency on the support group and the self-sacrifice his involvement with it entailed; these feelings would often cause him to withdraw for weeks.

His anger is also directed at the doctors and the health system. He complains that he sees a different psychiatrist each time he goes for counseling, and that he is tired of telling his story over and over again. There are periods lasting weeks when Mr. Mphahlele is more confused, absent-minded, and aggressive than usual. When this happens, he either goes to see a doctor more frequently or completely withdraws and refuses to engage with the doctors, Khulumani, or anyone else. He has always remained ambivalent about the doctors, though. At one visit to Groote Schuur Hospital, "the doctor treated me like a fool!" he told me angrily, imitating the doctor's manner. A little later he conceded that he was glad to have the medications. They helped him to control his anger, and to not go completely berserk when something or someone angered him. Like the week before, when a drunken young man took a picture of him with his cell phone in what must have been a shebeen in Langa Township, and Mr. Mphahlele grabbed the phone and smashed it against the wall. Only months before that he had stabbed someone who had provoked him by saying that he always hangs out with whites. Mr. Mphahlele ended up in jail for a few weeks before charges were dropped.

During these serious relapses, he completely retreats to places he normally tries to get away from during the day and which he openly detests: to the townships and the shebeens. Nobody can get hold of him until he re-emerges. He detests the place where he lives and feels utterly misunderstood by this family and community. Young people do not understand what he did for them and for the future of the country; they only laugh at what torture did to his face.

He is acutely aware of the damage the pharmaceutical industry that keeps him going allegedly caused in collaboration with the apartheid regime. He and I came together for a few reading sessions in the library of the Holocaust Centre Cape Town and exchanged views on what we had read. He usually chose books on Switzerland's collaboration with the Nazi regime, such as *Blood Money* by Tom Bower (1997), on the Holocaust reparation cases, or on Germany's redress policy. In one conversation we had about which sector was left out of the apartheid litigations, he said:

> I am talking what I'm thinking, in my mind, I think the other groups that must be held accountable . . . the pharmaceutical companies! Even here in South Africa . . . [t]he pharmaceutical industry never appeared in front of the TRC. I don't remember—even let alone the pharmaceutical industry—I don't even remember one doctor, medical doctor, coming to testify in front of the TRC. And they did lots of damage. They did lots of damage to our people.

When I asked him to give me an example, he said: "Biko! There are lots of cases. Poisoning . . . poisoning political prisoners!"

Mr. Mphahlele is, in a way, an expert about himself and he often tries to relate the new regulations, policies, and qualification categories to his own case. He knows the regulations for qualifying for a Special Pension by heart, for example, and often does the work the officials of the Special Pension Unit are supposed to do; that is, he helps other members to obtain the application form and fills it out with them. If their cases are rejected, he accompanies them to the Special Pension Office in the city center. His preoccupation with who qualifies for what is also apparent in his thoughts about the apartheid litigations. Given that the suits also define categories and classes of violations, he wondered whether the money would be distributed according to categories of injuries sustained. He would probably be in the "forcibly imprisoned and tortured" category, he speculated. Which company, he wondered, could be held accountable for that crime? But what about victims who were shot? They would be the responsibility of the arms and ammunition companies. "So I don't know what category I will fall into."

In various instances, the medical and psychiatric logic structures his account of himself. Having been in and out of treatment as a torture survivor, he has encountered numerous situations in which this discourse proves effective. Speaking about himself in medical terms gives him the opportunity to "try on" (Merry 2003) the medical coat, so to speak. It provides him with an objectified way of thinking about himself, the world around him, and the violations and injuries he has sustained. It asserts that he is a victim of torture and a survivor of the experience.

The ambivalence toward the medical profession may be due to the doctors' inability to completely relate to his experience of pain. As Scarry (1985, 13) notes, hearing about someone's pain is to have "doubts"; having pain is to have "certainty." The medical doctor, therefore, can never fully understand; he necessarily doubts. And the patient is always certain because she or he experiences the pain. Hearing medical explanations of how he feels can, I suggest, formalize and assert his sense of reality by giving a name to pain. This gives people like Mr. Mphahlele the opportunity to use words "that can be borrowed when the real-life crisis of silence comes" (Scarry 1985, 10). As mentioned, he has many other subjectivities.[22] The medicalized subject position may not be applicable in every phase of his life, in every situation, and may sometimes be worthless and even painful, and too close to or too far removed from his experiencing self, but at other times, it helps him to keep the pain in check.

Articulating Incorporated Injuries

Every person attempts in her own way to communicate her pain and share her suffering in her communities or with the larger society. However, the stories of pain in this chapter also yield the insight that victims, who live with chronic or more acute attacks of pain, or painful memories and emotions, such as anguish, rage, and grief, find it difficult to reconcile with the past in meaningful ways. Psychiatry would probably diagnose some of them with trauma or PTSD and would see proof of inter-generationally transmitted PTSD (Langer 1991). I am anxious not to pathologize the accounts on the basis of victims' silences and omissions,[23] and I suggest, at the very least, that we must acknowledge that experiences of violence may assume intimate and nonpathological presence in the lives of victims and their families.

The pain experienced by the people described in this chapter has not completely resisted articulation. They are all members of the Khulumani Support Group and had to claim and articulate a victims' subject position when they joined. As members, they are exposed to various discourses about what a victim of gross human rights violation is—as formulated by the leadership of the organization, the regional executive, their fellow members, the TRC or the Department of Justice, psychiatric institutions, and other victim-status-granting institutions (such as the South African Social Security Agency and the courts), researchers, and so forth. Given the context of a victim support group and the structural nature of state violence under the apartheid regime, the articulation of pain becomes a testimony to a collective victimhood, which also influences other members.

All the persons described here struggle to live in the present and to keep repercussions from the past at bay; yet their past experiences deeply encroach on their ability to find stability today. Chronologies that seem self-evident to others do not seem applicable in their lives—chronologies that suggest that the past is the past and that one can move on and overcome pain. The victims know this narrative well, and it shapes their expectations, but when they "try it on" (Merry 2003), it often lets them down.

People make various, often contradictory attempts to cope with pain. Some carefully embalm their experiences, cushioning them in silence to minimize the possibility of overwhelming and most upsetting setbacks. For others, using medical language helps them give expression to their pain. Others can only speak about their pain in the comfort of a much-trusted environment. Some use rage, anger, and a readiness to fight as a weapon to carry in everyday life. The promise of a life without pain and grief beckons to everyone, but only in rare moments does it seem achievable. These may be the moments when sharing pain seems possible and acknowledgment is effective.

> Full knowledge of the source of one's pain does make the suffering bearable. It puts one in a position to exercise one's right to make claims for historical wrongs done. These claims need not be exclusively material; they are, more importantly, claims for the acknowledgment of one's pain, and thus for its transformation into the arena of suffering worthy of social attention. Exposing one's wounds and having them acknowledged creates the possibility for the healing process to start from the base. (Ramphele 1997, 109)

Such attempts at sharing are always social, intersubjective, and embedded in the lifeworlds of those who suffer or are in pain. Being part of a community means, and here I draw on Schütz and Luckmann (2003), that one shares a lifeworld with others. The basic assumption is that we live our everyday life in the same world as those around us, and that we share this experience of living in the same world. With regard to intersubjectivity, Schütz and Luckmann establish several facts which we assume as unquestioned in the everyday reality of our lifeworld. Among the most important ones are the assumptions that I can enter into an interrelationship and engage in reciprocal actions with my fellow human beings, and that I can enter into dialogue with them. Furthermore, we rely on the validity of past experiences and on the stability of the world and our environment, and we situate our actions accordingly. We also rely on the ability to act *on* the world (Schütz and Luckmann 2003, 31). Living with pain fundamentally challenges all these assumptions. As Good and colleagues (1992, 7) note, "Something is at stake, frequently desperately so, in the lives of pain patients. Pain can be a massive threat to the legitimacy of the everyday world."

Those who suffer struggle to participate, and they find it difficult to relate their experiences to those of others. The more agency pain has in their lives, the less they give to their experiencing selves. Pain seems arbitrary and challenges notions of stability and agency. It threatens to unmake the world (Scarry 1985) and makes "past and present lose their order" (Good 1992, 42).

The arbitrariness of chronology is of particular importance in post-apartheid South Africa. Former liberation movements and today's political parties celebrate the new South Africa by declaring it distinct from the apartheid era. This is the founding myth of the country and the one assumption that cannot be questioned in the official discourse. The most prominent institution heralding the arrival of the new South Africa was the TRC. Ironically enough, it put victims at the center of its work and contributed to the upswing of victimhood in public, but it did not enable victims to become part of the new South Africa. People's lives do not easily fit into a pre- versus postnarrative. They perceive little transition or change in their own lives. The narrative of the new South Africa makes this all the more frustrating. It is so pervasive and tempting that it seduces victims to imagine themselves in a "post" world. But while their hopes tell us of a transition, chronic pain and unresolved grief do not.

The accounts here illustrate how people struggle to synchronize their lives with a temporal discourse of transition and change. Lungile Hlaise's account is the most telling in this regard: the denial of mourning, as it intrinsically pertained to the apartheid era, has not ended. She cannot mourn what her rapist inflicted on her because it is not publicly acknowledged. Neither can she mourn the aftereffects of her involvement in the liberation struggle, because it would be unpatriotic to question the sacrifice for liberation.

Publicly adopting a victim subjectivity is not without risks. People who adopt a victim subjectivity have to see that it is socially effective and not in too stark a contrast with their other ideas of themselves and the ideals prevalent in the lifeworlds they inhabit. We always try to synchronize our inner world with the outer world as it is socially organized and validated (see Schütz and Luckmann 2003, chap.1). In the same way, one's victim subjectivity needs to be acknowledged by the broader society in order to become socially and individually effective.

I want to stress the difference between recognition and acknowledgment, which are closely linked without being synonymous. As Axel Honneth (2003) argues, recognition is not possible without acknowledgment. To acknowledge someone means to have the knowledge that enables us to understand him or her. Acknowledging apartheid victims implies understanding what it means to have lived through the apartheid era and having come out injured. To recognize someone, in contrast, means to relate to somebody and to enter into a mutual relationship of respect. Recognizing apartheid victims thus means accepting and appreciating them in their injured personhood.

The vignettes in this chapter suggest that victims of apartheid-era crimes struggle to be acknowledged, let alone recognized, in today's South Africa. Their attempts to express pain are attempts to find acknowledgment and recognition as victims, in all their injured personhood. To achieve this, they try to relate their experiences to discourses around them that they find effective (such as the medicalized victim, the social victim, and the ready-to-speak victim), and they sometimes succeed in negotiating pain and recognition. But, and here we have to go back to the bodily dimension of pain, their experiences are not so malleable that they can be completely adapted to existing discourses.

Although Scarry rejects the idea that the experienced quality of pain can be communicated, she acknowledges that communication *about* pain is possible. One of the means of communication is the body. She suggests that the human body can be a "referent" for a person's suffering. It can be the referent for "felt-attributes" that are lifted "into the visible world" and thus become objectified attributes. Through these attributes, the "sentient fact of the person's suffering" can become "knowable" to a second person (Scarry 1985, 13). In short: Felt attributes undergo objectification and become knowable, but not sensible, to a second person. The body is the referent of such objectified knowledge. For Scarry, the body *refers* to something which is not transmittable in its original form and which necessarily undergoes translation (from sentient to knowable, from felt to visible).

The accounts in this chapter suggest that the body may be a referent and a means to communicate one's experienced victimhood to another. At some times during my research, the "sheer material factualness of the human body" (Scarry 1985, 14) played into the making and testing of a victim subjectivity. In moments when words failed, the factualness of the human body could speak for itself. People often showed me the scars from their injuries. However, I never had the impression that the demonstration was supposed to make *the* difference in people's victim subjectivity. Rather, it served to communicate a *subject position* in ways stipulated by various discourses. It seemed to refer to discourses the victim believed would require concrete bodily evidence to establish the credibility of someone's account. Generally, neither women nor men would uncover more than their shinbone or calf to show scars. The verbal reference to bullets in the chest or lack of scalp hair was sufficient *in its potentiality*. The words were trusted enough that they did not need to be complemented by physical evidence.

The body, in short, is not *the* argument for a victim subjectivity, but it is an *integral part of* that argument. We have seen in these accounts that victims do not dogmatically distinguish between body and "the rest," between visible and invisible injuries. The body absorbs exhaustion, stress, and sorrow, and injuries to bodies manifest themselves as confusion, fits, depression, uneasiness, inability to socialize, and so forth. The body is one of many communicative tools victims can use to reach out to the other—at all times, not only when they are communicating their pain and injuries. The body is not only a tool, however, and it often sends the most powerful messages when no communication is intended: grief intersubjectively affects the other without a word spoken, anguish leaves an impression on the face and in the posture of someone who has not found closure; one may recognize loss in someone's stance or see the desperate decades-long yearning for a loved one in another's gaze.

Sometimes the body is deployed consciously and deliberately. Marches to Parliament to convince the minister of justice to withdraw the government's opposition to the apartheid lawsuit relied on the impression made by a mass of bodies. Some forms of protest and resilience also tie in with ways the body was used as a means in the struggle. During one of my frequent meetings with several women from Philippi (see chapter 5), they told me how women were involved in the liberation struggle. At one point, they all started laughing naughtily and with the utmost pleasure: "One day when the police wanted to invade KTC [township], we all took our clothes off and we stand naked there. The whole KTC. They [the white policemen] run, they run! The women used to also think of plans! When the police see our big bums and our tummies . . . [then they would run away and leave us alone!]" and another woman added, "They haven't got big bums."

Reference to bodily injuries can thus be a possible modest way of articulating what Connerton calls one's *incorporated* injury to others. It is, however, a resort to "objective," what he calls *inscribed*, signs of injury (Connerton 1989). Only if this resort is understood in all its limitations, and *in its reference* to an experienced victimhood, can it amount to a genuine sharing of pain and a real recognition of the pain of the other. The vignettes in this chapter suggest that the injured body is more likely to raise suspicion because it is perceived as a sign of otherness. However, they also powerfully suggest that victims themselves have a model of the body that is historical and accumulative rather than biomedical.[24] Victims explicitly blame history for their current suffering. They thus directly challenge medical, anthropological, and psychiatric approaches to injuries and trauma.

Victims' bodies were targets of violence under apartheid rule and still are today, and this has left tangible traces. Ms. Hlaise and her daughter became victims of rape, and Ms. Hlaise lost some of her sight when the apartheid security forces dissolved the crowd of mourners at a political funeral, so that a body could not be properly laid to rest. In both political and criminal violence, the body is a target. Mr. Mphahlele speaks about torture that attacks the body directly or by deprivation (cf. Foster, Davis, and Sandler 1987). His face remains disfigured as a result of torture. Ms. Mgweba also shows how the raw control of the body and its movements has been at the core of apartheid policies. People living in squatter camps and other communities declared illegal by the apartheid state were periodically forcibly removed and detained.

Bodies left injured by these experiences of violence make it difficult for their owners to conform to the society's expectations, and may bring victims into a suspicious subject position. Mr. Mphahlele often tries to escape his community, where he feels utterly misunderstood. He partly anchors this feeling of misunderstanding is his deformed face; and even his attempts to overcome his injuries through his work for Khulumani single him out as different—because of this work, he has many white acquaintances. He is attacked, or feels pressure to defend himself, and responds with violence himself. His experiences seem to set him apart from his family and the community he lives in, and whose recognition he does not sense. Ms. Hlaise speaks most clearly about social exclusion of those who cannot deal with their painful experiences, those who set themselves apart: they are seen as bewitched, she explains. Happiness, Ms. Mgweba's daughter, has been excluded from school and has little chance of ever getting married because of her uncontrollable fits. Her mother traces this illness back to what her daughter witnessed as a child: the killing of people and burning of houses.

But physical and visible damage to the body cannot alone explain the nonrecognition of injured subjectivities. Social recognition is often lacking because victims cannot satisfyingly fulfill the social roles that have been reserved for them. The Trojan Horse theater performance shows how difficult it is for victims themselves to form alternative victim subjectivities. There is always the pressure to articulate one's experienced victimhood in ways that relate to established forms, be they therapeutic, political, irreconcilable, medical, or legal.

I understand the failure of recognition as an unsuccessful communication in both directions: from society to victims and from victims to society. Society seeks closure and it offers certain social roles to victims: the medicalized, the social (ready to reconcile) or the therapied (ready to talk). Victims try to be acknowledged by society and therefore try to take on the subject position offered to them. They fail for two reasons: either they cannot relate their experience of pain to a subject position that sits uneasily and does not offer any lasting relief, or, their injured personhood turns them into suspicious subjects. The failure is thus due to society *and* to the bodily memory of harm. It would not occur if the offered victims' subject positions fit the lived and experienced forms of victimhood; nor would it occur if society could recognize victims in spite of their injured personhoods.

This seems to suggest that "newness" can only come from victims themselves; when they come together, recognize one another, and work toward the emergence of alternative victims' subject positions that may take them beyond victimhood. The conditions and possibilities for another future and for new ways of relating to one another is the theme of the next two chapters.

Figure 7. Ethel Khali and Janet Ndeya, Philippi, Western Cape, December 2010

Figure 8. Lulama Lucia Mvenge, Alice Mvenge, and Janet Ndeya, Philippi, Western Cape, August 2012

Figure 9. Nolasti Twala in front of her house, Philippi, Western Cape, May 2009

Figure 10. Engelina Jama at the Nontsebenziswano Educare Centre, Philippi, Western Cape, November 2009

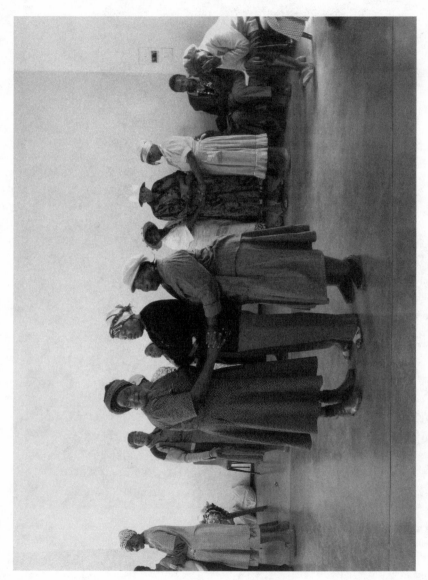

Figure 11. Khulumani members, Sebokeng, Gauteng, October 2010

Figure 12. In Eggie's Soup Kitchen, run by Agnes and Linda Ngxukuma, Ikwezi Park, Khayelitsha, Western Cape, December 2010

Figure 13. Ntombentsha Mdunyelwa in her stall at Ingulube Road, Philippi, Western Cape, November 2009

Figure 14. Elsie Gishi and her family, Nyanga, Western Cape, April 2013

Chapter 4

The Formation of the Political

THE SOUTH AFRICAN TRC was a governing institution.[1] It offered possibilities of political and legal action as an unintended consequence of its work, but it also imposed constraints on victims, who ever since have had to deal with a dominant societal idea of politicized, legalized, and bureaucratic apartheid victimhood. Under what conditions can a counterdiscourse of a different understanding of apartheid victimhood emerge in a hardened political environment?

Whereas sharing experiences of victimhood can foster sociality among victims, to be politically effective in the broader society, victims need to relate to the dominant victims' subject position. For individual victims, this requires emancipation from the bodily dimension of victimhood. In what follows, I examine the role the law can play in that process and, ultimately, in the formation of a political collective.

The Formation of a Political Community
Based on Joint Individual Dissent

In September 2009, Mr. Phelane (name changed) came to the Khulumani Western Cape office in Salt River to apply for membership and to ask for help with his application for a Special Pension grant. But he had not brought any documentation of the violations he experienced, so he was asked to come back the next day and bring along the relevant documents. An executive member informed me that a "direct victim" would be coming in the next day. On many days, the small ten-square-meter office is packed with people who would not qualify as victims in the office manager's and the organization's view. And many applicants were "indirect victims"—that is, they reported violations that happened to their spouses or children. When he came in the next morning, Mr. Phelane was angry and emotional, and was anxious to document his story. He spoke to the office manager, an executive member, and myself. Other people who applied for membership were present, and the office manager was also handling a couple of other cases simultaneously.

Mr. Phelane was in prison from 1994 to 2005, on what charges he did not elaborate. During that time, he made a preliminary statement to the TRC and received interim reparations. According to Mr. Phelane, his father gave the extensive statement to the TRC in his son's stead but without his son's authorization. Based on his father's submission, Mr. Phelane had also qualified for the individual reparations of R30,000. The R30,000 was subsequently deposited in his father's bank account because Mr. Phelane was still in jail. The TRC's statement taker never sought out Mr. Phelane to obtain his consent. At this point, the office manager interrupted and said that she had heard of this specific statement taker. It was his task to spread the information in the communities that a commission had called for submissions, but he did so very selectively. Living in the periphery of the City of Cape Town, township dwellers relied on word-of-month dissemination of the deadlines for submissions and the dates of the hearings. If the information did not reach them on time, they missed the opportunity to submit an application to the commission and could never be officially acknowledged as victims. It was because of this statement taker, the office manager continued, that she had not heard of the TRC on time and had missed the opportunity to give a statement. She further accused the statement taker of corruption: he teamed up with people giving statements on behalf of others and claimed his share of the deal.

Mr. Phelane resumed his story. His wife and other relatives did not have the money to make the journey to visit him in prison. Meanwhile, Mr. Phelane's father was busy spending his son's R30,000. He spent R15,000 on a car and divided R14,000 equally among his three daughters. Mr. Phelane assumed that the remaining R1,000 had gone to the statement taker, just what the office manager accused him of. On his deathbed, Mr. Phelane's father, evidently haunted by a guilty conscience, asked his daughters to give the money to their brother; but they never did so. They stick together like "the Three Musketeers," Mr. Phelane complained. He had many meetings with lawyers about trying to get his money back. It is hopeless, he said, one of his sisters had bribed the attorney in the Magistrate Court. He was also disappointed with the help he had received from LegalWise, the legal aid insurance agency. "I gave up on the judiciary," he said. Then he told us about his injuries: in 1976, he was shot in his chest. He still has the X-ray photograph of the wound. He also has thirty-seven rubber bullet shots in his back. He reflected on life under apartheid as a whole: "The system made us bad. "He made clear that he wanted to hold the statement taker and the First National Bank, which had transferred the money to his father's account, accountable. This is where he stopped, slightly out of breath.

Mr. Phelane's account was at times confusing and incoherent. His anger, accusations, frustration, and disillusionment with bureaucracies and legal institutions, was reminiscent of the accounts of many others who came to the Khulumani office, often to ask for assistance as a last resort after many failed attempts to receive what they thought they were entitled to. His account is also not exceptional in that real or promised payouts have caused rifts, jealousy, and sometimes threats and violence in families and communities.

The TRC has acknowledged Mr. Phelane as a victim, so officially, he is a "good victim" in the eyes of society. But he does not fit the description of a "good victim."[2] He spent the first twelve years of democratic rule in South Africa in prison. He is not only a victim but possibly also a perpetrator; he quarrels with his family over money; and he is not a useful member of the society that is rebuilding South Africa. This might be so precisely *because* he is a victim and struggles to integrate into a society from which he has been and remains estranged. This contradiction, which society prefers not to see, underlines the effects of the past and undermines sociability and solidarity with him.

Khulumani, however, offers solidarity with those who have in common both their victimhood and their difficulties in integrating and taking advantage of their supposed opportunities, who have not "made it" in the new South Africa. Mr. Phelane's probable delinquency is seen as part of a broader context of a fight for dignity and acknowledgment. The commonalities are therefore prioritized over the differences. Based on her own experiences of exclusion, the office manager could relate to Mr. Phelane's account because she thought she knew the statement taker who had collaborated with his family to appropriate his money. She identified with his victimization by allegedly corrupt state officials. The executive member, who also listened to Mr. Phelane's account, may have related to it because he has also been jailed a couple of times since 1994 on charges that he stabbed someone in an attack of rage. The ambivalence toward the part of society that has "made it" persists for all those who declare their victimhood from past experiences as an act of positioning themselves in the present time. It is an urge to belong despite victimhood and possibly perpetration. Khulumani offers victims a space in which to belong *because of* victimhood. Based on a common experience of an exclusive notion of victimhood, an alternative sense of community may emerge.

In the opinion of the majority of South Africans,[3] the question of victimhood was resolved in 1994, or, at the latest, in 2003, when the TRC published the last two volumes of its final report. There is strong pressure to comply with the approach to reconciliation and forgiveness endorsed by the ANC, for which the TRC is a pivotal reference (Borer 2003, 1092–95; Humphrey 2005; Wilson 2000). This approach holds that everyone should try to reintegrate and take his or her rightful place in society, and should become a useful member of that society to build the new South Africa's future. She or he should reconcile. Even survivors who are still suffering the long-term effects of apartheid-era violence, and are marked by them, should at least be willing to integrate. If victims try to foreground the ongoing consequences of past injuries and to render their suffering politically effective, these reminders challenge both South Africa's break with the past and its hopes for the future. The efforts are resented as a sign of the speaker's ungrateful egotism and seen as proof of the speaker's inability to integrate. The acknowledgment of a person's victimhood should instead be smooth, sociable, and generous—not threaten to evoke bad memories or to challenge the success of the so-called new South Africa.

For many victims, Khulumani is, at first, just another place to turn to find help with administrative problems. Once they make contact, however, many discover the possibility of sociability in their victimhood. A victims' subject position may, in some ways, be transformed into *conscious* victim subjectivity. Mr. Phelane had heard that Khulumani would help him fill out a Special Pension application. He was surprised to find sympathy and an articulation of shared concerns there as well. One executive member said to me: "Khulumani is a one-stop shop," and another added, "We are an advice office," marveling at the very different perceptions people have of what Khulumani will be able to help them with. The application for membership is not a quick bureaucratic process, and it is not completed by an employee who has little connection to his or her work and the lifeworlds of the applicants. It is received by someone who can relate to the experience of the applicant and intersubjectively engage with his or her story. In most cases, it is a very local story, with specific protagonists and incidents that only someone who has lived in the townships during the years of struggle can understand and put value to.

Despite the inconsistencies in his narrative, it was clear that Mr. Phelane had told his story before. He was emotional, but in his account, he touched on several institutions that he had approached in his capacity as a victim and which had accepted or rejected him on the basis of his victimhood. His account was thus not as raw as those of others, but he was more eloquent in articulating his frustration over the lack of acknowledgment and recognition. The bodily experience of victimhood shows through in the form of body-bound evidence (such as the X-ray and the bullet wounds). Although Mr. Phelane has had little success in making his victim subjectivity financially effective, he is not helpless when he approaches institutions for support. His claims are, among other things, based on the formal recognition of his victim status by the commission.

Dominant Notion of Victimhood versus Individual Dissent

The general notion of apartheid-era victimhood in South African today potentially clashes with individual dissent. The political in the daily lives of victims is formed in relation to the dominant notion of how victimhood should be lived and performed. The story of Amanda Mabilisa shows how an individual directly contests the effects of this dominant victims' subject position. Such acts of articulation are likely to be met with strong opposition and dismissed as unpatriotic, selfish, or weak. They are also risky because victim subjectivity is chiefly linked to the private and the intimate experiences of the individual.

Amanda Mabilisa, who lives in the province of Mpumalanga, ties her victim subjectivity to her active nonmembership in the ANC. In 2009, when we spent two weeks together, she had just stood for the Congress of the People (COPE) Women's League in the party's first national elections. In her own account, she chronicles the corrupt apartheid state and the biased post-apartheid state. She had left school in Swaziland in 1973 and was, as she emphasizes, the only female member of the South African Students' Organisation to be hidden and later smuggled out of the country after the 1976 Soweto Uprising. Her life in exile then took her to Lesotho, Botswana, Nigeria, and Germany, and she did not return to South Africa until 1995. The nursing certificate she earned in Germany in the 1980s and 1990s has never been accredited in South Africa. Her refusal to join the ANC is an expression of her self-image as a noncorruptible cosmopolitan thoroughly rooted in her community. She calls herself a "politician."

One night, Ms. Mabilisa took me to her neighbor's house, where he runs a shebeen in the outbuilding in his backyard called Theo's Place. Ms. Mabilisa and some of her male friends meet there to watch soccer, debate, and drink beer. She is ambivalent about some of the men who frequent the shebeen, saying that they are well-positioned in the ANC and enjoy a comfortable suburban lifestyle, and just come to the township on weekends to show off their cars. The four men who were present on the night I was there with Ms. Mabilisa were indeed dressed in suits and ties and had a worldly flair. The conversation at one point turned to politics, and one of the men, a senior ANC official, argued that a multiparty system does not work in Africa. As proof he cited the postelection violence in Kenya in 2007 and Barack Obama's *Dreams from My Father*, trying to impress us as a well-read man. He implied, and surely this was not the first time they had had this discussion, that Ms. Mabilisa excludes herself knowingly and deliberately from accessing the resources the cadres of the ruling party and officials have access to if she does not partake in ANC politics.

The conversation turned to a discussion of the ANC's integrity and Ms. Mabilisa mentioned a document that, she claimed, proved that the former head of South Africa's Communist Party, Chris Hani, was killed by his Umkhonto we Sizwe comrades.[4] Another man, a former mayor, was deeply upset by this accusation, exclaiming, "I think I am with the wrong people!" The senior ANC official mediated: documents, he said, are easily counterfeited. And anyway, he had read the "three volumes" of the TRC's final report, and nothing about this was mentioned. Ms. Mabilisa said triumphantly that this was part of the "unfinished business of the TRC" that her organization, Khulumani, had been trying to clear. The senior official warned her that engaging in such activities would harm her and her career. The conversation stopped, and everyone returned to drinking.

The advice Ms. Mabilisa received that evening was that she should let sleeping dogs lie. The men acknowledged that injuries of the past still impact the lives of South Africans today, but rejected individualized grievances, which they see as unreasonably holding on to the past. The TRC has dealt with apartheid. The senior official cited its final report as a canonical document with truth-value, substantiating the ANC's role as author of a transformation that, by now, is accomplished. Ms. Mabilisa, in turn, noted the TRC's shortcomings. She did not foreground her experienced victimhood but made her political victim subjectivity effective in a routinized political argument in a private setting in which the men's habitus, which often comes with being in a secure position of power, unfolded to the fullest. She made a structural argument and was confronted with an individualistic, liberal response. Feelings were strong on both sides; though the argument never threatened to get out of hand, nothing less than the recognition of individual choices was at stake.

I have seen Ms. Mabilisa in other situations in which she is readily listened to and easily finds favor—in youth and women groups, at COPE meetings, or at protest rallies over service delivery. Her victim subjectivity proves widely effective. Unlike many of the victims we saw in chapter 3, her status as a veteran of an important struggle allows her to express her point of view and assert her individuality. Her personal bodily experience of victimhood is in the background and gives way to persuasive argumentation about structural victimhood and biased politics. Victimhood as a personal experience is manifest as emphatic argumentation. It is not communicated in its raw and intimate form, which makes it possible to be on a par with a strong discourse of the past as finished.

The Law as Broker: The Formation of the Political

In the following account, victims and a representative of the law meet. In this situation, it is the law that facilitates the formation of political victim subjectivities. Legal ways of thinking about victimhood and personhood as such do not affect victims' personhood, though. Only when victims enter the political realm do they become tangible elements of victims' subjectivities. *What does this mean for my life and my future?* and *Am I socially and politically recognized in my state as a victim?* are questions that transform law-making into a tangible reality in victims' lives. In this form, law can be a basis for the formation of the political.

Khulumani Western Cape, unlike many other provincial branches, has held regular monthly general meetings since being consolidated into Khulumani's national structure in 1999.[5] Charles Abrahams, the South African legal adviser to the Khulumani apartheid litigation filed in the United States, was scheduled to speak at the October 2010 meeting.[6] Advance rumors that he was going to appear guaranteed that the Ashley Kriel Hall at the Community House in Salt River would be packed, and indeed, more than two hundred members attended. Abrahams's presence at these meetings is a reminder of the professional and international support that exists for their everyday struggles and suffering. His loyalty to Khulumani makes him an authority who can be trusted. On a more practical level, every announcement that he is going to speak sparks hopes and rumors that there might be a payout from a settlement in the lawsuit. His talks give short-term clarification of technical and political matters and tend to momentarily brush away rumors and accusations of misappropriation. Given that information at Khulumani is predominantly communicated orally, both among members and by the executive to members, there is room for misunderstanding and misinterpretation. In turn, such orality gives more authority to those who are chosen to speak or appoint themselves to speak. Mr. Abrahams is an effective speaker who has the ability to make complicated matters comprehensible to members—technically, conceptually, and discursively—without undermining the complexity and contingency of the law. All these qualities give him a certain monopoly of definition, in other words: normative power. The October meeting was unique in that, for a number of reasons, members articulated the most critical stance toward government I had yet heard in Khulumani meetings. I will show that, facilitated by the lawyer, their relation to the law allowed members to momentarily and temporarily emancipate from their embodied experiences by taking on a political perspective on their collective victimhood. This, in turn, offered a basis for collective action.

At the time, the apartheid litigations were still pending at the US Second Circuit Court of Appeals. Just a month before, on September 17, 2010, three Appeals Court judges had issued an opinion in a related case that was a blow to the international human rights community. In *Kiobel v. Royal Dutch Petroleum*, the Nigerian plaintiffs alleged that the Shell Oil Company was complicit in the torture and crimes against humanity committed in the Ogoni region of Nigeria because it had allegedly collaborated with the military regime of Nigeria in the 1990s. The majority ruling in the Appeals Court decision denied that corporations could be held liable for violations of international law.[7] The plaintiffs were expected to file a petition to rehear the case.[8] In short, as Mr. Abrahams told me before it was his turn to speak, he had the difficult task of conveying the negative impact this other ruling could have on the apartheid litigation without demoralizing members or understating the contingencies of such cases.

Abrahams opened his address to the membership as follows: "As most of you know, I always talk about the lawsuit. Sometimes I bring good news, and sometimes I bring bad news. Or sometimes I just bring news. Now today, I am going to bring just news. I am not sure whether it's good or bad; you must decide." He briefed the membership on the status of the defendants' appeal of Judge Scheindlin's ruling that the apartheid cases could proceed. Of the three judges who were hearing the appeal, Mr. Abrahams singled out Judge Cabranes: "He is a bit of a terrible judge." He is the very same judge who strongly argued against the liability of companies under international law in the *Kiobel v. Royal Dutch Petroleum* opinion.

The first comment from the membership was from a man who thanked Mr. Abrahams for not sparing them the facts. He said, as translated by provincial executive member Zukiswa Puwana: "It is encouraging to see that as lawyers you are not just sitting, you are looking forward and thinking of the appeal. We are behind you, 100 percent, we pray for you." Another man said: "I don't think we have any questions. You are the lawyer, we are not." This made the audience laugh, partly because they were amused by such a blunt handing over of authority, but also because they felt uncomfortable—questions should be asked to show appreciation and respect for the lawyer. Then it was Sakwe Balintulo's turn to speak. He is the first named plaintiff in the Khulumani lawsuit (*Balintulo et al. v. Daimler AG et al.*) and is always given a slot to speak.[9] He is old and his voice was so soft that members could hardly hear him: "It is important that we are patient. These things don't come easily. We have to wait. Mandela waited for twenty-seven years [in prison]."

Then a female member spoke, causing a small uproar. She joined in the general expression of gratitude, then asked: "My question is, I am not going to hold back: how much longer are we going to wait [for the money to be paid out]?" Her question didn't cause an uproar because it was irrelevant to members, on the contrary. It was considered rude, or, at best, brave, to question the lawyer's efforts. He, in turn, talked about the South African government's ongoing opposition to the cases. "Yes, tata Balintulo is right, we must be patient. But it's a real question of how long still?" He said that had there been "a government that was a little bit stronger behind us, perhaps it might have been a different outcome." He assured the membership that "if I look at all of you and also myself: My wish and desire is that this matter should be resolved as quickly as possible" and elaborated on the two approaches they always had: the legal and the political. "And when there was enough political will not just among Khulumani but among everyone, everyone, there may have been a different outcome."

A man responded that he had not seen any political will in the three administrations, from Mandela to Mbeki and Zuma. In the Groote Schuur Minute of 1990,[10] "Tata Mandela said there isn't going to be any reparations for victims and also no arrest for perpetrators. And then Thabo Mbeki came into power and he used our money." The membership was, at this point, torn between excitement and surprise. Some were visibly angry and tried to hush the speaker.

It is rare to hear Nelson Mandela being attacked for not thinking about the victims. The majority of the members are loyal ANC members and would evaluate successive presidents for their faithfulness to Mandela's heritage.

The fact that Charles Abrahams, as a lawyer, was talking about the need to critically engage with the government had given rise to such articulations. Then a young representative from the rural branch of Khulumani stood up and called for action, in English:

> Chief! . . . Is there any strategy in terms of dealing or strategizing around how do we engage with the current government? . . . Because I believe in a way we need a more militant approach in terms of reparations . . . We need to sit down and strategize how do we engage *militantly* this reluctant government. . . . A militant approach, chief!

When he was speaking, the members muttered and mumbled in agreement; when he finished, they applauded. Everyone was curious what the lawyer had to say in response to this youthful and well-spoken person. Such words were unheard of, and he clearly represented a new, second generation of members who advocated new ways to engage government on the issue of reparations. This young man had once worked for the government, and it was clear in his rhetoric that morning. Mr. Abrahams responded:

> I owe the chief a response. . . . I have got to be very wary about my position because first and foremost I am a lawyer. And you are asking me, and in fact all the other questions prompted, a political response. So accept my response not as a lawyer; so that you accept it was as an individual that's been involved in these lawsuits. I just want to make that clear. . . . As you know lawyers are very restricted in what they can say and what they can't say [*understanding murmuring from the audience*].
>
> Now, stepping outside the realm of being a lawyer: I think you are right. We need to up the pace [applause] . . . It is not militant in the sense of being destructive but we need to really show that we are very serious about this matter. . . . So that hopefully it is not another nine years before this matter is being resolved.

An elderly man took up the criticism of the government and was loudly cheered: "I think it is up to us to put pressure on government. Whenever there are elections coming up, [the ANC] will come to the communities and pick up old people to vote for them. Let's use that channel, let's make our voice heard and say that we are not going to vote because they are not considering what we are saying." He suggested that they actively oppose being instrumentalized for party politics. His suggestion, of course, also meant passivity in that he proposed abstaining from voting.

The next contribution showed that, at the end of the day, members are struggling most with the practical details that have a huge impact in their everyday lives. A man said, "People are dying without getting anything. My question is to you, Charles. Is there a provision for us as plaintiffs when we die that our dependents will get something when this matter is resolved?" Mr. Abrahams was then said good-bye as songs celebrating him and Khulumani were sung, making members dance and cheer.

In sum, upon provocation by a young member and in a move that only persons of law can successfully *perform*, Mr. Abrahams proposed a shift of perspective from the legal to the political *through his own personhood*. He drew a line between the legal and the political and temporarily left the one for the other. In effect, of course, he also confirmed the demarcation of the two. He offered solidarity that went beyond his professional advice and reasserted that legal action has to happen in parallel with political action.[11] This shift from the legal to the political realm facilitated various articulations from the audience that probed what he advocated. For members, the legal realm remained obscure in its technicality, but it became possible to engage with it publicly in the meeting and make it tangible for collective political action.[12]

The meeting was the result of years of conscientization. No one needed to explain to members what the apartheid regime had inflicted upon them and what the effects are up to today. But the formulation of one's own victimhood into a political victim subjectivity—that is, a critical quest for attention and for recognition from the former liberation movements and the current government—is a different thing. It could only come about by an emancipation of one's own victim subjectivity from an official discourse that clashes with the solidarity they feel with their respective political parties, with the search for reliable leadership, with hopes long held, and, most importantly, from one's bodily sedimented victimhood.

I suggest that a legal process offered a crucial possibility for members to momentarily see their elected leaders in a different light. In that meeting, the legal became tangible and personally meaningful *in the shape* of the political and started to form the basis for political collective action. Members' victim subjectivities successfully became politicized in this safe environment of a public realm shaped by familiar solidarity.

The condition the possibility of articulating one's victimhood politically requires is (momentary) emancipation from the bodily dimension of victimhood. Hence, bodily experiences are not only the basis for the formation of the political, as Mr. Phelane's account shows to a lesser degree and Ms. Mabilisa's shows to a greater degree; bodily experiences are also the dimension from which people have to be able to emancipate themselves, at least to some degree, in order to be politically effective

Habit Memories as the Basis for the Political

In May 2011, the Department of Justice (DOJ) gazetted regulations for assistance to apartheid-era victims with respect to basic and higher education and in relation to medical benefits for victims and their dependents, and invited responses. Only the 21,000 victims identified by the TRC would be eligible for this assistance. The payments would come out of the President's Fund, which has accumulated almost R1billion since it was established in the mid-1990s. Civil society was appalled by the proposal. For years, civil society organizations had tried get some say in how the Fund should be used in the reconstruction efforts, pushing the state to finally release the money and suggesting that community reparations and benefits be paid to *all* victims, not just those on the TRC list. They criticized the "closed list policy" and demanded that the current process be halted until "meaningful consultations are carried out with victims and interested parties." It was a setback for civil society after years of closed or public meetings with the DOJ, South Africa's president, and the TRC Unit and what was believed to be progress in making small steps toward a more inclusive notion of victimhood. The DOJ, notwithstanding the increased attention on its handling of post-TRC matters, had decided to use the officially recognized list of the TRC. It thus decided against using the Khulumani Support Group database to identify recipients and holding a follow up to the original TRC so that more victims could testify, and against a community-based approach that would not single out individuals.

The list proves to be persistent. Government had, almost two decades ago as a result of negotiations and by way of the Truth and Reconciliation Act of 1995, decided on a model for dealing with the past. I have shown above that this was, in effect, a form of governance that leaves traces and is not easily revised. But what does this form of governance mean beyond a list and inclusion in or exclusion from public benefits?

What is at stake here is the myth that post-apartheid South Africa is based on—that it has overcome its cruel and unjust past. The list is in essence a list of injustices redressed and abolished. By defining a category of victims and paying reparations to all that fall in the category, government does not only provide resources to a select few; it attempts to define and provide the public good of a postconflict political order. This governing process was at first a typical example of an interventionist measure. As many interventionist measures, it did not fully reach its aim but remains hotly contested and challenged. What is more, it influenced the formation of political subjectivities. An interventionist measure thus triggered the emergence of other less interventionist forms of governance. We can only understand the trajectory of governance if we take both into account.

I analyzed the scope and limits of forms of governance "from below," based on shared personal experiences rendered politically relevant by a categorization from above. For victims' agency in making a political victim subjectivity effective in their everyday lives, I emphasized *experience*, or *habit memories*, as one of the driving factors. Is the persistence of incorporated knowledge a source of resistance against governance? I argued, drawing on the last chapter, that the sedimentation of *habit memories* is not only the source of agency but also what puts limits to agency and a successful political articulation. Especially so when the body is, in various ways, injured. The outcome is hence contingent on the bodily dimension of victimhood—or of being human. I therefore suggest expanding any analysis of governance and agency to include the embodiment of experiences.

Including the embodiment of experiences in our analysis of the impact of dominant subject positions on lived subjectivities would also mean carefully rethinking the effects of such governing measures in terms of their outreach into social space. It would mean asking what are the effects of dominant discursive practices on the possibilities of sociability. In what ways do governing processes—through their discursive formation of differentiation—affect the possibilities of sociability?

In the public discourse, the bodily dimension of victimhood dissipates, to the advantage of more political forms of articulating victimhood. Does this formalization of articulation toward dominant forms of victimhood result in a distancing from one's own experience—or is it simply a learned way that may allow shifts in subjectivity away from an overwhelming victimhood?

Governing processes open up possibilities for political action, but they also impose constraints on social actors trying to emancipate from dominant definitions and subject positions. I tried to show that sedimented knowledge is the source of political articulation. But the developments in courts and the political reactions to legal actions also suggest that the political often emancipates, moves beyond, and develops a logic on its own. This, in turn, is effective in daily lives in contingent ways and forces the cementation of distanced subject position or fosters the articulation of new forms of political subjectivities. This process is at the heart of governance, which inevitably affects the relation between the individual and the political.

Judith Butler (2005) wrote that to be a subject is to be subjected. Of course, this is not where she stops, but it is her premise, just as it is Foucault's. I have shown how the dominant victims subject positions—the TRC's but also the law's—tend not to acknowledge a bodily grounded victimhood; in that perspective, lived victimhood is discursively detached from victim status. But I have also shown that lived victimhood is often a nonpredicated and bodily state. Then how do people come to make claims and relate their bodily experiences to dominant subject positions in the first place? Is there not a necessary gap between personhood and subject position, a gap that may be a reason to fail to claim a subject position in a politically successful manner? In other words, how do we have to understand the relationship between the political and the social? In Butler's line of thinking, the political dominates the social; it literally *subjects* the social to its logic.

The empirical data I presented in this chapter suggests a more nuanced view. First, governance is never complete (Förster 2015). Because interventionist measures are flawed, they may constrain, but they also leave room for contestation. Governance may be flawed in various ways. I point to governance's emphasis on status rather than experience. Governance measures often assign a status to a select few, which necessarily (and maybe intentionally) excludes others. People, however, do not understand themselves (nonpredicated or cognitively) primarily in the categories created through these forms of governance, or only in response to them. This is where I believe we need to better understand the role of embodied experiences through which people come up with creative alternative notions of selves (which may, of course, turn into hardened subject positions and may be appropriated for new governing interventions).

The political emerges where people with similar experiences recognize one another in their subjectivities. Such recognition, which is essentially social, may turn into collective action. The example of Mr. Phelane shows such a moment of recognition. The example of the lawyer speaking to his "clients" addresses the possibility of the formation of collective action. The case of Ms. Mabilisa shows that individuals who do not fit into the dominant narrative of the reconciled victim have to deal with challenges to their personhood. In her years in exile, Ms. Mabilisa learned to adopt and live multiple subjectivities and gained sufficient social mobility, which enables her to fend off attacks on her personal and political choices stemming from her experience.

It was the law, brokered and performed by the lawyer, which triggered the emergence of subjectivities as political. But it was the bodily or *habit* memories of the law's "subjects" that ultimately connected the political, the legal, and the social.

In this sense I disagree with the view of Jean and John Comaroff that the law is, increasingly, primarily a strategic avenue. In terms of class or group actions, they observe that people come together who have little in common but society's prescribed subject positions (Comaroff and Comaroff 2006, 26–31) and whose subjectivities are then jointly affected by a legal logic that makes political mobilization less likely. Victimhood, I would argue, is anchored in embodied knowledge, even if the law does not acknowledge it; for people recognizing similar experiences in others, even the joint relation to given subject positions can act as a trigger for political mobilization.

If discourses around victimhood in South Africa are as strong as I suggest in this and in previous chapters, and if it is such an enormous effort for victims to refer their personhood to these discourses in order to start establishing political efficacy, there is, I believe, still a missing link. How do victims come into the position of relating successfully to discourses? To answer this question, we need to look beyond discourses. The next chapter is in many ways the core of this book: I present practices I have found during my field research where victims produce the seeds of social change.

Chapter 5

Emancipation from Victimhood

I SPENT the major part of my research time with women from Philippi Township. From them I learned, in informal and unspectacular meetings, most about the magnitude of victimhood and the degree to which their past injuries continue to affect them in every aspect of their everyday lives. As I became more acquainted with them individually and blended better into their group, I also began to understand how much the meetings meant to the women, and the opportunity to transform their victimhood these meetings presented.

Suffering has bodily consequences, and painful experiences are remembered bodily. In what follows, I show how a shared social space, which is often constituted by non-family ties, can partly undo pain (cf. Shaw 2012). It is a space not defined by words but by lived sociality among victims. Personal pain can be contextualized in mutual support. As will become clear, my description of these relationships contains no sensational or otherwise eventful moments. They rely on a shared victimhood rooted in the past and are therefore fragile. However, it is precisely this anchoring that also makes change in the present and future time possible.

Tacit Practices of Mourning

On many a day, two to five women of Philippi gathered in one of their homes. Typically, they would choose a house (as opposed to a shack) and a household that could offer space to sit down and, hopefully, some tea bags. They would meet for an hour or more, mostly in the afternoon after the morning's chores had been completed. During the winter, the weather was often bleak; the strong Cape wind howled across the Flats and the room would be cold. Sometimes I was the reason for the meeting, the reason the women had dressed in layers of skirts and jerseys and braved the winter cold to be there (or, wearing the same layers of skirts, suffered the hot and humid summer weather). More often than not, however, they met of their own accord.

On the days I attended the meetings, I would pick up Ethel Nosipo Khali, and we would drive to the meeting together. Ms. Khali did not have many possessions, but she did own a cell phone, so I could contact her and announce my coming. It became our routine that I would go inside her two-room RDP house for a while before we left for the meeting. Her mentally challenged son lived in a room attached to the house, and she sometimes had tenants in the two backyard shacks. The house sits behind another shack, in the front yard, which was full of piles of building materials, such as corrugated iron, iron plates, cardboard, and bricks. This is also where the Philippi branch of the healing movement News of Salvation (uSindiso laku Tsolo; Indaba zuSindiso) had built a temporary prayer room. The original room, a few hundred meters away, was torn down after the owner reclaimed his plot. Ms. Khali is a dedicated member of the church that was founded in her hometown of Tsolo, Eastern Cape, by the late lay reader and healer Elizabeth Paul (1906–1964). Sometimes Ms. Khali would offer me an overly sweet drink and make me sit down to look at something she urgently wanted to show me: it might be a photograph of Elizabeth Paul or of Ms. Khali's three sons (one of whom has since passed away) wearing traditional blankets at the celebration that followed their initiation into manhood in the 1990s, or it might be the notes she had compiled as an election observer, appointed by Khulumani, in the 2009 national and regional election. After that, she would take the passenger seat in my 1989 Golf Sedan, and we would wind our way through the narrow streets of her neighborhood. We only have to cross the main street (Ingulube Road), but she prefers to be driven. This time of day, the early afternoon, is when she usually feels the best. Her chronic arthritic pain, which is worse in the mornings, exacerbated by spending windy nights in a drafty house, has subsided somewhat. She knows that by the end of the day she will feel exhausted again, and takes care to be back home by 5:00 p.m. The less she moves, the less pain she has. There were days when she could not get out of bed, and I had to bring her painkillers from the city center (she could not get them from the township).

We stopped next at the shack of Maureen Mazibuko, which stood next to her "new" house, which had been half finished and uninhabitable for years. She is "never at home," Ms. Khali routinely teased as we approached the front door.

"She likes to visit her friends." I would knock several times to make sure that she could hear me through the loud music blaring from the adjacent shacks. If there is no answer, Ms. Khali and I might drive on some hundred meters to see if we can find her at the shack of her closest friend, Janet Ndeya. Ms. Ndeya's nephew, the son of her late twin sister, greets me cheerfully, knowing that we are only there to collect his aunt and her friend. Sometimes Ms. Ndeya, who suffers from diabetes and high blood pressure, is too sick to join us; or, she has to attend to her husband. "She is the only one among us who has a husband," the women once told me. Ms. Khali was widowed in 1985. Ms. Mazibuko's first husband was also shot dead in the 1980s, when she was pregnant with their son. She also has a son with her second husband, whom she left a while ago.

Because of her ailments, Ms. Ndeya is frequently in pain. She is supposed to go to G. F. Jooste Hospital, in Mannenberg, every three months for a checkup and medication. Like Ms. Mazibuko, who also has diabetes, she used to inject insulin, but the injections had stopped working for her, and the doctor prescribed pills instead. Both women take pills now. Ms. Ndeya, however, gets tired of eating pills every day and deliberately misses appointments with the doctor. Ms. Mazibuko recommended Chinese medicine sold by an African lady as an alternative, which an old man had told her about: put the powder on the sole of a foot with the help of a plaster and it will instantly draw out all the poison. In addition to sharing health advice, the two women check on each other to make sure the other is following the doctors' dietary instructions (only one teaspoon of sugar in your cup of tea!).

Our next stop would be at the house of Alice Mvenge. During the day, Ms. Mvenge looks after her four grandchildren and other children of preschool and primary-school age. Her son, Vusumisi Goodman Mvenge, died of AIDS, leaving his son, Sixolile Dyaluvane, in her care. "He will be a lawyer one day," she proudly says when her grandson comes sprinting home from day care. The other women look up to Ms. Mvenge, who was born in 1932 and is the oldest among them. In the 1950s, as part of a widespread buildup of passive resistance to apartheid, she was one of the leaders of the protest movement against the extension of pass laws and the introduction of passes for women (Wells 1993). "She is the oldest, but she is healthy," Ms. Mazibuko says in awe. Ms. Mvenge welcomes us in the front room, an addition to her two-room RDP house. Although this room is also bleak, it is still more decked out than the stuffed and dark private rooms at the back. As these afternoons progress, the grandchildren will come home from school and the crèche and maybe ask for a snack or one of the cold drinks that I have brought along. Or Ms. Mvenge's daughters will come to help their mother with the chores.

We often settle in for the afternoon at Ms. Mvenge's house, but when she is not at home, we will go to see whether Ntombentsha Mdunyelwa is at home. She has a stall on Ingulube Road, where she sells pieces of pork or grills them for her customers to consume on plastic chairs under a corrugated iron roof. We started calling her Pork Lady when I first forgot her name; somehow, the sobriquet stuck. Her house is particularly attractive. It is spacious and there is running cold water. There is a kitchen in one corner, and she has enough cups to offer tea to all of us. It is not an RDP house but is part of a housing develop-ment project funded by the Bill Clinton Foundation. For years, Ms. Mdunyelwa put a small amount of money in a bank account each week to cover her contri-bution to the project. The house is still unfinished: under the corrugated iron roof, the ceiling is missing.

She buys pigs from a farmer and slaughters them in the backyard—one pig every two weeks suffices to meet the demand. If we cannot find her at home, we look for her around the corner, where her stall is. Business usually picks up later in the afternoon when people are returning from work. Ms. Mazibuko emphasizes that she always gets tea at Ms. Mdunyelwa's house. In the 1980s, though, they did not have time to sit down for tea: "We were on the run." Ms. Mdunyelwa's fourth-born son passed away from a lung disease caused by teargas, and her daughter was a trained underground soldier.

In the 1980s, most of the five women had lived in KTC or one of the ad-jacent informal settlements, such as Crossroads (to where many inhabitants of KTC fled during the unrest in 1986), Nyanga Bush, and Nyanga Extension (J. Cole 1987, 2012). Some had left their assigned homelands in the 1970s, or earlier, to find work in the Cape; some settled temporarily in the hostels in Langa (Wilson and Mafeje 1963). All were forcibly moved back to the Transkei or the Ciskei several times because they didn't have a valid pass, sometimes riding in the same police van. After being deported, they all returned to the Cape by any means and as quickly as possible. They often left their children with their parents in the homeland (Henderson 1999; Reynolds 1989). As the women became more involved in the liberation struggle, willingly or not, it was safer to leave the children in their grandparents' care. Constant harassment by the police; nights spent in police stations; frequent searches of their shacks by the security forces; staged road blocks, marches, and sit-ins; and frequent destruction of their dwellings followed by weeks of living in churches allowed for little stability in their lives. During this period, houses were often set on fire and the people inside were burned alive (Platzky, Walker, and Surplus People Project 1985). Inevitably, however, their children were sometimes with them during these years—toddlers affected by the fire and teargas, young children exposed to the sight of destroyed communities and suffering parents, or teenagers involved in stone throwing or gang activities.

At these afternoon meetings, nothing really happens. We talk. Often, I just listen; or sometimes I stop listening and play with the children, and the women revert to isiXhosa and stop translating for me. They share the latest news, such as cases of death and criminal incidents in their families and acquaintances, both in the community in Cape Town and in their respective homes in Eastern Cape. They exchange news from Khulumani, advise each other, to the best of their knowledge, on how to navigate the bureaucratic maze of social grants, and always ask about each other's health.

Most of the older women suffer from diabetes, high blood pressure, arthritis, or other chronic illnesses. If one or the other of the five is unable to attend an afternoon meeting, it is usually because she is at the clinic in Nyanga, where they go to receive free basic health care. At the clinic, their illnesses are attended to periodically and episodically, and they come home with pills or instructions to change their eating habits. All the women link their poor health, being overweight, and their chronic illnesses to problems in the past: hard physical work; exposure to the wind and the cold and other harsh weather conditions; untended injuries; and constant mental stress, in some cases even physical torture, beatings, and unlawful detention. They could not afford to pay for the operations they needed. Ms. Mvenge, for example, had long needed an operation to remove a cancer in her stomach,[1] and Ms. Mazibuko's shoulder had been dislocated ever since she jumped over a fence and fell when trying to flee the security police in the 1980s. In those days, the women didn't go to clinics as often as they do now. As she explained:

So we didn't go too much to the clinics, we put herbs on our legs and bandage our legs ourselves. Here I was struck by a tree (showing her thigh), by a tree, here. The tree branch went in here. And that we pulled out. And I never went to a clinic, Rita. Here I jumped in KTC (showing another scar), the dogs were chasing me. This was never stitched. It's got no stitches. It just healed on itself. Put medicine, herbs, and it gets better. We were frightened even to go to a clinic. They just take us and call the police, there is somebody here with a bird shot.

Ms. Mdunyelwa's nephew was shot in the back during that time. When she took him to the clinic, the nurses phoned the police, who came to arrest him.

The frequent visits to the clinic today also need to be understood in the context of the grant system: in order to receive a disability grant, one must see a doctor a couple of times a year to confirm that she or he is still disabled and maintain coverage.

One time, Ms. Khali and I left Cape Town together to go visit her village in the Eastern Cape. On our two-day journey from Cape Town to her home village, Tsolo, in the former Transkei, Ms. Khali and I stopped for coffee in Komga. It was in this tiny place, she remembered, that she and other women were "dumped" in 1981 after being deported from Cape Town for not having passes. Komga was then at the border between the Ciskei and Transkei home-lands. The police did not care that their homes were another 200 kilometers northeast of Komga. The deported women thus decided to go straight back to Cape Town. "We were stupid that time. We were tortured a lot." They relied on each other and on the leadership of some women to find food and transport to eventually get back to the Cape. Ms. Khali pointed out that children were not well nourished back then. The women could only afford to feed them maize meal, soaking it in water instead of milk. Ms. Khali is sure that this affected many children's development and health. As late as at the age of five, they could only say "mama," she remembered.

All five women had grown up in rural areas. To survive on small plots of poor farmland was difficult, so families had to rely on relatives earning money in the towns. The daughters went to the cities to find work as domestic work-ers. They had little protection from the law: there was neither a minimum wage nor fixed working hours or guaranteed holidays. Women workers often did two jobs: they did wage work during the day and went home to do the domestic work for their families at night. Their time to rest or to organize in unions or politically was very limited. Given the large number of fatali-ties, confinements, and disappearances of the fathers of their children, and the general instability of families, women often became heads of households. This has not changed.

Most of the women have the former Transkei as their main point of refer-ence. Many inherited a house from their parents or their in-laws, which they try to attend to. However, these houses are often even more dilapidated than their dwellings in the Cape. Some have just gotten electricity, and having run-ning water in the house is the exception throughout the rural areas. The graves of their family members and the spirits of their ancestors are believed to rest in those villages. Funerals typically take place in the villages, as well; the women frequently travel from the towns to attend the ceremonies, which last for several days.

Returning home is a dream deferred. To their lived habit as a rural person in an urban environment, the city poses a constant challenge. In the apartheid years, it was the struggle for an income; for the children's survival; for legal status; and for a better life, free from degradation, discrimination, and violence (Reynolds 1995). Having left the harsh environment in the homelands, they had to make the areas outside of Cape Town habitable. Philippi (or Brown's Farm, as it was originally called), for instance, was forest, they say, when they first settled, and it was they who conquered nature and made it inhabitable. Their children went to a school their mothers had helped to build with their own hands.

For the generation of women in Philippi and other townships who are nearing or in their sixties, or older, finding regular employment is not an option, often because of their damaged, tired bodies. For the past eighteen years, they have had to get by on an unreliable income from petty, informal jobs (with the exception of the Pork Lady, who can at least buy pigs), on disability grants for their disabled children, or on child support grants for their grandchildren. If they are lucky, they can prove that they are eligible for a special pension. Above age sixty, they receive an old-age pension, which often becomes the only steady income for a large extended family (Ferguson 2015). But the money is so little that they cannot put anything aside into savings. Their wish to return to their villages is put on hold. As Ms. Khali put it: "I'm not going to . . . I'm not thinking to go to home. Because it's not nice to go home with . . . you have got *nothing*!! How can I go there without money? When I got no money I . . . my, I can't go there, Rita." So, they come home to attend the funerals of family members or family friends. But the mourners always return to the city, even more determined to return to their villages one day.

Today, life in the city has changed insofar as police harassment and deportations have stopped.[2] Notwithstanding this change, the women experience the "limits to liberation" (Robins 2005) in the post-apartheid era on a daily basis. Liberation has not brought redress for the deaths of their husbands, their lost belongings, or their ruptured lives. And it has not resulted in a significant change in their lives. Liberation has failed them by not keeping its promise to substantially transform the everyday lives of ordinary South Africans.

Even though all five women belong to Khulumani, they rarely talk about their victimhood there. To be sure, talking about poverty or about the manifestations of poverty, for instance, is not easily distinguishable from talking about victimhood. Nor is it easy to draw a conceptual line between poverty and victimhood. One perpetuates the other, and vice versa. But it is safe to say that these women feel no need to emphasize their apartheid-era victimhood among themselves; it is part of a shared self-image requiring neither explanation nor confirmation. There is a *tacit knowledge* among the women that they are victims (albeit for the context of expert knowledge; see Collins 2010; Polanyi 1967). This knowledge is rarely made explicit, nor does it need to be, as victimhood is part of an *us*-understanding. On these afternoons, they do not need to assert themselves as persons with a victimhood status.

The women's precarious physical condition refers to the brokenness and heaviness of their lives. They are exposed to contingencies stemming from the fact that the injured body does not let them forget. Their experiences were not one-off beatings, which a person may be able to forget. Their experiences were decades long: being deprived of medical care, subjected to physically strenuous, undignified work and ill treatment, and, finally, enduring the frequent ruptures of social relations.

This brokenness becomes, among other things, a bodily condition that is jointly lived with others who have a similar condition—without being articulated. The brokenness is the condition for their sociability, not its overt content. But it is its *silent* content because it is the reason for their shared sociability. What emerges in these meetings is the solidarity of people who have shared, and continue to share, similar experiences. The women support each other in their everyday lives, help each other out as much as they can, and offer one another company.

The meetings keep this tacit knowledge alive and make it bearable. At the same time, they allow the women to live their victimhood in a context of acute awareness of their experiences. Forming new social bonds that are not family ties but originate in the similar condition of victimhood may hold out to these women the possibility of changing their victim subjectivity.

Their social roles in society do not change, though. They find some safety among themselves, but it does not really reach beyond their circle. Their sense of community thus contains the risk of isolation if it is not translatable into a sociality that reaches the broader society. There is no real point from which the women can embark on something new that will take them beyond their victimhood. This chronology of pain has a strong economic dimension. Their economic situation is the same as it was before 1994. And they are even less able to work now for low wages because of their age and their brokenness. In that sense, apartheid-era victimhood starts merging with a more general experience of marginality.[3]

The women practice a mutual acknowledgment of their ruptured, hard lives; in many ways, their being together is a mourning practice. Such social experiences allow them to slowly and silently work on their individual and shared grief.

Habituation and Emancipation

If certain memories of systematic injustice are embodied and habitual, how should we view the possibilities of becoming emancipated[4] from them? As we have seen, not much has changed for these women of Philippi since 1994. And although their tacit practices among themselves are central in their lives, they ultimately are precarious. Their community is fragile and requires being in the physical presence of one another. It can easily be disrupted by changes in a woman's circumstances, illness, or relocation. The question of how things can change if so much of the past is embodied and habitual is thus a troubling one.

In what follows, I provide some empirical material that deals with the reconcilability of the body and with the social conditions for change of an injured subjectivity. *Emancipation*, as I use the word here, can happen through various processes, such as repressing, forgetting, or confronting, as long as it represents a step toward the assertion of a self that is not primarily dominated by victimhood. This, as I will show, makes the assumption of a new social role in society possible.

By focusing on daily life, I seek to understand changes in practices that are related to past experiences; my aim is to draw some conclusions about the possibility of changing bodily sedimented experiences and on its limits. I rely on Connerton (1989, 22) who distinguishes *habitual memory* ("a class of memories [which] consists simply in our having the capacity to reproduce a certain performance") from *personal memory* ("those acts of remembering that take as their object one's own life history"). I will show that changes in habitual memory necessitate changes in personal memory, and vice versa. Changing (bodily) practices may bring about a new (social) position from which to reflect on one's own life history. The possibility of looking differently at one's life may spark changes in what has become habitual.

Certainly, a person acts out of various (conscious or unconscious, self-chosen or imposed) reasons, and not every action can be empirically related back to his or her victimhood. How, then, are researchers to know which actions to trace back to painful experiences, particularly when these experiences have taken on a habitual form? This question is at the core of anthropological knowledge. Social scientists determine what is "normal" or "typical" in a particular social setting by looking at a break with a custom or a sanctioning measurement (see Popitz [2006], for instance, or, in a different vein, Garfinkel's [1967] "breaching experiments"). The irregular should tell us something about the regular, just as trespasses should tell us something about the norm.

To understand a person's effort to liberate him- or herself from the habitual means first paying attention to what has become habitual. *Habit memories* have gone through a process of habituation and become part of the embodied knowledge of a person or of a group of people. Hence, *habit memories* give stability and continuity to learned ways of doing something or of being. From these, I believe we need to differentiate habit memories *based on injuries*: although these, too, are embodied and part of a person, they are not stable or settled memories.

In the case of *habit memories* of repeated and normalizing experiences of violence and subjection, emancipation is highly contingent. Attempts to emancipate oneself from them are as likely to fail as to succeed. This is because they are unstable: they typically sit uneasily with the person and are in constant conflict with her or his current social role and self-image. They demand to be dealt with in some way; they haunt the injured person. Very often, habit memories of injuries run against an acquired self-image. To use a graphic example: a person who has grown up with two arms learns to perceive himself or herself as a person with two arms; if one arm is amputated, this leaves practical capabilities and self-image in contradiction. It also runs counter to a societal image of normality (which, in this example, is the expectation that a "normal" person has two arms and functions accordingly). Similarly, experiences of pain and suffering sit uneasily with the self-image and the social perception of a person. Hence, the establishment of stability and normality may precisely be the goal of everyday agency—and not its condition (as we usually think about habits).

Emancipation from *habit memories* depends on personal and individual attempts to change and overcome them. However, just as these memories emerge in a social context, emancipation from them can also play out socially. But what kind of social ties do people seek, what role do family bonds play, and what kind of sociability emerges from them?

In the context of World War I and its aftermath, Winter (1998, 30) draws a direct link between social bonds and the support systems that were created in those times of loss and suffering (such as the Red Cross or church initiatives): "From consolation and support, it was a short step to commemoration. The bonds shared by those in mourning, by widows, ex-servicemen, the disabled, the young and the old alike, were expressed openly in ceremonies of collective memory."

The Great War resulted in an immense number of deaths. During and after the war, the fallen soldiers and their bodies became a tangible target on which to focus the survivors' grief and mourning practices. Support and lobbying groups formed and requested that the bodies of the fallen soldiers be brought home for reburial. Many war memorials were built in remembrance of the war's atrocities and the sacrifices made by the soldiers. Indeed, war memorials are prominent institutionalized sites of mourning, and scholars have been drawn to them as carriers of political ideas. But they are also places in which people grieve, invest meaning, and experience healing (Winter 1998, 79).

There is ample scholarly literature on the responses to extreme forms of violence such as massacres, genocides, and wars (Gewald 1999; Krüger 1999). To the individual mourners, institutional responses often seem flawed and biased, but at least they produce tangible results, such as monuments, memorials, reports, speeches, events (commemoration days), and so forth. But what mourning practices do people develop and seek if their grief does not stem from extreme forms of violence and they cannot project their grief at institutionalized mourning sites? What kind of responses do people develop to routinized forms of suffering?

Responses to Routinized Forms of Suffering

In his book *The Spirit of Mourning*, Connerton (2011) focuses on two kinds of suffering—*episodic* and *routinized*. He differentiates these experiences of violence from other forms of suffering for the lack of a societal repertoire for responding to them in a meaningful way. There is, he holds, no repertoire of shared practices with which to mourn the losses people experienced, no rituals or rules to draw on. In other words, we lack a culturally learned response for coping with the experience of episodic or routinized violence. There is nothing that can take up the immensity of that bereavement, Connerton (2011, 17) suggests. "[T]he emotional responses of the bereaved lack the formalized channels which might, to some extent, ritualize and contain those responses of loss and grief."

For *extreme* or *episodic* conditions, Connerton (2011) cites as examples the Holocaust, the atomic bombs dropped on Japan at Hiroshima and Nagasaki, and the depredations of the Chinese Cultural Revolution. As examples of the more permanent and subtler *routinized*, suffering, he lists experiences of deprivation, exploitation, degradation, and oppression in situations such as apartheid, enforced migration, or chronic unemployment. They mostly affect the poor and "the defeated," who are "especially exposed" (16). The two types of suffering tend to blend with one another, and Connerton summarizes them in one broad category: *historical catastrophe or trauma.*

Of course, mourning practices are being invented in response to trauma (he calls them "sites of mourning"), and new forms of responses to loss and grief necessarily emerge. But they remain imperfect—and this is where their importance and topicality lie.

Connerton (2011, 25) turns to literature and the arts to show what kind of responses have been developed to cope with an otherwise "uncontainable experience of loss." Some sites of remembrance also have a legal status. In criminal trials and tribunals, mourning is channeled through a system of retributive justice, and the trial provides a ritual framework for both the public and the affected families.[5] Public prominence of criminal culpability for crimes "assigned to the category of the unjustifiable" is an important element in the mourning for historical catastrophes. He thus includes both the Nuremberg trials and truth commissions, and specifically mentions the South African Truth Commission, which he says attempted "to engage in a collective ritual process of mourning past losses so that the conditions might be created for a more liveable society and more desirable future." According to Connerton (26), the South African TRC "permitted the making of a public apology."

Apartheid, just as the horrors cited by Connerton, left people with the need to find forms of mourning. The truth commission was the most prominent institution that facilitated the creation of a history of mourning (Sanders 2007). However, it focused on the most extreme examples of decades-long discrimination, deprivation, and episodic suffering. It considered apartheid "in terms of excess phrased as violation of certain rights" (Ross 2002, 163). It neglected the everyday occurrence of violence and offered few ritual forms for mourning routinized suffering.

Routinized suffering requires a complex response. Typically, this kind of suffering does not end automatically. There are reasons for that. What characterizes routinized suffering is its "integration" into daily life (cf. Farmer 1997, 2004; Galtung 1969; Scheper-Hughes 1997). *Normalization* in this context does not mean that people stop trying to protect themselves from violence. However, the constant threat and reality of violence and the struggle against it are real and, over time, become part of a person's knowledge. This sedimented knowledge in turn shapes the person's capacity to act in the world, and this affects the person's social status in society.

There is no prescribed or imposed moment at which it can be said that routinized suffering is past. In contrast to episodic and extreme suffering, routinized suffering lacks instantaneousness and exceptionality. Even in the event of sweeping political change, such as the toppling of an ideological regime (communism, apartheid), for the individual and for certain social groups in that society, some forms of suffering do not end. Overt discrimination may end, but people's economic conditions tend not to be instantly alleviated, despite, for example, the expansion of a social security system. Also, the social reintegration into society of war veterans or otherwise socially stigmatized groups often does not happen in a lifetime. Surgery and orthopedic devices can replace limbs or repair internal and external damage to the body. But they cannot undo damage that has turned chronic—and *habitual*. Nonetheless, gestures and concrete measures on a societal level, or therapeutic treatment on the individual and group levels, do attempt to address habitual suffering. More so, people often search for ways to deal with their situation themselves.

This is where the body becomes an important focus of analysis. For which experiences of violence is redress possible, and which resist any attempt at healing? In what follows and in the example of the women of Philippi, I look at victims' attempts to give a form to what has no form yet. I privilege the nonverbal side and the potentially *collectivizing* dimension of bodily experiences, approaching mourning as a bodily practice and analyzing its sensory nature (Förster 2001; Jackson 2004, 2005; Stoller 1995, 1997).

As the Body Weakens

Coming back to the five women of Philippi, I only fully understood what the meetings meant to them when one of them, Ms. Mazibuko, could no longer participate. In 2006, when I first met her, she was at the forefront of efforts to build up Khulumani's regional branch. As a founding member, she was the vice chairperson of Khulumani Western Cape from 2000 to 2003, and the chairperson of the province from 2003 to 2006. She served as a guide for the traveling exhibition "Breaking the Silence: A Luta Continua" when it was hosted by the Apartheid Museum in Johannesburg, the Slave Lodge in Cape Town, and the Slough Museum in Slough, England. In 2007, she stepped down from her executive position because of health problems, but she remained a Khulumani leader in her community. She was still instrumental in distributing information and motivating other older and weaker members. When I saw her again in 2009, she was weak from her high blood pressure and diabetes, and the challenging gaze in her eyes, her strong and determined voice, and the sharpness of her arguments had dulled. She became, for Khulumani advocacy, emblematic of what happened as a result of the government's disastrous delay in paying out reparations and of the effective slow death of unacknowledged victims. She continued to live in the shack next to her unfinished brick house and to participate in Khulumani activities on a smaller scale, mostly only in her community. And she invariably kept meeting with the other women.

The real rupture in Ms. Mazibuko's and her friends' lives happened in 2010, when she moved to Mfuleni, a twenty-five-minute drive away, to be closer to her son. A few months later, on her birthday, I visited Ms. Mazibuko in her new home. Talking to her son that morning, I realized that the move had been very sudden. He said he had seen his mother sitting in her shack in Philippi one day, alone and without food. He was no longer comfortable with her living on her own and had the impression that no one cared for his mother. He felt bitter. After all that she had done for her community during the years of the struggle against apartheid and for Khulumani more recently, he thought she deserved more care now that her health was declining. And that very morning, he was angry again, he told me. He had received a call from Khulumani Western Cape, which did not only send his mother birthday wishes but requested that she be one of the representative plaintiffs for a new lawsuit (the *Consumers Case*, see chapter 2). He saw no reason that she should be the one to do it.

Now her son and the in-law family cared for Ms. Mazibuko. They monitored her diet to help control her sugar levels and encouraged her to attend a weekly meeting for elderly women in the Mfuleni community. Mfuleni is a new settlement and quite peaceful in comparison to Philippi and the townships that are nearer to the city. But there was not much happening there. Her son had thought it was best to bring his mother to his family. Plans to move to the former Transkei, to his father's family, would materialize, they hoped, as soon as his business took off. Her son had initially insisted that the interim reparation money she had received from the Truth Commission should go into building a house in Philippi. But when the R30,000 was spent, and the house only half built, what was supposed to be a source of pride became a source of shame and a constant reminder of how true change in post-apartheid South Africa remained outstanding. Ms. Mazibuko's son had been involved with several NGOs. He felt that Khulumani's focus was too narrow; they want individual reparations, he says, and forget that structures need to change.

The move, however, may have been a mixed blessing for Ms. Mazibuko. His mother may have been somewhat relieved to be closer to people who would take care of her, but she had also been forced to give up her central position in her community and among the five women of Philippi. The absence from her familiar environment weighed on her even though she was safer now. Her family did not acknowledge her leadership position in Khulumani and in the Philippi communities. If her son blamed Khulumani for the deterioration of her health, for Ms. Mazibuko, her work with Khulumani and participation in activities around her victimhood was what had kept her going. The dramatic deterioration of her health speaks much more to the irreconcilable body, on which the injuries and torture she had experienced in the 1970s and 1980s had finally taken their toll.

Her son's feelings about the exemplary role Ms. Mazibuko had had at the forefront of the victims' movement were, in fact, highly ambivalent. His view was that Khulumani had exploited her. But this is not how his mother felt. She had loved the traveling with the Khulumani exhibition and the frequent meetings at which she had argued with the authorities. Her survivor status in her community and Khulumani's advocacy work were pivotal—they enabled her to assert her personhood, again and again. For her, the saying that victims can turn into survivors had real value for long time.

Certainly, it was not only her son who put an end to that. Her body was catching up with her. Nonetheless, as tired and weak as she had been in the last few months before the move, the meetings had allowed her to offset that pain with sociability. The women and her colleagues at Khulumani took seriously both her sacrifice and the necessity of asserting her victim's subject position.

The tacit knowledge of victimhood she shared with the five women of Philippi, which was reaffirmed at every meeting, had created a community that could not easily be replicated. Neither Ms. Mazibuko's son nor his wife's family understood its importance to her or that her activism, though taxing, was essential for Ms. Mazibuko. Her sudden, unexpected move completely cut Ms. Mazibuko off from the other women, who, in turn, sorely missed her and made several fruitless attempts to get in touch with her.

I negotiated with her son that I could take his mother to Philippi for a day. En route to Philippi, Ms. Mazibuko hesitantly inquired about Khulumani's activities and slowly shook off her apathy. In Philippi, we visited with the other women, just as she had done in the past. All of them were very happy to see her again. Her moving away was accepted as a fact; no one wanted to openly question her son's decision. Her son had asserted her weakness and her victimhood, and his decision was respected. The women understood that the capacities of their family structures could always change and cause a rupture with their communities. Their children try their best to care for their mothers in old age. Relocation or the death of a family member may put an end to the women's shared practice of mourning.

During our visit, some of Ms. Mazibuko's curiosity about what was happening around her and in the world, her life, and Khulumani began to return. But instead of talking, she mainly listened. From being the link between the Khulumani executive committee and the members, she had gone out of the loop of information shared in everyday life. This visit in late 2010 was the last time Ms. Mazibuko would see the other women before her death in August 2012.

Making New Social and Bodily Experiences

In November 2009, I visited the Nontsebenziswano Educare Centre, a crèche in Village 2 in Philippi. Khulumani members Engelina Nomarashiya Jama and her younger sister Nomatoza Irena Jali run the crèche together with seven other mothers. The small Educare premises are neat, in some parts bleak, but there are also green patches where the center has started a garden with the help of Abalimi, a Philippi-based association that supports dozens of gardening and agriplanning projects, providing training and intervention, in the Cape Flats. The two Khulumani members from Philippi who had accompanied me and I were welcomed by the sight of at least fifty children, separated by age group, quietly napping after lunchtime. None of the center's three painted brick houses had electricity; water was scarce, and so was rain to fill the containers for watering the garden.[6] Child-oriented motifs were painted on the outside walls, and the children's paintings covered of the inside walls; purple, yellow, and green fitted sheets covered the tiny mattresses, and the purple curtains on the windows billowed gently in the breeze on this warm, early summer afternoon. There was no ceiling, but patches of carpeting covering the floor gave the rooms a warm and cozy atmosphere. I was interested in the crèche and the story of such a place run by two Khulumani members. As we sat down with the sisters to talk, a handful of children slept quietly on the floor around us. The sisters explained how they had come to Philippi in the first place. I learned what Ms. Jali meant when she said that her sister's suggestion to set up a crèche in August 1991 had improved her life.

In their thirties and looking for work, the sisters had arrived in the Cape Town area in 1976, when thousands of other passless and poor migrants from the homelands were also arriving. They had no close relatives in the city or, more precisely, in those primitive structures in the bush and sand dunes. Ms. Jama was arrested on her second day in Philippi and taken to Langa police station. Ms. Jali had arrived at Nyanga but soon left for Crossroads, where an acquaintance lived. Numerous resettlements, crowded into an area about 10 kilometers in diameter, followed. Ms. Jali and Ms. Jama built shacks in Crossroads, an area that later became one of the main sites of the rioting that followed reforms and repression from the mid-1970s onward. Unsurprisingly, the black squatters constituted a threat to the apartheid regime's vision of separation along race and into ethnic territories. This is when the raids started. The sisters were repeatedly forced to flee the police, returning to the squatter camps only to see that their shacks had been destroyed. They had no avenue of appeal.

Both were arrested by the security forces several times and held in Langa before being loaded into a police van and deported back to Transkei. But they had almost no money and therefore no intention of staying in there voluntarily. After they were dumped in a town then called Umtata, they headed straight back to Cape Town. They looked for work in the white suburb Mowbray. It was a hostile environment, and finding work was not easy. Ms. Jali recalled an incident when a white child had started crying in fear upon seeing Ms. Jali passing by her house. Being employed, however, was the condition for obtaining legal status in the city.

In these years, many Crossroads dwellers lived under the rule of a strong-man and headman called Yamile. In exchange for a tribute, they were promised protection from feuding groups led by other strongmen, such as Ngxobong-wana[7] and Nongwe (see J. Cole 1987). These strongmen shifted their alliances with the ANC and the PAC frequently, depending on what furthered their personal interests—that is, helped them maintain political and economic control over their communities. They were supported by their own "armies" in their efforts to establish hegemony over the older and the newer parts of the Crossroads area. They were often called *witdoeke* and were primarily made up of young black men from the communities (see J. Cole 1987): in order to identify themselves, members of what was called the "Ngxobongwana's army" and other groups wore white pieces of cloth. "Witdoeke" also came to stand for residents who were agents of the state and who participated in the arson and killings. It became difficult for ordinary residents to distinguish the violence erupting from clashes between the feuding groups and the violence coming from the security forces. Most residents were not directly involved on either side but their presence in one or the other community made them targets. In 1985 and 1986, apart from constant incidences of shooting and the burning of each other's strongholds, the armies of the feuding groups descended on Crossroads several times, armed with spears, guns, and *pangas* (machetes), while the police watched and did nothing.

When there was fighting, Ms. Jali and Ms. Jama and hundreds of others were forced to abandon their dwellings and had to sleep outside. Mothers and fathers lost their children; many either disappeared or were killed. The sisters also bemoaned the actions of the police in other incidents, when they crushed all apartheid resistance activities, even those in which school children were involved, but also the in-fighting among the squatter camps. Many children either died at the hands of the security forces or were caught in deadly strongman rivalries. Although the churches could provide shelter in these months, they could not offer protection from the police, who would throw teargas bombs into them. Once, a tent was burned down and many people died as a result. Men and boys patrolled during the nights to protect and warn their communities about the police and criminal activities; some of them never came back.

Left homeless, the sisters went to the squatter settlement KTC, a subsection of Crossroads. However, the *casspirs* (mine-resistant ambush protected vehicles) followed swiftly and flattened the settlement's makeshift housing; the security service fenced off the area. Along with many others, the sisters spent eight days in the Pollsmoor prison. Their possessions were lost or stolen.

By the mid-1980s, the squatter camps in the Cape Flats had become a source shame for South Africa. Not only had the flow of new immigrants not ceased, it had increased, and every raid or riot in the camps turned into an international media event. After 1986, when the pass laws were scrapped, partly in response to international pressure, the Cape Flats area experienced an overwhelming influx of people from the homelands. Apartheid's defenses began to crumble. By the end of the 1980s, the sand dunes were covered by shacks that seemed to stretch on endlessly. The regime had allocated new land to the dwellers, which was much farther away from the city, and promised to provide basic services for the thousands of new residents. Many of the newcomers moved to Khayelitsha (isiXhosa for "new home"), but many mistrusted the regime's promises and refused to be pushed farther away from the job opportunities in the city.

The two sisters decided to go to Brown's Farm to what was still scarcely inhabited private land. They collected pieces of plastic to use as building material for their dwellings. There were negotiations involving the owner, the state, and community leaders and headmen Yamile, Toise, and Siphika around the largely uninhabited land. Also Sindiswa Nunu, who was the secretary of Siphika in the early 1980s and who is considered a city woman, was deeply involved in these negotiations.[8] She was the chairperson of Khulumani Western Cape for a few years, and then became the office manager, and is now a field worker for Khulumani Western Cape.

Back in the late 1980s, the Legal Resource Centre had tracked down the land's owner, Mr. Brown, and the family sold Brown's Farm to the government for R2million. R1million of this money was raised overseas, and the government contributed the other half. The upgrading of the land started in 1988, and in 1990 it was opened for occupation. It was only in 1997 that the RDP kicked off; shack residents could then apply for housing subsidies to build the modest two-room houses. The RDP had problems, however, and many houses were never completed; or, people had to invest their own money to finish building them.

It was here, in the early 1990s, that the sisters and seven other mothers started offering to look after working women's children. During those troubled years, children who became separated from their parents often got lost or were stolen. The crèche would provide safety by taking them off the streets. And it would relieve the women running the crèche from having to look after white people's children in the suburbs instead of helping to build their own community. At first, the women set up the crèche in their homes. And even though three of the nine mothers have since passed away, the remaining organizers have moved the crèche to another plot and expanded it.

The two sisters and the other mothers literally built the crèche by hand; a limited amount of governmental and nongovernmental support came only much later. The women now make up the staff of the Educare Centre, which receives some of its funding from state subsidies and some from donations from individuals or in practical support, such as interns from other organizations. However, the state subsidies are minimal, and the crèche also heavily relies on the fees it charges the parents. Not all parents can afford to pay the R100 per month fee; the center then accepts whatever they can give.

The gardening project came later. Despite the extensive farming experience the women had gained growing up and living in the Eastern Cape, the sandy ground and the harsh climate in the Cape area posed challenges at first. But then they received training from the Abalimi gardening center, and they started growing vegetables for the children meals and to give to the needy of the community.

The Department of Agriculture recognized the garden and donated a container for tools and a fence; this recognition has helped grow the resources for the crèche and the Educare Centre as a whole. Moving to the new plot was also difficult at first. Homeless and unemployed people occupied the land. Even today, skollies (gangsters) break in to steal equipment and vandalize the center. Two men sleep at the center and act as guards to keep them away.

In the early 1990s, the sisters looked at the scattered and destroyed communities in the Cape Flats and found both meaningful work and a way to help other women that contributed to a more peaceful and stable community in Philippi. More so, their lives—like those of thousands of others' during apartheid—were defined by the pattern of not living in or being able to provide a stable environment for their own children. They needed to emancipate themselves from those experiences. Starting the crèche emancipated them from the frustrating search for work in a hostile environment and from being forced to take unsteady, unappreciated, underpaid jobs doing undignified work, with no social security and daily exposure to discrimination and degradation. Life under apartheid for women like Ms. Jali and Ms. Jama meant suffering various forms of corporal discrimination as well. These ranged from being jailed by the police for nothing more than being in the wrong place to feeling the disdain of a white child in a white suburb to being unable to care for their own offspring because their only way to earn a living had been made illegal. These injuries were not always executed through words. They are neither exclusively inscribed *as* words nor necessarily retrievable *in words*; they are nonpredicated. People's dignity and humanity were violated through the body, and the body was both a means and a target of deprivation. To transform such experiences—but also to transform their social status, and generate income, of course—these women directly lent their bodily care to children. It is an attempt to emancipate from a control (executed partly but not exclusively through the body) of how to be viewed and judged, how to care, and how and where to live.

In the story of Ms. Jali and Ms. Jama, I have focused on the bodily manifestations of verbally or structurally inflicted injuries and identified their habitual and gradual incorporation. We saw how the two sisters dealt with this incorporated knowledge and changed it by making new experiences. These experiences have a strong bodily dimension: caring for others, actively establishing a home for many, nourishing themselves and others, and settling down. They are, obviously, very gendered and draw directly on dominant discourses. Nonetheless, they offered the chance to create new experiences.

It is neither compensation nor restitution that these women directly seek.[9] Theirs is an attempt to make new experiences. These new practices in turn have the potential to slowly overwrite past experiences. But instead of using the term *overwriting* (which connotes a textual understanding of remembering), we may better understand these new experiences as *acting out*,[10] thus putting the emphasis on practice. The performative aspect of such practice has direct consequences for the person herself.

Parallel to personal processes of acting out new forms of being and relating to others, the two sisters obtained a new social position. Establishing and codirecting an education center gave them a recognized and respected status in the community. Before anything else, the sisters are staff members of a center and gardeners, mothering the children of the community. Only secondarily are they victims. The two women who accompanied me on my visit to Ms. Jali and Ms. Jama had particularly wanted me to meet them. They were proud of having such industrious and strong members in Khulumani.

Hence, the having the chance to act out a new form of social relations carries the chance to obtain a new social status in society no longer dominated by victimhood. Whether people actually do get this chance, of course, is not only up to the person but is chiefly dictated by the person's economic situation. Generally, people who live a reasonably comfortable life in economic terms have more opportunities to achieve a new social status. They have the means to pursue activities that make a shift in subjectivity possible. An economic status that allows greater freedom to make choices is, of course, not the only requirement for a successful emancipation from victimhood, but it certainly is conducive to it.

For the two sisters, contingencies remain high: even if crèches are now fairly established institutions in the communities, they nonetheless depend on a stable political and economic environment. State subsidies may dry up, or an NGO may have to withdraw its support. Or a sudden debilitating health problem might make it more difficult for the women to continue this reconstitutive practice. Both an injured body and memories that remain too strong may betray them.

The sisters, the two Khulumani members, and I chatted for more than two hours, at the end of which the sleeping children started to stir. Their soft breathing turned into grunts and stretching, and soon we were surrounded by awake, chattering children. Ms. Jali and Ms. Jama went to the garden and returned with big bunches of spinach and onions for each of us to take home.

Transformation through the Performance of Victimhood

The situations I have analyzed so far were characterized by victims' implicit attempts to change what victimhood meant for them. In what follows, I use two different scenes to look at the codifications victimhood undergoes in a situation where two women actively addressed their victimhood vis-à-vis a public, searching for a way to articulate their mourning. Instead of sharing the tacit knowledge of victimhood, as did the five women in Philippi, or actively pursuing a different bodily and social experience, as did the two sisters, these two women searched for a different perspective on their victimhood by "trying on" forms that they hoped would be legible to the broader society. They relied on a performance of their victimhood that they hope will break its habitual dimension. In contrast to the Philippi women and the sisters, their attempts were the most directly shaped by the TRC process.

In the first incident, a victim initially "tried on" a form of enacting her victimhood that she had been taught by the leaders of Khulumani. She ultimately could not do it and fell back to her own coding of her victimhood. The two codifications clashed—one habitual, the other explicit and influenced by organization's desire to render victimhood politically effective and legible. In the second, another member of the support group performed the end of her habitual victimhood and the beginning of a new way of perceiving.

The national office of Khulumani in Johannesburg had invited representatives of the Vaal Triangle branches (Evaton, Sharpeville, Sebokeng) and Soweto to an event to commemorate World Trauma Day (October 17) at the Khotso House, on Marshall Street in Johannesburg. The office staff, field workers, and

program coordinators of Khulumani, together with some ten representatives
of the branches, met in the chapel of the South African Council of Churches,
a few floors below Khulumani's national office. It was a curious mix of a public meeting and an internal Khulumani meeting. In the small group, everyone knew each other, but the placards and other decorations placed around
the room were also commemorative enough to give the event a solemn atmosphere. During the first part of the meeting, the persons responsible for various
programs Khulumani had launched reported on the progress that had been
made. Then the seven staff members in turn went to the front of the room to
speak. Although a storytelling time had been planned for the second part of the
commemoration, storytelling entered in earlier, as the members in their coor-
dinating capacities integrated their own subjective experiences and personal
growth into their reports.

One member, Ms. Selota (name changed), spoke about the efforts to establish a trauma counseling facility at the Sharpeville police station. She sounded
like a preacher; her voice was thunderous and strong, and she was clearly proud
of their success. "I have been fighting with the government, with the police.
But now I am right there, inside the police station. It is what we needed, all
of us." She explained how she became involved in counseling work. With the
help of Khulumani, she recounted, she had taken counseling courses at the
Centre for the Study of Violence and Reconciliation. She began working as a
counselor and specialized in helping victims of rape and domestic violence. "I
volunteered for fifteen years without no pay," she told the group. Among other
things, she accompanied the rape victims when they appeared in Magistrate
Court to obtain a protection order. At first, relations with the police were bad.
She tried to counsel the women before they had to give their statement to an officer. Because, she explained, "policemen would do just the same," that is, rape
them again, especially during the night. "Even men were raped. . . . They used
to call it sodomy. But now it is just rape, not sodomy anymore." Over time, she
managed to build a relationship with the police at the station. "I even counsel
them. Many policemen commit suicide." She was good at her work. "It was my
dream to be a social worker," she said. In 2008, she received the award for the
Best Trauma Centre Worker in Sedibeng. Her work was so successful that the
Ministry of Safety and Security recently opened a one-stop trauma center in
Sedibeng. Although Ms. Selota is old and sick now, she is still involved. "They
still call me, especially for the elderly women cases; and the widows who are
abused by their children, their in-laws and the police." The effort to establish

a counseling facility in the police station, for which she was the driving force, was tightly connected to and directly grew out of her own experiences. "Politics is in me," she said, recalling a formative experience: "My parents were tortured in front of me."

Ms. Selota described herself that day as a "widow" and as a "victim" of both domestic and political violence. Her child had been killed. "I was tortured [by the security forces]. My house was burnt. I am still blamed of killing my husband. My husband blamed me with everything; for killing my child." Despite his accusations, she stayed with him "until his last day," when he, too, was killed by the security forces.

But as she spoke, she was overcome with emotion. She had started off using a learned vocabulary of victimhood, speaking in clear, orderly sentences, sometimes looking at notes written on a small piece of paper. Now, as her emotions took over, her speech became different. She was communicating her victimhood directly and with emotional intensity. "I will never forgive apartheid for what it did to me," she exclaimed. "It is the monster! All my dreams were blown up because of apartheid."

Like other speakers that morning, Ms. Selota had started off using a script. Pamela Whitman, a volunteer from Australian Volunteer International and a trained nurse, who led Khulumani's so-called Victim Empowerment Program, in which these members participated and the community initiatives were embedded, not only provided them with counseling but also scripted their public presentations. It was part of her job, Whitman told me later, to help members speaking in public settings to not get "lost in their stories." Indeed, her contributions became obvious whenever the speaker departed from the script—or "lost herself in her story." After each person spoke, Ms. Whitman would say that it was another "lovely example" for the "transformation from a victim to a survivor" or from "a victim to a victor." She was anxious to acknowledge both the hardships the person had gone through and the progress they had made because of their work with Khulumani.

Here, we see two different forms of coding victimhood, both of which are in a relation to the person's experience. Both went through processes of interpretation; hence are both learned. The script provided by the organization was the more tangible codification of victimhood. It was directed to a public that is supposed to understand how to interpret the codes of Ms. Selota's experiences and her victim subjectivity today. It employed familiar notions such as "widow" and "victim," the witnessing of torture as a child, and the process of politicization that results from that. The second form of coding victimhood is more complex. It looks raw given its emotional and more sensory expression. But it has been transformed through Ms. Selota's personal bodily and social experiences since when the violations occurred up to that day.

Neither form is truer or more authentic than the other. Nonetheless, I can safely say that the external form, the script, aimed at addressing an (imagined) audience that has most likely not gone through similar experiences of harm, was unfamiliar to Ms. Selota. It sat in an unstable relationship with her own experiences. It had offered her a new form for looking at herself, at her *personal memory*, but on that day, the external form and her real experiences could not entirely be reconciled. She had to switch codes.

During the second part of the meeting, the designated commemorative part, a woman from Sebokeng spoke. Unlike Ms. Selota, she had received no guidance on what to say and made no effort to follow a particular protocol. She spoke seSotho, and no one jumped in to translate. She spoke in a breathless manner, sobbing. Others tried to comfort her, bringing her tissues and a glass of water.

She was the third person that afternoon to openly mourn her loss and pain. A member of the Khulumani staff, seeing this despair, suggested doing a healing exercise that he had learned in a trauma course. He gave each speaker a piece of paper and asked her to write a sentence: "Write something like: I don't want to think about this anymore, because . . ." he told them, "because you can't live with the trauma every day. . . . Then we go and throw it away." They left the room, along with another staff member who was filming them with a digital camera. We sat still and waited, talking in low voices. When the speakers came back, we all stood up and joined in their prayer song. A bit later, when the commemorative part of the meeting was finished, I talked to the woman from Sebokeng, who exclaimed: "Now I am healed!" The force of her own performance—her public performance of her victimhood—seemed to have relieved her of a burden she had been carrying for a long time. She created a new experience of victimhood when she stepped in front of the small group and started to speak, and everyone listened. The other people in the room, as witnesses and by our mere presence, acknowledged her pain. But we also asserted the possibility of change, which she was ready to undergo. After her bodily performance of embodied knowledge of victimhood, the "healing exercise" offered a form with which to *de-inscribe* her experiences. She could write her pain onto another surface. It was a reversal of inscription because she was allocating painful memories to a new place. It was also an embodied place, but it was ceremonially separated from her own body. She wrote off her experiences from the place where her memories had been all along.

It was a ceremony without drawing on established rituals and it was performed with no relation to a ritualized form (except the reference to the field of professional trauma intervention). Nonetheless, the ad hoc character of the process, and the presence of a receptive audience that was very supportive of such transformations had led the lady to feel changed. She needed the audience to witness and partake in her transformation. We were witnesses to her shift from a "victim" to a "healed" personhood.

It is difficult to say how long this shift will endure. To be completely successful, it probably needs societal embedding. She will go back to Sebokeng, changed perhaps, but the question remains, can this new subjectivity be sustained in an environment that has not witnessed—and acknowledged—her performance?

Transformation of Habitual Memories

The concern here is with the question of whether it is possible to forget or deal with individual and societal memories of injustice if those memories have a strong bodily dimension. That memories are embodied is important because it gives the question of reconcilability a new urgency. How can memory change if it is already part of one's being in the body and thus of one's being in the world? This is a broad question, and I tackle it at the level of painful memories stemming from gross structural violations of socioeconomic and human rights.

To better understand how injured people cope with their experiences of violence, we need to look at the practices in their daily lives. Connerton argued that in the case of routinized forms of violence, victims often have at hand a quite limited repertoire of responses with which to deal with their suffering. It is in this context that I ask about ordinary and everyday but also formalized attempts with which harmed people seek new ways to relate to their memories. The ethnographic data in this chapter demonstrate that practices of mourning encompass both a strong societal *and* a bodily component. I elaborate on each.

The experience of violence is social. In any act of violence there is an agent who harms and another person who is harmed. The harmer may be invisible in a largely anonymized system of injustice, so that his or her social character may be difficult to identify. But what ultimately makes violence social is its effect: the exposure to violence changes social relations. It changes the victim's position vis-à-vis the perpetrator, and vice versa. More importantly, it may shatter or severely challenge the victim's social position more broadly. In the aftermath of violent acts, which can range from torture to humiliation to the repeated burning down of one's dwellings to the disappearance of a loved one, we find social consequences. After the loss of her husband, a widow has to renegotiate her social position in a community and in society. A person who lost a limb has to learn that he attracts stares and has to deal with the expectation of encountering curious glances or disgust. A mother whose children witness her being beaten by the police has to live with the knowledge that they are confused about her vulnerability. These are somewhat tangible examples. It is more complex when experiences of humiliation, discrimination, or exclusion are the rule and turn into a habitual assumption about the world. For this, violence does not have to be accepted as a norm if it has reached a condition of constant possibility.

Violence impairs the social position of a person. My ethnographic material suggests that this impaired social status needs to be re-established socially, too. To do that, victims of violence seek to create new social ties, which often lie outside their family bonds. People who have experienced similar events (tacitly) know what the other person went through. Apart from sharing the resulting suffering, they also better understand why a person acted in this or that way in circumstances that are familiar to both of them but not necessarily to their family members.

Winter looked at new bonds that were created among victims during and in the aftermath of the Great War:

> Families were torn apart by war. Nothing could have reversed completely this tide of separation and loss. But after 1914 there was as well a gathering together, as people related by blood or by experience tried to draw strength from each other during and after the war. The bonds thus formed were powerful and in many cases durable. (Winter 1998, 29)

In the case of the women of Philippi, such ties were formed between women who have gone through similar experiences of suffering and loss. All five had grown up as rural women and had come to the city for economic reasons. In the city, they were more or less willingly involved in the struggle of their new communities against the apartheid regime, and found themselves in the line of fire between the feuding groups in the squatter camps and the illegal communities of the broader Crossroads area. They all lost their makeshift homes and minimal belongings several times, were victims of police violence, and experienced the everyday hardships of raising a family and trying to earn a living in such an unstable environment.

They share all these experiences as part of their habitual bodily knowledge. This tacit knowledge of victimhood is what brings them together in their informal meetings. They are getting old together and monitor their respective health conditions. They do not have much power to improve their living or health conditions and are, on top of this, responsible for their unemployed or handicapped children, as well as their grandchildren. However, they support each other by creating a space in which the hardship of past times as well as its effects on their social and physical conditions today are acknowledged. Based on their local leadership in the liberation struggle, they still hold a social position of respect in the community that is not easily challenged by youngsters. They are the mothers and grandmothers of the youth and have a certain authority over moral questions. They disapprove of criminal activities and jump in when the child of an acquaintance needs their financial support and care. Of course, they complain about the erosion of a communal morale; but as they get older and weaker, they can no longer do as much for the community. In the 1980s, they helped to build the first school on Brown's Farm; today, they are barely strong enough to serve as election observers for Khulumani in that very school. Ironically, they hope that this community they have helped to build will not be their final one. They all aspire to return to the villages of their ancestors in the rural former homeland of Transkei.

The sisters Ms. Jali and Ms. Jama are directly and actively shaping their community by running a big day care center, which they have built through hard work guided by their vision. Their everyday practice today is to help care for their community's children. Their older embodied experiences of violence, as painful as those of the five women of Philippi, may slowly be overwritten by new social experiences. For one, the children demand their active care; it is a kind of work that is chiefly social, but which provides the two women with new ways of using and perceiving their own bodies. Secondly, the community respects them for their work. They managed to build a stable home for themselves and for the children and even to grow vegetables in an arid and sandy area. All of this serves the community, but it also allows them to make new social experiences.

Social recognition and the possibility of changing one's social status was also an important feature of the commemoration of World Trauma Day in Johannesburg. Unlike the more habitual practices of the Philippi women and the sisters, the instant performative dimension here was central. The leadership of Khulumani had taught Ms. Selota an external, codified way of talking about her victimhood. In the middle of giving her testimony, she had to abandon that script to express her victimhood in a way that felt truer to her lived experiences. Both versions are interpretations of her victimhood. The former was shaped by the desire to increase the political effectiveness of her testimony in forums that are not accustomed to relate to such testimonies. The latter was the personal expression of her victimhood as it has gone through processes of embodiment and habituation over the years. The women who spoke later in the meeting felt the sudden relief of a burden after she had spoken to the meeting's participants and was taken through a short "healing exercise." The social recognition of her suffering was the constitutive part of her healing experience.

Just as an injury impairs the social status of the harmed person, it may also have long-term effects on the body of the harmed. In the case of the women of Philippi, I showed that there are forms of chronic suffering that remain in the body. The women experienced violence on a daily basis for years. They had to live their lives knowing that violence was a constant threat and a brutal reality. The routinized violence they were subjected determined their movements, their thoughts, their well-being, and their health conditions daily. It became a condition in itself. This thin, precarious state cracked when even more severe incidences of violence happened: murder, the death or disappearance of a loved one, torture or severe physical impairment, and so forth. These ruptures had to be integrated into their already precarious lives.

Such experiences have long been incorporated into and left traces on the body. These traces are not necessarily cognitively accessible or translatable into language. That they are incorporated means that they have become part of the person's manner of being in the world.

It is, of course, immensely difficult to say anything systematic, let alone predictive, about bodily effects of injuries. Do certain forms of violence lead to this or another form of incorporation, and if so, why? Are some forms of violence easier to redress because the victim's body is more easily reconciled, while other forms of experienced violence ultimately remain in the body of the harmed? What role does individual resilience play—different preconditions and learned ways of coping?

Without minimizing these limitations, we can certainly say that incorporated experiences are not static or fixed and that they can change over time. If the injured person has the opportunity to make new experiences that are different from the ones she or he had been subjected to, the chance of transforming habitual memories is much higher.

The activities the two sisters who lead a crèche and a gardening project chose as the center of their post-apartheid life are corporeal. It is hard physical work to run and oversee a crèche, to educate fifty or more children, and to run a gardening project. Their work does not directly address their past experiences of forced removals, homelessness, death, unemployment, and the undermining of a sense of dignity. However, for the children they live and practice values that they came to through their experiences. In this exemplifying capacity, they can also acquire new experiences. By building a day-care home for the children, they also built a home for themselves. By growing vegetables to feed the children and the hungry in the community, they also practice a kind of solidarity that could only have been temporary during apartheid. They are slowly changing their *personal memory* by occupying a new subject position that is not directly related to their victimhood.

The two performances of victimhood that took place at an internal support group event can also be explained along these lines. Why did the woman tell me that she was healed after she had deliberated on her experiences of suffering? Through her body, she acted out her victimhood in a fierce and powerful manner that caused her to collapse. Then through the exercise of "writing away" her experiences, she gave them a place of inscription outside herself. Here, the enactment of incorporated knowledge and the ceremonial description of her painful experiences worked hand in hand and led to provide (at least temporary) relief.

These three vignettes strongly suggest that reconciling incorporated memories of harm needs to involve a bodily dimension of acting out, be it an impulsive performance of the body or the slow and steady pursuit of self-chosen practices of mourning. The more durable and routinized new experiences are, the greater the chance that they can indeed become a basis for emancipation.

In sum, the practices draw on personal habituated and embodied memory. With variable emphasis, they attempt to establish a new layer of personal memory and a new layer of habit memory. Practices that rely on the continuous performance of a new subject position (such as caretaker) address the habitual side of memory. Practices that rely on an exceptional performance address the personal-life-narrative side of memory.

By presenting three different attempts by the women to emancipate themselves from the painful bodily memory of harm, the vignettes also illustrate the different ways people try to make their victimhood social. Teasing out the differences can help us to understand some of the conditions that make change possible. The women of Philippi are, in a way, the most creative ones. Their daily gatherings constitute a form of sociality that does not rely on grand discourses of overcoming experiences of violence. They tacitly share their bodily knowledge and undertake small and repeated attempts to support each other—in a situation in which they do not have the strength and the capital for change. The meetings may slightly change their perception of the world and make their current suffering more social. But they are not likely to have an effect on others besides themselves. It is a very fragile community they fostered, one easily ruptured by more illnesses, relocation, or death—all ever-present possibilities because of their precarious economic situations, poor health, and unresolved memories of violence.

The second vignette looks at how two sisters found a way to build some social capital by making new bodily experiences, and vice versa. With outside support, Ms. Jali and Ms. Jama managed to build a crèche. Their daily work keeps them from becoming preoccupied with their victimhood. The interplay between the promise of a new social status in their community and the bodily experiences they are making as part of their work with children and in the garden is a path toward emancipation. It potentially is an economic, social, and bodily emancipation from past experiences. It is difficult to say which of the three dimensions—bodily, economic, or social—is the prime condition for emancipation. Compared to the women of Philippi, the sisters' story seems to suggest that a degree of economic stability is a prerequisite for being able to "seize" the possibility to create social and bodily experiences. In that sense, apartheid-era victimhood will be perpetuated for people who cannot emancipate themselves economically to a sufficient degree. Redress is one means to address this dimension of victimhood. You can buy a house and move out of your shack, for instance, or you can bury a deceased family member properly. But once apartheid-era victimhood has assumed a life of its own that is increasingly disconnected from the legacy of apartheid and shaped by more current experiences, structural changes are needed. It is difficult to say when this turning point is reached (and it should definitely not be misused to repudiate the necessity of redress and its potential for real social change).

The third vignette illustrates an attempt to achieve emancipation from victimhood that relies most heavily on the victims' subject position that emerged from the TRC process. At the commemoration of the World Trauma Day, the two women from the Vaal Triangle had hoped to find closure through speaking. This is what the TRC had advocated, practiced, and even imposed on those who wanted to formally be acknowledged as victims. Khulumani builds on this notion of articulation; there is no other option, in fact, if the organization wants to address the public and change the perception of victimhood in the public mind. In all its activities, the lawsuits, the demands to government, and so on, members' articulation of victimhood is the first, necessary step in being acknowledged at all.

Hence, if Khulumani is a space where victims find recognition of their suffering, it is also a space that actively tries to shape their victims' subject position. By teaching members how to articulate their pain in public settings, the leadership plays a constitutive role in coding members' victimhood. This is part and parcel of the process of professionalization described in chapter 1 that many growing organizations undergo. I understand it as straddling of what it needs to do to achieve its political goals and the hampering effect that process can have if the resulting victims' subject positions do not fit the experiences of the members.

As we saw in chapter 4, this form of articulation is limited—and dominant, thanks to governing processes. In the third vignette, we see that it did not sit easily with Ms. Selota. At first, she recounted her experiences in the given form: she "tried on" the victims' subject position that had been generated by the TRC and subsequent governing processes. But she dropped it in the middle of her speech, when her bodily memory took over and she had to change code to something discursively closer to how she sees herself. Necessarily, the second form is also a verbal codification of her victimhood, already transformed from the non-predicated into the predicated.

This brings us back to the problems of how to become emancipated from the bodily memory of violence and how to communicate nonpredicated bodily memories.

The women of Philippi and the sisters running the crèche represent two kinds of attempt victims make in their everyday lives to slowly create new social and bodily experiences. For both, victimhood largely remains in the non-predicated realm; these women do not have to articulate their victimhood and communicate it to someone *who has not experienced what they had experienced.*

In contrast, the third attempt, the public performance of victimhood, tries to do exactly that. The two ladies try on given forms of acting out their victimhood. It is the only way of relating their experiences to a public that does not have the bodily knowledge to decode their alternative forms of articulating (or practicing the emancipation from) their victimhood. They will not understand the reference to something they do not tacitly know themselves. (In the commemorative World Trauma Day meeting, however, most of the people present could relate to it. I read the meeting as a safe space in which the women could try out a public victims' subject position.) Victims, for their part, cannot necessarily translate their bodily knowledge into a language that will be accessible to the society at large. It is for this reason that victims have to relate their experiences to established forms of victim subjectivity. Many try to do so and fail. The various ways of trying to cope with victimhood are thus often private, or limited to a small group of people who share similar experiences. Here, alternative subjectivities may emerge. But the vignettes also show, some form of societal acknowledgement is necessary for a transformation, even if it is only the chance to assume a new subjectivity by way of societal support.

Seclusion among victims holds the danger of creating a sociality so unique that it is inaccessible to the rest of society. Some degree of articulation is needed to push for a public discussion about redress and about the responsibility of society to help victims who are coping with a bodily memory of violence, or else victims die without recognition. The exclusive dimension of social communities is also a question that concerns ethnography; the methodological aspect of which I pursue next.

Chapter 6

Ethnographic Experience and Anthropological Knowledge

THE BODILY DIMENSION of victimhood shapes the boundaries of what people can communicate and to whom. What consequence does this have for ethnographic research? What are the preconditions for understanding each other? Here, problems of ethnographic method are closely linked to the difficulties victims face when trying to make their bodily experiences socially relevant. Linking methodological and theoretical discussions, this chapter offers a methodological reflection and makes a strong case for why the body matters in ethnographic research (Kesselring 2015c).

Ethnographies originate in everyday interactions with others, but anthropologists' analysis and interpretation of a social world is often restricted to people's words and identifiable actions. As in every social setting, much of the knowledge we acquire during fieldwork remains unarticulated and habitual. We often lack the tools to even become aware of it, let alone to bring in into the predicative realm. Still, its existence is the only basis we have for recognizing the unarticulated experiences of others. Here, I propose avenues for using our own bodily experiences to intersubjectively recognize those of others.

"Her Body Always Felt Much Better Whenever She Sees You"

I start with a small scene that describes a key moment, far into the second period of my field research in 2010, which made me better understand how I had been conducting my research all along. This key moment progressively changed my perspective on what was important in my informants' lives.

I frequently met with Nolasti Twala, an elderly Khulumani member who lives in Philippi Township. I never met with her one on one, but always with other women. She would welcome us into her house. Her English was very poor, and my isiXhosa negligible, so that we could only exchange warm greetings and give each other the comfort of being happy to seeing one another. Ms. Twala has a very strong and warm manner, and it always made me feel good to be in her presence. The fact that we could not communicate verbally did not discourage her from now and then speaking to me in a flow of words; and without understanding the words I believed I could still grasp the essential part of what she wanted to communicate. Indeed, this type of interaction characterized many other situations during my research, as well. Often, I just listened to my informants, sometimes trying hard to catch some words, sometimes less concerned with that. I was generally keen just to be around the women. I didn't want to overwhelm them—or myself—by aiming to understand everything they said. I actually often preferred just to be present.

Similarly, people mostly did not seem to mind my presence and allowed me to partake in whatever they were doing. What they were doing was limited. Anthropological methodology insists on participation, but in these gatherings there was little real activity in which I could directly participate.[1] Daily life for the women was not structured as life in a village is. They did not work the field or go about pursuing activities that might generate income. These elderly women were unemployed or beyond working age. Their activities mainly evolved around their children and grandchildren, with whom many shared their small houses or shacks, and around trying to survive on the meager monies coming in from social grants and their children's occasional jobs. Their active days were over; having sometimes ended too early according to the age on their identity cards. Whether a day was good or bad depended on their sugar levels and how much pain they were having from their arthritis or old bullet wounds or injuries from torture, for instance. They would occasionally attend Khulumani meetings, and I would accompany them. It was not always clear what kind of data this research environment could generate. Because both conversation and shared activities were limited, and there was no easy access to my research questions: how discourses of law shaped people's subjectivities. I was shy, and careful not to ask my informants to put their experiences of victimhood into words. On the one hand, I did not want to cause them any harm; on the other hand, I wanted to understand which discursive forms they themselves chose for their victimhood.

In one revealing moment, however, Ms. Twala told me something that changed my perspective or, rather, sharpened my awareness of something I had practiced but not been capable of understanding cognitively. I was about to leave on a longer research journey. As I was hugging Ms. Twala and saying my good-byes to her and the others, she spoke and someone translated: "She says that her body always felt much better whenever she sees you, Rita." In that moment, I was just very moved; it was only over the following days and weeks that Ms. Twala's words made me think about the bodily dimension of social interaction. I slowly started to realize that victim subjectivity has an important bodily dimension, one that goes beyond the physical signs of injury. In the months that followed, when I was still spending some time in the field, I realized that my informants' bodies had importance beyond being a site of strength or fragility, and that, methodologically, the body was more to me than just the venue of inscription of a discourse or one element of a (material) argument for victimhood.

Methodological literature in anthropology gives us many tools to unearth information, but it tells us little about how we specifically generate knowledge in our everyday lives as researchers (for an exception, see Okely 2012, 107–24). Among scholars who have reflected on this question, it is often a consequence of their interest in the body and its role in relating one's being to the world and participating in the formation of the social (Featherstone, Hepworth, and Turner 1991; Förster 2001, 2011; Hastrup and Hervik 1994; Jackson 1989; Okely 1994; Stoller 1989; Wacquant 2004; Wikan 1991). In the course of the formalization of an anthropology of the body in the past three decades (Lock and Farquhar 2007; Mascia-Lees 2011), we have not come very close to a social scientific understanding of the bodily dimension making up our agency and shaping our lived experience (cf. Csordas 1990, 1993; see also the introduction to this book).

Hannah Arendt argues that what may be articulated in the public realm, and what fails to be heard or seen, is predetermined by what is considered socially relevant in a certain context (Arendt 1958, 51–52; Jackson 1998). However, she insists that the impossibility of articulating one's experiences in the public realm when they contrast with dominant discourses does not mean that such experiences do not exist or matter. They may undergo ideological shifts due to their interplay with the public sphere, but they do not have to. Things left unsaid continue to matter. If they matter—and anthropology certainly is sensitized to things left unsaid and to experiences that resist predication—how do we find methods that take the bodily and nonpredicated[2] dimension of experience seriously and access individual and social experience grounded in the body? In what follows, I propose practical avenues to access the experiences of the other, and tentatively suggest what this access entails for anthropological research in general.

Noting Ethnographic Experience

After my experience with Ms. Twala, I searched for notions of the body in my field notes, and found that there were indeed few direct indications to it apart from references to the injured body—to wounds, experiences of torture, chronic illness, and so on. Had I not jotted down my "headnotes," I wondered. And if not, how could I then retrieve them? Or had I not noted such experiences at all because the body had not been the focus of my research questions? Only after several rereadings of my field notes did I realize that they did contain information about the body, after all, although it had been jotted down in an untrained and unsystematic manner.[3]

Here I was, twenty years after Paul Stoller (1989) had published *The Taste of Ethnographic Things*, a work in which he explores how doing research changes the researcher. Stoller conducted research among the Songhay in Niger from the mid-1970s onward, and later wrote about his conversion from hard-core linguistic anthropologist (equipped with "a language attitude survey, a census, and tape-recorded linguistic data" [4]) to practitioner of experiential anthropology: "Slowly, I uncovered an important rule: one cannot separate thought from feeling and action; they are inextricably linked" (5).

Writing Culture: The Poetics and Politics of Ethnography, a work which is primarily concerned with the *notation* of ethnographic material, had also been published more than twenty-five years ago (Clifford and Marcus 1986; see also Sanjek 1990). The editors' concern was textual theory and textual form. The essays in the collection focused on power relations and the extraction of readable knowledge, but also inquired into the conditions under which "data" are "collected." But despite this concern with the production of ethnography, the essays scarcely reflected on the bodily dimension of generating knowledge.

The two questions that the early writings in the anthropology of the body and the *Writing Culture* project raised seem to persist today: how to *take note* (through cognition and the senses) of what is beyond the verbal, or the non-predicated; and how to *note down* perceptions and experiences of what is neither verbal nor a clearly distinctive action. Field notes, the basis for ethnography, are often devoid of such sensory experiences (see also Ottenberg 1990). As Hastrup notes:

The almost mythological status of field notes as recorded observations has obscured the pertinence of the highly emotionally loaded "headnotes," the unwritten recollections. This has fostered a view of intentionality as located in a disembodied mind, and a view of agency as the outcome of cognitive rationality alone. (Hastrup 1994, 174)

The question of what precedes notification of ethnographic experiences thus deserves more systematic reflection. How do we even come to note certain ethnographic experiences we make?[4] In other words, how do we come to "attend" to something? Phenomenologist Maurice Merleau-Ponty ponders the notion of attention and suggests that paying attention turns something that has been there *as horizon* into a new object.

To pay attention is not merely further to elucidate pre-existing data, it is to bring about a new articulation of them by taking them as figures. They are performed only as horizons, they constitute in reality new regions in the total world. . . . Thus attention . . . is the active constitution of a new object which makes explicit and articulates what was until then presented as no more than an indeterminate horizon. (Merleau-Ponty 1962, 35)

Merleau-Ponty does not indicate through what kinds of processes such a "new object" is constituted. Thomas Csordas (1993) draws on Merleau-Ponty's (and others') work and attempts to look at the operationality of what Csordas calls "somatic modes of attention," which, according to him, are "culturally elaborated ways of attending to and with one's body in surroundings that include the embodied presence of others" (Csordas 1990, 138). Attention implies both "sensory engagement" and an "object," and he therefore suggests including in a definition of attention both attending *with* and attending *to* the body. In other words, it is prominently one's own body that is the means to connect to others' experiences (see also Widlok 2009). This is similar to Kirsten Hastrup (1994, 227), who understands the body as a medium that gives access to what may still be nonpredicated: "The feel for ethnographic relevance to a large extent is mediated by the bodily and sensory experience that may precede linguistic competence."

Although readily comprehensible and indeed revolutionary for anthropological scholarly literature as a whole, the notions of such scholars as Hastrup and Csordas are also slightly tautological: it is through our own bodily experiences that we can come closer to experiencing the experiences of others. But how do we then decrypt our own bodily experiences? *How precisely do we attend with our bodies and attend to bodies?*

Field Research as a Maussian Experience

The question of how we attend relates to the ways in which we grow accustomed to a new research field. In the literature on anthropological methodology, the habitual dimension of the researcher's knowledge is a major concern. Knowledge acquired in our (first) socialization has to be revised in anthropology's rite of passage: the second socialization. Here, habituation can be seen as an obstacle to accessing foreign forms of sociality (cf. Girtler 2001, 65–67). How can a researcher take on his or her informants' perspectives if the environment in which the researcher has grown up and lived for most of her or his life has shaped him or her culturally and socially? Förster (2001) suggests that "seeing" (a sensory activity) instead of "observing" (a cognitive activity) is a way to acquire (habitual and nonpredicated) knowledge that avoids "looking for" cognition, as predefined by our own categories of knowledge. In order to observe, we need to direct our cognitive attention to a predicative subject. Seeing, in contrast, does not condition the predicative or the normative. Hence Förster pleads for a rehabilitation of the everyday act of seeing. He attributes a habitual dimension to seeing and participating, but nonetheless grants the possibility that we can resume attending. What we, with hindsight, try to understand predicatively, he argues, is closer to lived experience than what we would have had we started with predicative intentionality at the first place (22).

While I certainly agree with the benefits of "seeing," my concern is a different one. There is a distinct quality to what is experienced through the body. We always see *something*; there is thus a third element to which one can refer when (discursively and thus predicatively) exchanging experiences. A bodily experience, in contrast to the sight sensory experience, does not take a straightforward object. Embodiment of experience means that subject and object have merged into a way of being in a world. Embodied experiences do not as easily have a referent in the world. It is thus much more difficult to refer to embodied experiences in a social exchange. While "seeing" refers to something external one can have a conversation about, "being" necessarily refers to something internal that first needs to be externalized—that is, predicated. This, though, entails a shift in consciousness that is probably more than making something visible into an object.

General literature on fieldwork practice not only argues that our (first) habituation shapes our outlook, but says that we need to go through a (second) habituation as quickly as possible. A quick "immersion" into the new environment is typically aspired to. The sooner one learns the daily ins and outs of a place and a particular community, the sooner one can start focusing on the "real" issues. During the first months in the field, anthropologists need and want to become streetwise, active, and somewhat self-sufficient agents in a new environment (Gupta and Ferguson 1997). We are anxious to overcome, as quickly as possible, newness and relegate it to the habitual space of our being. Necessarily, there is a degree of habituation in this process as well. We cannot constantly reflect on everything and disallow everything from becoming part of what is normal.

A familiarization with the field and the sedimentation of certain routines are necessary (but not sufficient) preconditions for research. The process of habituation is precisely what makes the anthropological approach unique (cf. Herzfeld 2009). It is our prime technique, and it gives us unique access to the lifeworlds of others. But, as necessary as this may be (for knowledge production and, sometimes literally, survival), it also has a downside in terms of a thorough generation of anthropological knowledge. Habituation may turn against us: on the way to becoming habituated to a new environment, we lose attention.

To better understand this (normative and technical) problem, let us apply Marcel Mauss's (1934) notion of techniques of the body, not to the object of anthropological inquiry, but to the researcher him- or herself. Mauss wrote that once a technique is mastered, attention recedes into the horizon. This is a problem for anthropology. It means that as soon as we have acquired a technique (anything from movements to wordings), our attention to it dwindles. In gaining habituation, we lose attention. So how can knowledge that has been habitual or nonpredicated reenter the realm of cognition? How precisely can we resume attention? Mauss does not say that we lose the ability to access newly acquired knowledge upon habituation. But we need something that triggers our attention. In his lecture, he uses the example of the difference between French and English soldiers' ways of marching during World War I, something the Englishmen realized when a regiment set out to march in time with French buglers and drums. The tempo of the English marching and the French music could not be aligned. The "wrong" combination triggered a recognition of the difference between a trained gait and a habituated gait. Heidegger ([1953] 1996), in turn, uses the example of a hammer that is "ready-to-hand," (*zuhanden*) that becomes "present-at-hand" (*vorhanden*) in a moment of "breakdown"—that is, when the hammerhead comes loose from the handle (cf. Zigon 2007, 134–38).

Moments of Dislocation: How We Come to Attend

We can distinguish two processes through which we come to attend to something. The first is the move from ignorance to (cognitive) knowledge: we notice something we did not note cognitively before; we learn something new because we are exposed to something new, what phenomenologists Alfred Schütz and Thomas Luckmann (1974, 187–91) call "a new theme." We then relate this new experience to a relevant structure and content that we have previously acquired.

> We can state generally that the less familiar a total situation is the greater the attentiveness will be with which one turns to it, so to speak, "on one's own." . . . In other words, if one cannot be routinely oriented in a situation, one must explicate it. And if one knows that in advance, then he also in advance turns to it "voluntarily." (Schütz and Luckmann 1974, 191)

But themes do not necessarily have to intrude, there is also what the phenomenologists call "motivated thematic relevance": both "imposed" attentiveness and "motivated" attentiveness are triggered by a "theme change." All of this happens in the cognitive-reflective realm. In other words, the kind of knowledge we acquire through this first process, moving from ignorance to knowledge, is cognitive.

The second process through which we come to attend to something takes us from (cognitive, habitual, or nonpredicated) knowledge to recognition. We attend to something to which we have grown accustomed. That means that something has been present in our experience habitually or nonpredicatively (but possibly also cognitively). In a specific (yet to be defined) incident, the habitual or routinized dimension is unmasked, so to speak, and we recognize something "anew." The kind of knowledge from which we move to recognition can be nonpredicated, cognitive, and habitual. Of these, habitual knowledge is particularly interesting for my analysis here. It has not yet become a "theme"; yet it is knowledge. In order to disentangle this seeming contradiction, I draw on Schütz and Luckmann's definition of habitual knowledge:

Habitual knowledge is on hand in situations, not simply at hand from case
to case. . . . It is not necessarily cogiven in the horizon of every situation, . . .
rather it is only continually "ready to grasp." . . . [I]t is not thematized and it is
rather automatically included in situations and acts. Habitual knowledge presents "definitive" solutions to problems, which are organized in the flow of lived
experience without one having to give them attention. (Schütz and Luckmann
1974, 191)

Habitual knowledge has thus gone through a process of sedimentation
(cf. Ostrow 1990). It "flows" precisely because it is not a theme. Marcel Mauss,
Pierre Bourdieu (1977), and Paul Connerton (1989) confirm that the acquisition of habitual knowledge requires sensory experience. It is only through a
process that addresses the senses that something can recede to the background
of our attention and assume a habitual dimension in our perception of the
world. Recognition of knowledge that has turned habitual or that resides in the
nonpredicated realm can happen in different ways. The first way, and one that
is immediately apparent in a scientific tradition that privileges recognition as
a largely cognitive act, is recognition based on new cognitive knowledge that
helps me to recognize a new element of my (nonpredicated) knowledge about
the world. An activity such as reading or reflection directs our attention to
something that thereby enters the realm of the predicative. This is indeed crucial for anthropological interpretation. For example, reading what other scholars have written very often gives us a completely new understanding of things
we know from the field without ever having thought about them.

But given our bias toward the textual, verbal, and visual, we tend to forget another form of recognizing: through sensory and bodily information.
A sensory or bodily experience is one important possible way to access habitual knowledge. It can give us access to what has resided in the nonpredicated realm. Examples are experiences involving taste, touch, smell, and sound
(cf. Howes 2005; Leder 1990). Even the environment shapes our perception of
the world and is therefore a source of recognition. Drawing on theories of place,
scholars suggest that we are not only embodied but also "emplaced" (Casey
1996; Ingold 2007); there is thus a "sensuous interrelationship of body-mind-
environment" (Casey 1996, 7). On a more methodological note, Pink (2008)
draws our attention to the fact that we the researchers, too, are "emplaced" in
ethnographic contexts and engage in place-making practices.

A sudden recollection through one of these sensory channels, and our attention is drawn to something we have never thought of consciously. This kind of recognition enters our corpus of predicative knowledge about the world upon sensory stimulation. Just as new pieces of knowledge can help us to recognize previously made experiences as such, new experiences can help us to recognize what we have previously known in a nonpredicated manner. Mauss's example of the English military gait that is incompatible with French military music is one such incidence. The resulting confusion may be the beginning of a cognitive reflection on the respective gaits. In any case, both sensory and cognitive stimulus, if successful, result in a *moment of dislocation*. We halt. We stop. And something in what we understand about the world changes.

In anthropological field research, creating the conditions for the possibility of recognition—that is, for *moments of dislocation*—is particularly important. In other words, we have to acquire a new stock of (habitual, nonpredicated, and cognitive) knowledge from which we can then potentially learn something new about our informants' lifeworlds and the world in general. Typically, we enter a new field with our ready-made knowledge about it. We have research questions in our mind; we have read literature and come with our theories and concepts, and many other ideas of how the world functions or is supposed to function. This kind of cognitive knowledge often very stubbornly resists change, as much as we would like to be open to its overthrow by new experiences. But we sometimes do make new experiences that contradict our taken-for-granted notions about the world.

I follow a small number of scholars who have tried to systematize stumbling as a moment that leads to insight. Fabian (1995) writes of making mistakes and of ethnographic misunderstanding as a source of insight. Agar (1985) examines the researcher's own taken-for-granted ways of acquiring knowledge. Similar to what Zigon (2007) calls "moral breakdown," Agar identifies "mandated breakdowns," hence the failure to understand, as the source of knowledge. These scholars have primarily looked at the cognitive and sought to understand the predicative. My own inquiry is complementary to theirs in that it focuses on moments in which the researcher's habituated being confronts nonpredicated knowledge. I thus not only shift the focus to the nonpredicated but also approach the theme from a positive angle: we begin to understand because we have been acquiring nonpredicated knowledge that we have not even been aware of. Certainly, the predicative and the nonpredicated always interact and condition one another.

In what follows, I lay out two ways in which we can recognize nonpredicated knowledge that we generate as part of our research experience as information about our informants' experience of the world. Of course, we cannot assume that the researcher and the informants—or any two persons sharing a social situation—can ever make an identical experience. Or, in Husserl's (1929, 177) words, "Each person has, from the same place in space and with the same lighting, the same view of, for example, a landscape. But never can the other, at exactly the same time as me (in the originary content of lived experience attributed to him) have the exact same appearance as I have. My appearances belong to me, his to him." Habitual knowledge shapes our perception of the world. People have a different stock of knowledge when they encounter one another (on the interrelations of difference; see Okely 2005). Even if we share an experience as banal as walking together (cf. Gilbert 1990), we do not experience it in the very same way.[5] We can thus only look for ways through which we can recognize other people's experience without having experienced the world in an identical manner.

Imagination: What We Can Share

Most would agree that the participatory dimension of the anthropological method produces some kind of shared experiences. This is not to say that observing, or seeing for that matter, cannot result in shared experiences; but, as many have argued, mere observation potentially produces distance. Doing something together with others is, by default, a sensory and bodily experience that leaves impressions on the researcher (cf. Spittler 2001). These impressions often are and remain nonpredicated. For that reason, not everyone subscribes to the notion that sharing experiences is a valuable ethnographic method. Geertz, for instance, rejects any possibility that knowledge production results from shared experiences.

> We cannot live other people's lives, and it is a piece of bad faith to try. We can but listen to what, in words, in images, in actions they say about their lives. As Victor Turner . . . argued, it is with expressions—representations, objectifications, discourses, performances, whatever—that we traffic. . . . Whatever sense we have of how things stand with someone's inner life, we gain it through their expressions, not through some magical intrusion into their consciousness. (Geertz 1986, 373)

Judith Okely (1994) is one of the few scholars who has tried to clarify what Geertz dismisses as "magic." She conducted research on elderly people and elderly people's homes in rural Normandy, France. Just as I confronted elderly and sick people who had lost much of their mobility and agility, both because of age and because of the bodily manifestations of their suffering under apartheid, Okely was faced with inactive informants and had to find creative ways to connect her own lifeworld and theirs. Her fieldwork thus partly consisted of working in the fields—something her informants had done all their lives before they were transferred to a retirement home. Okely suggests substituting what Geertz (1994, 48) calls "magic" with sensory knowledge, "one which is gained through experience of the everyday rather than confined to distilled external representations." She criticizes the authors of *The Anthropology of Experience* (Turner and Bruner 1986) for understanding experience as events and expressions. As a way of accessing the everyday experience of others, she suggests working through what she calls "vicariousness": "The anthropologist cannot replicate others' experience, but she can use her own [experience] for a vicarious understanding to surmise others' experience" (Okely 1994, 47). As such, the "having been there" assumes a quite different meaning from anthropologists' typical assertions of authority as regards their interpretation of happenings in a particular locality.

> My cumulative experience in the field and a familiarity with aspects of the subjects' past or present through participant observation were conveyed back to them, not just through words but through their recognition that I had "been there" and had experienced something similar through bodily presence, action and sight, sound, taste, touch or smell. I had engaged in agricultural labour of the kind they had once known. Here a distinction can be made between subjective experience which is individual, and creative understanding which is an approximation to empathy but never complete. (Okely 1994, 47)

If we include the possibility of sharing experiences vicariously in both directions between the researcher and the researched, the grounds for potentially accessing informants' experiences must be rethought. Sharing experiences, then, does not mean that something is experienced together, but that the time and place of a shared experience may be different for each of the persons. Whether directly experienced together or not, it becomes much more clearly tangible as a joint experience in the act of sharing it than in the act of experiencing it. Shared experience may result in *shared imagining*.[6] Shared imagining may include experiencing something vicariously, as when in Okely's research she physically experienced what her informants had been doing their whole lives. Imagining, then, refers to an idea of how something is done or is supposed to be done (which may result in a shared intention; see Gilbert 1992, 2009). It is normative for the persons who share an imagination, but it is not necessarily in compliance with dominant discourses. Imagining is mostly non-predicated, but it may also emerge in an articulated form when it seems conducive or necessary.[7] For it to enter the predicative, it needs a (verbal or sensory) trigger to be *recognized*.

My argument that shared experiencing is possible even if removed in time and space may sound counterintuitive especially when considering the criticism against nonethnographic methods and its assumptions of what is being shared (e.g., bridging intercultural differences). However, by making this point, I want to emphasize the fact that there has to be something to mutually refer to for shared experiencing to work.[8] Engaging in agricultural practice per se does not, of course, suffice to recognize every other farmer's personhood.[9] Gaps in time and space need to be bridged through a direct exchange, for instance, about the ways the respective hands are equally marked by the work with soil, and "thick knowledge" to contextualize the exchange. We do not only have to be contemporaries but also share a face-to-face (ideally "thick") encounter. Duranti (2010, 21) makes a similar point when outlining Husserl's idea of intersubjectivity not as "reading the mind of the other" but as "trading places": "[Husserl's] idea is not that we simultaneously come to the same understanding of any given situation (although this can happen), but that we have, to start, the possibility of exchanging places, of seeing the world from the point of view of the Other."

My research entailed numerous instances of shared imagining. As with Okely, my research with elderly or injured people meant that I often lived "aspects of [their] former lives" (Okely 1994, 53). I witnessed how members became too ill to attend Khulumani meetings, for instance. When I went to the township subsequently, they inquired about what had been debated at the meeting. As time passed, I became the person who went to the meetings for them, to report back, but also, in my own right, someone who did what they could no longer do themselves though they still had a clear idea what doing that thing had meant to them. With many of the more active members, I shared the experience of trying to make Khulumani's work and members' concerns and needs legible to the state. Without romanticizing this (my and members' ideas of social justice and social equity most likely differed widely), we jointly experienced our respective daily attempts to work toward them. I had a very close relationship with one executive member in particular, Zukiswa Puwana. Our shared concern was national and regional governance within the organization. This meant that we regularly talked for hours about what the problems were and how they could be addressed. By doing so, we learnt a lot about the other's imagination, which, in turn, helped us to clarify our respective understanding of what was and of what needed to be done. Another dimension of experiencing vicariously cuts across time. My travels to different branches of Khulumani, which is a nationwide organization, took me to places where, in the 1970s or 1980s, people had been as domestic workers or for visiting their relatives. My visits to Soweto, to Mthatha in the former homeland of Transkei, and to Zwelethemba in the rural Western Cape, for instance, came to mean a visit to what my interlocutors remember of and associate with the place (activism, work, family, imprisonment, etc.).

Intersubjectivity: How We Come to Recognize

So far, I have shown that shared imagining can be the basis for something else: a shared reference to an experience. But how does this shared reference turn into a shared perception, and the possibility for recognition? Ms. Twala, by telling me how my presence influenced her being, made me aware of the intersubjective dimension of conducting research. Intersubjectivity means that two or more people share a judgment of aspects of the world they inhabit and that they understand this as a given in their interaction, but also as part of their world. In the case of Ms. Twala and myself, we could not share much content with words. Even if this may be why we came to share much sociability nonverbally, I am, of course, not suggesting that lack of linguistic mastery is generally beneficial for intersubjectivity to emerge (cf. Duranti 2010; Throop 2012).[10] The best possible field situation is probably one in which mastery of linguistic and nonlinguistic registers can be combined.[11]

Surely, as Förster (2011, 11) shows, the emergence of intersubjectivity entails a sensory and bodily dimension. When Ms. Twala commented on her well-being and attributed to me a role in the fluctuations of her health, she was also commenting on how she saw me. She expressed and reinforced an intersubjective relation and commented on it through the expression of a bodily experience that directly resulted from our interaction. This is very close to Michael Jackson's understanding of intersubjectivity:

To recognize the embodiedness of our being-in-the-world is to discover a common ground where self and other are one, for by using one's body in the same
way as others in the same environment one finds oneself informed by an understanding which may then be interpreted according to one's own custom or bent,
yet which remains grounded in a field of practical activity and thereby remains
consonant with the experience of those among whom one has lived. (Jackson
1989, 135)

I would certainly not go as far as Jackson to say that the self and other become one in a research situation (or ever). Geertz clearly reminds us of the
limits to our ability to access one another's experiences. But where exactly do
we perceive these limits? Do we stop at the possibility of sharing experience
through actions? Or do we acknowledge the possibility of the overlapping or
even merging of each other's *horizons* in a way that is similar to what Lévinas
([2003]; see also Throop (2010b; 2012, 87) suggests?

Without having a ready answer to these questions, we can nonetheless say
that it was only as a result of intersubjectivity—which Ms. Twala so plainly
called to my attention—that I came to attend to what I finally thought of as
relevant in terms of apartheid-era victim subjectivity. As we have seen, for victims, the legacy of apartheid-era violence is difficult to articulate, partly because strong discourses determine which experiences are publicly relevant and
which are not. At the same time, most experiences of violence are embodied
to the extent that victims need more or less radical social and bodily changes
in order to emancipate themselves from them. Ms. Twala's comment fell on
the horizon of my subjective and sensory experiences in the field. That horizon had prepared me to attend to the embodied dimension of victimhood,
but only her remark made a shift from *knowledge* to *recognition* possible. I had
known that my informants had been harmed in various ways. I had known it
cognitively before even starting my research. I had known it habitually because
my informants' states of being had greatly influenced my research experience
and had regularly left me tired, worn out, and deeply sad in the evenings. I
had partly learned to deal with these experiences in what I described earlier
as the researcher's habituation: trying to adjust to the research environment
in order to focus on the "relevant topics." And I had known all this in a nonpredicated manner, I believe, because I had somehow known that I had been
missing much, without being able to put my finger on what it was. I had tried
to grasp victims' subjectivity by employing a discursive approach that relied on

signs of injury and utterances of harm. Ms. Twala finally gave me the chance to look at the injured body in its lived experience, beyond inadequate notions of discourse and inscription.

One is never exempt from all predicated notions, and I am not suggesting that, in my research environment, victims are not conscious of their victimhood. But victimhood is much more than its public performance or the predications we give to it, and our ethnographic methodology should be able to guide us toward this "more." In every social environment, certain experiences are not "a discursive object or a subject of articulation" (Förster 2011, 12). In my case, the embodied nature of experiences of violence had let me sense people's victimhood, but had also hindered me from accessing it predicatively. Ms. Twala's utterance was the trigger that made it possible for me to recognize it (cf. Jackson 2011; Stoller 2008).[12] It was a verbal action—as outlined earlier, a preferred trigger momentum. Nonetheless, her words would have fallen on (my) deaf ears had I not acquired a habitual and nonpredicated understanding of her and other people's victimhood over many months. It was only by way of our shared experiences (of their daily activities, the being together, the public and private meetings, etc.) that I was able to grasp the relevance of what she had told me. The object of recognition was thus not her well-being and my presence alone; it was an element of my previously habitual and nonpredicated knowledge about victims' subjectivities that turned into cognitive knowledge. Cognition—partial and forever limited—again, only came later once I started engaging with my field notes, read literature about the body and injured personhood, and looked at photographs and other ethnographic material (cf. Pink 2008, 190–91; 2009, 129–31).

Intersubjectivity is the basis for attendance to what is relevant in informants' lifeworlds—for *recognizing* an element of the stock of knowledge that we have acquired as part of our engagement with the world and with our informants' lives. Intersubjectivity is based on experiences we make jointly. It goes beyond empathy because it allows for mutual recognition and a redefinition of what has been.[13] It will always remain difficult, as Geertz reminds us, to prove the similarity of shared experiences. However, when we consider the possibility of sharing, we should leave the door ajar. Shared experiences can be the basis for something else: a shared *reference* to an experience that, in turn, is manifest in a shared *perception* of the world. The fact that it is possible to intersubjectively recognize an overlapping of perception is a step toward proving that a nonpredicated access to the experiences of others is indeed possible. If we deny this possibility, we reject the possibility of socialization more generally, unless one argues that socialization is only based on words.

Compensating the Unequal

With regard to the ethnographic method, Roger Sanjek (1991, 617) notes that "anthropologists have done a better job of using than articulating it." In this chapter, I have tried to articulate what largely remains in the nonpredicated realm in reflections on the ethnographic method and in ethnographies themselves.

Participant observation, if taken seriously, results in a degree of habituation to a new environment. We engage bodily with new forms of doing things, speaking, and relating to new people, objects (cf. Napier 2014), landscapes, and the like. However, as we grow accustomed, we lose attention to the new. I have suggested that there are ways through which we can recognize an element of the knowledge we have acquired bodily, which, in turn, gives us clues about what is relevant to our informants. These moments of dislocation trigger a process that helps us to cognitively access knowledge that was previously in the realm of the habitual or nonpredicated. The moment of dislocation at which nonpredicated and habitual knowledge enters our cognitive realm can happen in different forms. We tend to privilege the visual and the verbal, but it can as well be a sensory experience that dislocates us.

For moments of dislocation to occur, habituation is a necessary if not a sufficient condition. It is important to point out that what shifts from the nonpredicated into the cognitive realm may again recede into nonpredicated realm—namely, by way of renewed habituation. This is why I used to term *nonpredicated* as opposed to Husserl's "pre-predicative." The latter could be misleading in that it suggests that the formation of predication is linear rather than circular. Even if Husserl's notion of "moral breakdown" differs from my own argument, Zigon makes a similar point.[14] Zigon (2007, 140) sees the possibilities for a transformation of the everydayness in the aftermath of a "moral breakdown"—that is, when "persons or groups of persons are forced to step-away from their unreflective everydayness and think-through, figure out, work on themselves and respond to certain ethical dilemmas, troubles or problems." It is a return to a new state of familiarity, so to speak, that is different from what it was before.

This chapter is a search for a form of knowledge that helps us to understand other people's experience when we haven't experienced the world in an identical manner (which, of course, is impossible, or at least unprovable). I have never lived under apartheid rule and can never nonpredicatively share the experiences of those who have, which still shape my informants' lives.[15] But with the help of intersubjective research experiences, I could still start recognizing the particularity of the apartheid's legacy. For intersubjectivity to emerge, we need two things. The first is what Schütz and Luckmann (1974, 62) call "we-relations": "[t]he immediate experience of the other['s]" condition so that the other "appear[s] to me in his live corporeality: his body is for me a perceivable and explicable field of expression which makes his conscious life accessible to me." Second, we need to know that we share parts of the social worlds. By imagining together, we create a shared reference to how we see the world. Such a perception often emerges from doing something together without putting into words what we are working toward. This overlapping perception is a form of nonpredicated access to the experience of others. Hence, if we cannot experience something identically, we can at least come to a shared perception of the world, which gives us clues as to what is relevant in our informants' lifeworlds.

The ground for such knowledge and moments of dislocation is intersubjectivity. Intersubjectivity guides the researcher's interest toward the important questions and sometimes enables recognition, because it both sediments experiences and directs our attention toward them. Formulated differently: if we take ethnographic experiences seriously, the intersubjective nature of research implies that our informants often lead us to what is relevant for them. This can be a conscious and even strategic decision on their part; but it has a subtler side, in which nonpredicated intersubjectivity draws us to experiences close to theirs, and later draws our attention to "themes." Spending sufficient time with our informants to allow processes of habituation, intersubjectivity, recognition, and imagination to happen is central to accessing this predicative and habitual knowledge.

Throop is interested in a similar process through which we come to understand; according to Throop (2010a, 281), the *ethnographic epoché* (a state of suspended judgment) is an "*unwilled* shift in attention that is enacted in the context of the ethnographic encounter, an encounter that is often defined by the recurrent frustration of our attempts at achieving an intersubjective attunement with our interlocutors." In other words, "experiences of estrangement" and "confrontations with alterity" are the source for a moment "where we feel some form of empathy with our interlocutors." The point of entry is an interplay of inaccessibility and vulnerability through which we are compelled to view the other "as a subject and not an object of experience" (ibid.).[16] I contrarily argue in this chapter that the basis for recognition can also be what we *share* by way of doing things together and developing a shared perspective on parts of the world. Dislocation does not occur in "the between" but *within myself*. We enter into a state in which moments of dislocation become possible by participating bodily in the lifeworlds of others, and not by willingly or unwillingly suspending our judgment. Recognition emerges from the shared experience of being-in-the-world, not from ontological difference.

It is only upon a sensory engagement with others' lifeworlds and lived realities that we have a chance to understand what it means to be (in a body). Encounters between the researcher and the researched have an impact on their respective subjectivities; both emerge changed. How these shifts can be shared—and whether they should be shared (in a fieldwork context, see Borneman 2011), is another question. Analytically (and hopefully, politically; see also Herzfeld 2009), the researcher and the researched come to be on the same level. This sensory and bodily ethnographic experience should then also be reflected in the ethnography and the ways in which we write about the subject and forms of subjectivity.

In this sense, this methodological postscript is also an attempt to renegotiate the relation between the researcher and the informants, taking forth what the *Writing Culture* collection (1986) have started. If we acknowledge that all generation of anthropological knowledge happens intersubjectively, the exclusive authority of the researcher is bound to dissolve. This corresponds to the communication between victims and the broader society (Chapter 5) and the possibilities for a shared idea of the future. For it to be possible, society has to find ways to intersubjectively interact with victims; and victims have to relate to the social roles society offers and thus partially bridge the gap between lived experience and discursive practice.

The Embodiment of Experiences of Violence as Seeds of New Forms of Sociality

MOST SOCIAL SCIENTISTS today would agree that some of the experiences we are making "become embodied" (Csordas 1990, 1995; Das and Das 2007; Farmer 2004; Kleinman and Kleinman 1994; Jackson 2002). Many, however, are vague about exactly how experiences are sedimented in our bodies; even less clear are the conditions under which people manage to emancipate themselves from their embodied experiences. Furthermore, most of our scholarly knowledge about embodiment draws either on situations where the body is in an exceptional state, such as spirit possession (Lambek 1993; Stoller 1995), manipulation of body matter/parts (Butler 1993; Lock 2001), torture (Scarry 1985), or severe illness (Biehl 2005), or, to the contrary, on situations of smooth, constant, and successful habituation, such as crafts apprenticeship (Marchand 2008; Sennett 2008; Sudnow 1993; Wacquant 2004), or societal skills (Bourdieu 1977; Elias 2000; Mauss 1973).

In this book, I have looked at the embodiment of routinized and episodic experiences of violence made over decades, and at its consequences for the possibility of emancipation from these experiences under a new political order. I have found that a major part of the knowledge of violence is indeed embodied, and have asked what this means for the possibility of becoming emancipated from painful experiences. How does bodily knowledge translate into new forms of sociality, and into political effectiveness?

I looked for answers to these questions among people who experienced structural and episodic violence under apartheid rule, and who, for various reasons, continue to struggle to cope with their experiences today. Victims find it difficult to relate their embodied experiences of violence to the broader society, and the social roles it offers, and they experience exclusion and marginalization as a result of that. I have tried to understand their attempts to create new forms of sociality and thus emancipate themselves from their bodily knowledge of harm.

Some who suffer either manage to overcome their experiences of violence or to integrate them in such a way that they no longer disrupt their social and bodily being in the world. For many others, however, the sedimentation of experiences of violence results in neither smooth integration nor complete habituation. For them, experiences of violence continuously emerge as restless memories not easily integrated into their habitus—even ten, twenty, or thirty years after the actual incidents. Their experiences and the self-image they (would like to) live come into a conflict they struggle to solve. Hence, embodied experiences of pain (as I define them broadly in this book) and suffering work against what we normally understand as habitual, even though they are bodily and mostly nonpredicated.

The violence people were subjected to during the apartheid era had a routinized character. It determined their movements, many of their thoughts, and their daily well-being and health. The experience did not leave people unchanged. Bodily knowledge resulting from decades of discrimination and marginalization often became part of their perception of the world, while severe and episodic violent incidents— the murder, death, or disappearance of a loved one; torture; severe physical impairment, and so forth—ultimately ruptured an otherwise precarious life.

It is difficult to communicate such experiences of violence—and how they persist—to those who have not experienced them. Elaine Scarry has argued that pain radically destroys the capacity to communicate. According to Scarry (1985, 6), pain is the experience that is most intimately bound to personhood and the "most radically private of experiences." Drew Leder (1990, 74) finds that pain "is marked by an interiority that another cannot share," and Kirsten Hastrup (1994, 238n2) believes that "pain strikes one alone." Several scholars have in their work become resigned to the understanding that the experience of bodily pain resists articulation (Arendt 1958, 50–52; Scarry 1985). According to these scholars, the reason pain is isolating is not only the experience of it but also its lack of a discursive form. In this view, pain is not a "discursive object or a subject of articulation" (Förster 2011, 11) and is "perhaps the only experience which we are unable to transform into a shape fit for public appearance" (Arendt 1958, 50–51).

However, intersubjectivity and a shared intentionality can emerge without a discursive form. Bodily memory of harm hampers a person's efforts to enter into certain forms of sociality and engage in some forms of articulation. But the bodily memory of harm can also create the conditions needed to relate to others who share similar experiences. Victims relate to one another by way of their bodily knowledge of harm. It is in such social encounters that new forms of sociality can slowly emerge. Among themselves, relying on intersubjective knowledge of their shared experiences, victims make new social and bodily experiences.

Silence is an important option for many victims trying to cope with past but lingering experiences. However, not to speak is too often viewed as deficiency by both scholars and practitioners, a dogma that was present in the liberation struggle but peaked with the TRC. However, in order to speak safely, one needs a receptive environment that is ready to take on the responsibility of someone opening up, and to give him or her the chance to assume a new social position in everyday life.

I have attempted to understand how victims relate their lived experiences of victimhood to the social and the political. I thus traced the shifts from *non-predicated* to *articulated* to *politically articulated* victimhood. What happens when a person takes his or her victimhood, which is a nonpredicated and genuinely personal and intimate experience, into the predicative realm and publicly articulates it? The role of victimhood in the person's subjective experience necessarily changes. His or her personhood comes into a relation to other articulated forms of victimhood. I call the resulting state *victim subjectivity*. Those articulated forms of victimhood also stand in relation to what I call *victims' subject positions*. Victims' subject positions are discourses—often dominant discourses—prescribing ideas and ideals of what a victim is or is supposed to be. Hence, victim subjectivity is necessarily political, because any articulation of one's subjectivity takes place in a context of discourses. In sum, as soon as victimhood enters the predicative realm, a connection between experience and societal discourses is created, which, in turn, can influence what a socially effective discursive form will be.

Practices of nonpredicated solidarity, such as those described earlier, do not offer spectacular changes in victims' social status or forms of embodiment. But in an often modest way, they do offer new experiences. They are emancipatory in the sense that they try to find new forms of sociality based on lived experiences that are not directly related to dominant victims' subject positions; and they are highly creative in the sense that they lay the ground for new socialities.

These practices are and often remain nonpredicated bodily experiences and do not necessarily become articulated in a way that is accessible to the wider society. The necessary condition of their effectiveness is shared victimhood. It is precisely this particularity that holds the danger of renewed exclusion from the wider society and a withdrawal from the more general political discussion of victimhood. What victims share in these spaces may be too particular to be effective in a broader societal situation.

Such tacit and bodily socialities can sow the seeds of new sociality among victims, which the victims can relate to the dominant victims' subject positions. If victims resist articulation in the political realm, tacit and bodily socialities remain everyday practices accessible only to those who tacitly share a knowledge of suffering. Not only can this further isolate victims, it can also cement victimhood as a political discourse *about*, not *with* victims. Under these circumstances, a transformation to a way of being in the world that goes beyond victimhood is much more difficult to achieve. If we are to create conditions under which victims can make truly new experiences, changes in the legal, economic, and symbolic realms have to happen. For changes to become reality, people have to engage with the dominant victims' subject position.

Dominant Discourses as Limits to the Transformation of Victimhood

Any transformation of subjectivity is a social process. Embodied experiences of harm may be rather stable, but they are not fixed forever. One way for them to change is the embodiment of new experiences. If the injured person has the chance to make bodily and social experiences that are different from the ones she or he had been subjected to previously, the status of those older experiences can change. Such new experiences are necessarily social. Consequently, a successful transformation of bodily experiences needs social acknowledgment and a societal space for new forms of action.

We have seen that bodily experiences can fragment the possibilities of intersubjective recognition of the other's suffering. If we ask how new social experiences are possible for victims, the crucial question becomes, what kinds of experience can be effective in the public realm and what kinds cannot. Arendt (1958, 51) writes that "only what is considered to be relevant, worthy of being seen or heard, can be tolerated [in the public sphere], so that the irrelevant becomes automatically a private matter."

Since our feeling for reality depends utterly upon appearance and therefore upon the existence of a public realm into which things can appear out of the darkness of sheltered existence, even the twilight which illuminates our private and intimate lives is ultimately derived from the much harsher light of the public realm. (Arendt 1958, 51–52)

I showed in my work that whereas sociality among victims can happen intersubjectively and without any predetermined discursive form, victims can only find acknowledgment in the broader society if they relate their experiences to the dominant victims' subject position. Making one's victimhood public (or publicly social) is, however, a risky step. As with any attempt of "trying on" a subjectivity (Merry 2003), it means exposing oneself to the risk of not being recognized. If one cannot adhere to a dominant discourse of victimhood, one likely will not be heard in one's injured personhood. Worse, one might be exposed to various sorts of allegations, from antipatriotism to witchcraft.

Any articulation is an abstraction from one's experiences. It is a translation of an experienced state into discursive forms that are available in a society. These forms may be actions or words; analytically, I do not limit "articulation" to the verbal realm. These forms shift over time and space. They constrain, but they also *enable* articulation. They constrain if a person cannot relate what is in the nonpredicated to a given discursive form; then, his or her experiences become incommunicable. But a discursive form can enable communication when a person is capable of abstracting from his or her own experience in order to discursively connect to broader society.

Such an abstraction entails a degree of detachment from one's bodily experiences. This detachment is, in turn, the condition for emancipation. It is no guarantee, to be sure, of a successful transcendence of one's painful experiences. The discursive form available might be so far removed from the experience that neither victims nor society can bridge the gap. But—and this is the important point—in order to become socially effective and transformative, embodied experiences do not necessarily have to be conveyed in their full meaning. People try to relate their experiences to available discourses because they want to be *recognized*. This recognition does not necessarily entail full understanding of the other's pain. Its necessary precondition, however, is an intersubjective recognition of the victim's victimhood and its consequences.

In South Africa, apartheid-era victimhood has assumed a discursive form over the past twenty years. In particular, the South African Truth and

Reconciliation Commission pushed for a public acknowledgment of the injuries of the past. But while it has catapulted victimhood into the public attention, it has also produced a very limited understanding of apartheid-era victimhood. The commission's work and the government's inadequate follow-up on the commission's recommendations are governing measures that have had a direct impact on lived victimhood in South Africa. To be recognized by society as a victim, people, subsequently and consequently, had to relate to the TRC's notion of victimhood. This notion has not become fully exclusive; it has also triggered alternative forms of articulation and creative responses by victims. But it is no longer possible to find one's own, but socially effective, ways of living one's victimhood without reference to the TRC's notion.

For victims, victimhood and its effects remain a problem. Not only does the experience of violence sit uneasily with one's self; experiences of violence also often isolate people. They alienate a person from others, be it as a result of a disruptive social experience or be it due to the effects of violence. Under apartheid rule, injury and exclusion were often a collective experience, but their effects today are lived individually rather than collectively, and victims in today's South Africa often fail to be recognized in their injured personhood by the broader society. On the contrary, they occupy a suspicious subject position. In other words, apartheid-era victimhood has not received sufficient and sufficiently differentiated public acknowledgment. In this situation, the dominant victims' subject position promulgated by the TRC becomes all the more powerful. It shapes the dominant social discourse and makes the social acknowledgment of different forms of living one's victimhood either more or less likely.

The social roles society offers victims do not take the persistence of embodied memories into account, and victims receive little instruction on how to assume those roles effectively.

In post-apartheid South Africa, the TRC process has given the state the power of definition over what and who an apartheid-era victim is. Only ready-to-reconcile personhood fell into this category, and only those 21,000 survivors who testified before the commission can (legally) claim that victim status in the commission's aftermath. The social role of the healed personhood emerging from the TRC process is "available"; but there is little indication of the way to a healed personhood.

In only a few cases could the commission convincingly perform a reconciliation between a perpetrator and a victim and the transition of a victim to a "survivor." Nelson Mandela embodied the image of a healed personhood. But he was too removed and too exceptional to be more than a myth and a moral obligation; his personhood is beyond the reach of ordinary people. Since heroism is reserved for and occupied by a few cadres in the African National Congress or given to some persons who were killed as a result of their involvement in the struggle, it is a highly exclusive subject position. Apart from heroism as the road to a healed personhood, it is wealth as a lived lifestyle of the new black elite in South Africa that is portrayed as a path toward healing. But, yet again, this is an exclusive economic, and thus social, position that is unavailable to the majority of black South Africans today.[1]

In other words, the wider society does not see victimhood in the light of the persistence of embodied memory and the difficulty of making new experiences. The role of the "healed"—that is, of the rich and the hero—turns into a demand placed on victims, whose nonadherence to the role becomes proof of their inability or unpreparedness to change.

Instead of facilitating change, the offer of heroism and wealth as roads to healing creates new and insurmountable boundaries between people who (at least discursively) were united in their struggle against apartheid rule. Today, discourses of heroism and wealth disable solidarity between victims and those who "made it"—those who can *afford* to abstract from their experiences. As a result, there is an increasing schism between persons who struggle to overcome their victimhood and those who have managed to reap the harvest of the "new South Africa." The legal developments outlined in the following sections are manifestations of this tension.

Here, Victor Turner's (1969) figure of the social drama can help us understand that the tensions in South African society between those who sit with their victimhood and those who managed to emancipate themselves from it have to be addressed performatively in order to be successfully remedied. If the performance fails, there will be schism.

The Possibilities of Change as Advocated by the State and as Practiced by Victims

The empirical material presented in this book suggests that a main concern of victims is that the state, the legitimate authority to which both the capacity and the authority to address past wrongs are ascribed, address past suffering *in any form*. For victims, concrete measures can take many different forms, as long as they are a first step toward dealing with subjective and embodied experiences of violence. At least three measures have been tried out globally in "transitional

justice" processes: symbolic redress, prosecution of perpetrators, and reparations. All of them are proxy measures. They are necessarily incapable of undo-
ing past wrongs; and instead of transforming experiences today and offering
new subjectivities that are livable in practice, they perform redress.

Under the form of symbolic redress, I subsume not only tangible acts, such
as renaming streets, erecting memorials, and burying the remains of killed
family members, but also less tangible acts, such as commemorating fallen heroes in public events. Symbolic redress is an act that *substitutes* an experience
with something that relates in its meaning to that experience. It is vicarious
by nature, as the substitution is, at first, merely a reference to experienced injury and can easily fail to become effective in actual realities. In South Africa,
symbolic redress has largely been an ANC-driven project; it thus privileges a
certain kind of narrative, so that it often produces biased tales of heroism.

The second globally applied measure of dealing with the past, the prosecution of perpetrators, fulfills another proxy function: proxy by person. The murdered son does not come back, but his killer is prosecuted. The South African
state has done little to remedy the fact that very few perpetrators came forth
to testify to the TRC and apply for amnesty from prosecution for the atrocities they had committed under apartheid rule. It was owing to initiatives taken
by victims' support and lobby groups that the issue of perpetrators' indemnity
began to attract attention, several years after the TRC had finished its work.

Nonetheless, my research suggests that victims are not primarily interested
in the prosecution of perpetrators (of what had been a largely anonymous system of violence). Their main concern is that leaving perpetrators alone results
in the ultimate loss of valuable information about what happened, and the impossibility of finding graves, knowing the truth about disappearances, or reha-
bilitating victims of injustices. This information could help to start a process of
facing up to what actually happened, and to potentially and slowly overcoming
it. In post-1994 policy making, perpetrators' privacy and safety has always been
rated higher than the victims' quest for information. For instance, the ANC
has tried to not disclose its responsibility for human rights violations in the
training camps in Angola and other countries. Even information that has been
divulged by perpetrators can be difficult to access: at the time of publication,
the archives of the TRC are still closed, which prevents victims from learning
information that came out of the amnesty hearings.

The third measure for addressing past injustices is payment of financial
reparations. In the fight to acknowledge victims in the post-TRC years, the

question of reparations has played a major role. The TRC only named roughly 21,000 victims, who then qualified for payouts. The government has so far objected to any expansion of "the list." South African victims' support and lobby groups demand the inclusive payment of reparations to all victims of apartheid-era crimes. Apart from the (often understated[2]) fact that many people need financial support today, reparations would, they feel, also be a form of acknowledgment that could help them in dealing with pain and loss. Reparations are also a substitute—in kind.

All these measures for dealing with the past are vicarious at best; they might be able to ease the burden of what happened, but they cannot undo it. This is often given as a reason to dismiss such measures completely. But measures of redress nevertheless have the power to transform lived victimhood from unacknowledged marginalization to social recognition.

In chapter 5, I examined victims' attempts to make new experiences and showed how these may lead to forms of sociality that take victims beyond their victimhood. These everyday life practices are creative because they try something that the traditional measures of redress (symbolic redress, prosecution of perpetrators, and reparations) do not: they directly address the social and the bodily dimension of victimhood. They emerge from experiences of violence and the quest to make them social. They do not primarily seek a discursive form but begin as bodily and nonpredicated activities. The fact that their experiences are not part of the dominant discourses does not mean, as Arendt (1958, 51–52) also emphasizes, that they go away. But it is precisely because of their particularity and their nonpredicated character that they not only can emancipate victims but also potentially isolate them more.

State measures and victims' daily attempts at emancipation are not mutually exclusive. But it is clear when we look at victims' subject positions and lived victimhood in today's South Africa that these two forms of instigating social change have not started interacting with each other. The reason for this nonrelation is sedimented bodily experiences: the dominant victims' subject positions do not acknowledge the bodily dimension of victimhood, and victims find it difficult to relate their bodily experiences to the dominant forms of victimhood and redress.

Among other things, the state's unresponsiveness and its flawed policy measures have caused victims' groups to seek recourse in the law. The two official measures of redress that civil society and victims' groups have begun to demand more explicitly, and in politically more effective ways, are financial reparations and ending extended amnesty for those who committed apartheid-era crimes. Both demands have been met with skepticism by both scholars and politicians because they chiefly rely on the law.

Legal Recourse as Path toward Recognition and Emancipation

The juridification of issues of transitional justice as a response to initiatives by victims' groups in the 2000s has to be seen in the context of the slow and lingering post-TRC decriminalization of apartheid-era crimes. Here, I synthesize my argument by teasing out the difference between the political avenue and the legal avenue to finding recognition for experienced injustice.

The South African "transition" to democracy has come to stand for a reconciliatory approach to dealing with the past, one that relies on political negotiations and a national healing project instead of courts of law. South Africa thus stands in marked contrast to many other countries. Globally, we are currently seeing a greater number of cases referred to international criminal tribunals and an increase in both political and legal efforts to deal with the past. But also in South Africa things did not stop at the TRC. Victims' support and lobby groups have pursued legal remedies since the TRC finished its investigations and issued its final report, in 2003. What started as a political process now has a legal character—thanks to the initiatives of civil society groups. This seems to support the assumption that victims demand that the violent past be addressed in the courts. I want to question this assumption from a victims' perspective.

Even if the South African Truth and Reconciliation Commission is generally perceived as a reconciliatory body, the work of its Amnesty Committee is typically associated with a legal handling of apartheid-era crimes. The amnesty component of the TRC reflected a compromise between the National Party, which had demanded blanket amnesty, and the liberation movements, which had called for a full investigation into the workings of the apartheid regime. The result was that, upon full disclosure of their crimes, suspected perpetrators could be awarded amnesty. In keeping with its mandate, the commission exclusively investigated apartheid-era crimes that had a political objective. The granting of amnesty had legal consequences for the perpetrators: amnesty freed them from all future civil or criminal liability. Requiring perpetrators to confess to their crimes in effect rendered a moral judgment against the perpetrators, but it did not prosecute them.

After the TRC, the South African judiciary was left with a huge amount of unfinished work. The conditional character of the TRC's amnesty process meant that perpetrators who had not testified or who were not granted amnesty (because of failure to fully disclose their crimes, for instance) were and still are liable for civil or criminal suits. Also, crimes that were not committed with a political objective and that should have been investigated during the apartheid regime in the first place were now supposed to be investigated by the post-apartheid government through its ordinary courts and the National Prosecution Authority. But far from launch investigations into these potential criminal cases, the National Prosecution Authority has failed to follow up on most of them. This represents a process of slow and lingering decriminalization. It is in this context that the legal actions undertaken by victims' organization and other civil society groups in relation to liability, impunity, and indemnity have to be looked at.

Victims' support groups and other organizations have lobbied government for a speedier payout and for the implementation of community reparations, but also for further investigation into newly emerging cases of apartheid-era crimes. They have repeatedly invited business to enter into a dialogue about what corporations can do to contribute to the reconstruction of the country. Business proved unresponsive, as did government.

In 2002, the apartheid litigations were filed in US courts (*Balintulo et al. v. Daimler AG et al.* and *Ntsebeza et al. v. Daimler Chrysler Corporation et al.*). The South African government opposed the litigations from an early stage. It argued that they would pre-empt the South African government's ability to handle domestic matters of reconstruction and reconciliation internally and transgress its sovereignty, and that they would discourage investment in the South African economy. Only in 2009 did the South African government half-heartedly withdraw its opposition.

South African civil society organizations also intervened to bring about domestic policy changes. The Ministry of Justice, for example, had, in 2005, suggested amendments to the Prosecution Policy that would grant the National Directorate of Public Prosecutions discretion in whether to grant indemnity to perpetrators of politically motivated crimes committed before 1994. Civil society organizations filed a challenge to the amendments. In 2008, the High Court in Pretoria found that the proposed policy amendments amounted to a "copy cat" of the TRC amnesty process and struck them down. In the same year, South African President Mbeki created a reference group to make recommendations with respect to which of these pre-1994 offenders should receive a presidential pardon. Civil society groups submitted an urgent application, arguing that the process unlawfully excluded victims. The court ruled that before granting a pardon, the president must consider "the inputs of victims and/or families of the victims."

From this brief summary of cases related to the TRC process and issues of liability for apartheid-era crimes, we can gain a clearer understanding of juridification. On the one hand, victims' and civil society groups are involved in generating new law. Backed up by the international human rights community, the apartheid litigations in the United States push for new standards that will recognize corporate liability for violations of international human rights law. On the other hand, the South African domestic cases insist on adherence to already established standards. The South African cases are an attempt to counter the decriminalization of apartheid-era crimes.

Going to the courts for "transitional justice issues" does not necessarily mean legalization—an increase in the law's grip on social reality. It may simply mean the insistence on the rule of law—testing an existing social space instead of increasing it. Victims' support and lobby groups did not primarily try the legal avenue in an attempt to "criminalize" the conflict around apartheid-era crimes and their evaluation. The law presented them with a promising option for obtaining some form of recognition, and a chance to become emancipated from embodied memories of harm.

This decriminalization of apartheid-era crimes has signaled two things: it is an indirect nonrecognition of the experiences and memories victims still live with, and it results in the loss of information about what exactly happened. In both aspects, it undermines the possibility of victims emancipating themselves from experiences of harm. Similarly, reparation payments and symbolic forms of remembering or overwriting the past are often flawed because they are based on the dominant victims' subject positions, thus helping to further entrench victims and to exclude and marginalize the majority of them.

For victims, the distinction between the political and the legal avenues to social justice and social equality is largely irrelevant. Recognition of injuries is important in making emancipation from embodied experiences of victimhood possible. If the political avenue fails because victims cannot successfully relate to dominant subject positions, the law is a viable alternative. What is it, then, that makes law seem more responsive than politics? What, in other words, is the characteristic difference between politics and the law?

For victims, the most important difference lies in the notion of procedure and responsibility. Courts are charged with dealing with what is brought before them. Even if they determine that, for procedural or substantial reasons, the court is not responsible for a specific issue, this results from engaging with the cases. The proceedings are prescribed and the responsibility of courts to at least hear them is clear. For plaintiffs, to file a case with a court means to rely on this abstract protocol. Only then can legalization "happen."

This is in contrast to the political path. Part of politics is *not* to react: to forget, to let things rest or to grant amnesty. Responsibilities and procedures to bring about a political solution are not clear from the outset. Both leave much room for unexpected actions, but also for nonaction. A government can simply decide not to address a certain issue, and demonstrators or petitioners can hurt themselves against a wall of silence. This, at least, is not the case for the legal avenue. One may not like or even understand a decision taken by a court, but one can at least follow the process through its stages and demand recognition as a plaintiff. Procedural rules cannot secure success, but if a claim is made compatible to the law, they do secure a modicum of recognition.

Of course, I do not suggest that the law and politics are completely separate realms. They are connected in many ways and can greatly influence each other—as is obvious in the US and South African cases. Importantly, taking recourse in the law often confers new negotiation power in the political realm, too, and has consequences for political organization.

By making claims readable to a wider public, going to court draws attention to the concerns of the plaintiffs. The apartheid litigations are a good example for this. They have grown out of international concerns for debt release and debt relief by the turn of the millennium, which for a time revived the support of former anti-apartheid solidarity groups worldwide. The litigations have not only emerged from these long-standing relations between South Africans and civil society across the world, but have in effect also regenerated some of these ties in a broader human rights community. Together with other international cases filed under the US Alien Tort Statute, the apartheid litigations epitomize the core concerns of this lose community: corporate liability, accountability for gross and structural human rights violations, and the commitment of postcolonial and Western states to ensuing social equity and social justice.

Furthermore, having recourse to the law has produced new social spaces within South Africa. For one, the Khulumani Support Group's membership has grown dramatically since the filing of the suits. People hope to benefit from payouts, but this alone cannot explain why many victims become active, not simply nominative, members. As a civil society group, Khulumani has partially emerged from the interaction with a legal logic, but it has generated political action that is the result of similarly situated people relating to one another, recognizing each other's experiences of violence, and trying out new forms of sociality among themselves. In many instances, they have managed to successfully articulate their perspective in the public space and modify dominant victims' subject positions. Ultimately, new forms of the political have grown out of legal actions. The reason for the emergence of the political can also be disappointment with the law. This confirms that recourse to the law is not inescapable; it is one possibility of articulation in the relation between the law and the social.

Theories of Legalization Revisited

Over the past decade, new forms of social and political organizing have come into the focus of the social sciences. How do people organize in a world in which political decisions have become more and more globalized and old patterns of organization (from liberation movements to class struggles) can no longer be taken for granted? In this context, social movements have emerged as a driving factor of (and a prime venue for the analysis of) social change (Beinart and Dawson 2010; Goodale and Merry 2007; Keck and Sikkink 1998; Robins 2009). While concentrating on political agency, scholars have also convincingly shown that under the current conditions, social actors increasingly take the legal route in seeking social justice and social equality.

The findings of my research contribute to our knowledge of why people turn to the courts with what are essentially social concerns: they turn to courts because the political path has not been successful. Having recourse to the law is a countermovement to decriminalization and marginalization. If recognition by political means fails, people search for it in courts, where procedures guarantee a degree of recognition.

My findings show more, though. I believe that they revise the conclusions scholars have drawn from these new forms of social action. They ask what kinds of new forms of sociality emerge from this increased litigiousness around the world (Comaroff and Comaroff 2006; French 2009; Goodale and Merry 2007; Griffiths, Benda-Beckmann, and Benda-Beckmann 2005; Hastrup 2003; Robins 2009; Roux and Van Marle 2008). They argue that taking a legal avenue produces particular subjectivities. If issues that are chiefly collective and structural are brought before courts rather than fought through political channels, they say, this may result in a situation that is contrary to the intention of the actors. Using the legal avenue for social action individualizes the structural and the collective. Furthermore, what is an inherently political concern is very likely to be depoliticized as a result of this turn to the courts. This view suggests that the law presents a specific way of looking at sociality, and that actors are quite likely to fall prey to this perspective if they engage with it—despite or precisely because of their attempts to request support from the very societal institutions, the courts, that help producing the legal perspective in the first place. In other words, social actors resist an unresponsive political situation that does not condemn collective and structural injuries resolutely enough by turning to the courts. This form of resistance is not emancipatory, though, because it replicates what the actors are fighting against.

This view supports a social theory that juxtaposes the system and the actors as opposing entities and seeks to understand the interaction between them. Some scholars emphasize actors who act within and in relation to a system, others privilege the system that impacts on the actors' actions, but both groups tend to view social action in reference to a system. They draw conclusions about the power of the system by showing the actors' unintentional replication of their subjected selves.

In short, scholars have adopted a Foucauldian approach to litigiousness by arguing that everyone who engages with the law is consequently, and necessarily, subjected to the legalization of his or her personhood.

Drawing on my findings on embodied experiences and discursive forms of articulation as formulated above, I suggest turning Foucault on his head: Recourse to the law does not produce subjection to a discourse, but it is the consequence of the attempt to emancipate from a discourse—under conditions in which the law is more promising than the political avenue. The search for emancipation stems from lived realities of victimhood; in the example at hand, it originates where recognition is necessary because it has the potential to transform embodied experiences. If victims seek recognition, they have to relate their experiences to socially effective subject positions. The legal developments in the post-TRC years are a consequence of this inescapable relation. Legalization of conflicts is thus the consequence of subjectivities' entanglement in society and societal structures, and not, as the legalization theory suggests, an entanglement in the logic of the law that results in subjection to a discourse.

Embodied experiences of harm are not (and cannot be) completely absorbed by legalization. Embodied knowledge of harm runs counter to a legalization of subjectivities precisely because the legal logic does not relate to a lived experience of victimhood. Legalization becomes effective as a discourse some can successfully adopt to relate their concerns to a public. But the legal view on victimhood is too distanced from any lived experience to capture one's perception of the world. One's perception of the world is a result of lived socialities, not of discourses alone. Any discursive form of seeing oneself loses relevance when it is too far removed from one's lived experience.

Of course, experiences are shaped by discourses. My focus here has been on the positioning of one's subjectivity in an environment of existing discourses; in other words, on a reinterpretation of experiences that are already sedimented. Sedimented experiences balk much more at discursive reinterpretation.

If a person cannot emancipate her- or himself from subjection to a dominant subject position that is disconnected from his or her perception of the world, however, we have a situation where a discourse indeed *subjects* in the Foucauldian sense. In this case, a person tries to adhere to an ideal that does not further his or her integration into society but instead results in social isolation.

My findings based on a bodily and sensory understanding of victimhood have consequences for how we see the "force of the law" (Bourdieu 1986). The law has, in some aspects, far less effect than legalization theory suggests. Plaintiffs often know very little about court procedures, and they do not relate their everyday lives to the legal actions. In this way, the apartheid litigations differ from conflicts between neighbors, for instance, who try to settle their disputes in court or by quasi-legal means (Merry 1990).

I am, however, not suggesting that a legal discourse does not have any effect. But legal discourses only become effective in specific realities and lived socialities, and we can only determine the law's effects empirically.

In my study, I have identified two major effects the legal discourse has had. First, even though legal actions draw attention to victims' groups, the lived experience of victimhood continues to be excluded from a socially effective victims' subject position. This is paradoxical because victims benefit from the procedural nature of the courts, which is lacking in politics.

In order to effectively present and represent the concerns of the victims and to engage with national and international actors, such as the state, the courts, lawyers, and other civil society groups, the Khulumani leadership has also had to draw on dominant discourses. This is a dilemma for an organization that is undergoing processes of professionalization. The work done by professional leaders is also guided by their experiences, but these experiences often differ from those of members. Leaders have managed to emancipate themselves from bodily memories to an extent that enables them to take on representative functions. Even members and leaders of a victims' organization may thus come to embody different socialities and find it difficult to recognize each other's experiences; their shared intentionality, however, attenuates the problem, as long as it persists.

Second, the individualizing nature of the law hampers solidarity among victims and thus works against victims' attempts to make experiences social. Given the particularity with which the law operates, it potentially isolates individuals. The law typically seeks proof for injury on an individual level. Whereas class actions (such as the apartheid litigations) are an attempt to make structural injury actionable, the law still needs to differentiate injury. Class actions therefore need individuals to function as class representatives who represent degrees and kinds of injury. This process of reading injury (which values the injuries of some more than the injury of others) may result in "individuation." In a society defined by shared structural suffering, to be singled out can only mean unfairly distancing oneself from others. The logic of the law thus generates a suspicious subject position: the victim who uses his or her experience to become different from other victims. Witchcraft accusations, or witchcraft fears, are a logical means to keep such victim representatives from breaking rank.

In the case of out-of-court settlements, this differentiation kicks in again. This happened in the apartheid litigations when there was a settlement offer by one of the defendants, General Motors, in early 2012. The twenty-three named plaintiffs are said to have received a cash settlement, whereas all the other members of the class of plaintiffs (in terms of the settlement, approximately 70,000 members of Khulumani) are promised to benefit from community projects. The law can leave traces in victims' subjectivities. The proxy function of legal action—the representative dimension in class actions in particular—works for victims insofar as their concerns are presented and represented by one of their own. But a class action reaches its limits when injury is measured and differentiated according to a legal logic; this is when differentiation among the plaintiffs is created.

The critical moment is thus not the legal action per se or the course the procedures take but the moment of a settlement or a payout. It is in relation to the individualization of injury that recourse to the law has implications in people's lives and impacts the possibility that victims will achieve solidarity. Solidarity is the necessary condition for the transformation of experiences that are immensely difficult to articulate. Experiences of solidarity are also the seeds of collective political action. Hence, social individuation as promoted by the law may work against politicization based on shared experiences of violence. By way of its individualizing dogmatic approach, it may endanger the seeds of political action.

The Body in the Social Sciences

Working at the intersection of the law and the body, I have attempted to show that we need to take the bodily dimension of being into account if we want to understand the effects of legal discourse or, for that matter, any discourse. Too much of what is analysed under the discourse paradigm simply sees action as *resistance to structure*.

A perspective on action and sociability that juxtaposes structure and agency (even it if acknowledges its dialectical interaction; see Giddens 1986) ignores one important dimension that lies at the foundation of social change: embodied memory. Embodied memory is an area we need to focus on in order to see the possibility of emancipation from a system. Pierre Bourdieu rather than Michel Foucault has given us the foundation for thinking through resistance to a system by elaborating on the bodily dimension of social action. Bourdieu, however, was primarily interested in the determining effects of processes of habituation and has not devoted too much thought to the emancipatory possibilities anchored in the body. I have argued that, under certain circumstances, people embody experiences of harm—a point close to Bourdieuian processes of habituation. On the other hand, experiences of harm do not necessarily result in habitual embodiment. On the contrary, embodied experiences of harm often sit uneasily. They may be nonpredicated and embodied, but they do not necessarily manifest themselves as habitual and smoothly integrated into a way of being in the world. In this, experiences of harm are different from many other experiences that lead to the integration of something new into the everyday perception of the world (Mauss 1973; Schütz and Luckmann 1974). Experiences of harm tend to disrupt everyday life time and again. In consequence, the relation between structure and agency is even more complex than the smooth, partly creative reproduction of structures through a habitus that Bourdieu describes (cf. Kesselring 2015b).

Much of the current literature that takes the body into account focuses on illness and illness narratives (Das and Das 2007). Didier Fassin (2007, 2008), for instance, understands collective history as embodied in individual biographies, in which shifts in health and illness patterns are indicators of societal shifts (cf. Biehl 2005; Cohen 1998; Desjarlais 2003; Kleinman and Kleinman 1994). It suggests that we can analyze the social by "(medically) reading the subject"—for social structures are inevitably inscribed in bodies and lives. This draws on bio-political thinking as initiated by Foucault in ways, I believe, he never intended to suggest. If we understand the formation of the social as a one-way, always successful, process from the "system" to the "subject," we miss what is happening on the side of persons, both predicatively and non-predicated. Hence, what Lock and Scheper-Hughes (1987, 6) noted in their synthesis article, in 1987, may still be accurate: "[W]e believe that insofar as medical anthropology has failed to problematize the body, it is destined to fall prey to the biological fallacy and related assumptions that are paradigmatic to biomedicine."

It was hoped that the new paradigm of "embodiment" would be a way out of this dead end. Csordas (1990) claimed that "the analysis of perception (the pre-objective) and practice (the habitus) grounded in the body leads to the collapse of the conventional distinction between subject and object" (Csordas 1990, 39–40). The embodiment paradigm indeed moved us away from former perspectives that merely saw the body as ritualized and symbolic object. However, I believe, the body instead became medicalized; that is, the anthropologist extrapolates from his or her technical and professional knowledge about illnesses and psychiatric states onto the social being. Anthropology would of course explain the medical with—and through—the social, but the social would only provide the context within which to situate the individual body. In other words, in the mission to renegotiate the mind-body duality, what happened was that the social became corporal; everything turned out to be bodily or embodied.

A significant number of studies since the early 1970s have attempted to overcome the old dichotomy between the mind and the body, whose cementation is usually traced back to Descartes (cf. Bergson [1994] for an early work). While I do not contend that my findings can resolve the monism/dualism problem, I think that they can be used to show the questionable effects the new preoccupation with the body in social sciences has had (Lambek 1998, 109). What we find in most of today's anthropological literature on the body merely represents a shift in the mind-body dualism: whereas the polarity was previously assumed *in* a person and his or her personhood, today it separates the researcher and the researched. The researcher has come to be the mind, which is knowledgeable and has acquired cognition about the (social, political, medical, etc.) body of the researched. The researched is more and more seen (again) as an embodied object with little agency in a "biopolitical" world, an object on which the researcher can "read" the symptoms of (social or political) illness.

The scholarly tendency to theoretically abolish a doctrinal separation between mind and body only to separate the "cognizant" (the researcher) und the "cognizable" (the researched) comes at the cost of a failure to understand what it means *to be*; what it means *to be embodied*; and what it means to act upon knowledge that can be cognitive, habitual, or nonpredicated.

Instead of influencing the subfields of anthropology, the anthropology of the body is in the process of becoming a subfield in itself. In the work at hand, I have tried to bring a perspective that takes bodily experiences seriously in the anthropology of law. To understand legalization, we have to understand what it means to be a victim; and this necessarily includes understanding bodily experiences.

Through the experiences we share in long-term field research, we can establish a ground of (bodily and sensory) knowledge upon which we can start understanding what is relevant for those whom we interact with. Ultimately, this implies giving up on the ethnographer's exclusive claim of the authority *to know*. It replaces this claim with the ethical, political, and methodological premise that we need the other not only to *acquire* new knowledge, but also to *recognize* the knowledge we have acquired intersubjectively and, often, in a nonpredicated manner.

In some ways, our efforts to then communicate our shared experiences to readers resemble victims' attempts to find recognition for their pain: in order to be heard, we have to relate our knowledge to dominant discursive forms. Looking back on my own writing, I find that my experiences, too, sit uneasily between embodied memories and discursive forms. I have attempted to write an objective ethnography—not in a naively positivist sense, but in the sense that describes a quality no scientific work can do without: the attempt to transcend individuality without negating it, to critically reflect on our own partialities, and to analyze commonalities and differences in contingent experiences, until we reach a level of abstraction that makes understanding possible. The quest for this kind of objectivity is inscribed in the scientific project. It asks for an analysis committed only to truth and meaning.

At the end of this book, I realize how far I am from achieving such objectivity. My account remains both partial and partisan. Both, partiality and partisanship (or whatever parts of them are not due to my clumsiness, lack of insight, or stupidity)—both have their roots in my encounters with victims. They marked me in ways I could not ignore, even though I would often have liked to do without them. Had I fully succeeded in objectifying these encounters, I would prove untrue what I have written about victims. If it were possible to engage suffering and pain *sine ira et studio*, no difference would exist between them and us—and they would not have to spend their days seeking redress for experiences that continue to haunt them.

Notes

Introduction

1. Even earlier, at the turn of the century, two social scientists took interest in the body and its social significance while working on ritual and death; these were sociologist Robert Hertz (1960) and the folklorist Arnold Van Gennep (2010).

2. In 1939, sociologist Norbert Elias published, in German, his two-volume *The Civilizing Process* (2000). In the first volume, *The History of Manners*, he also used the term *habitus* to describe how we internalize certain standards of civil behavior. Beginning with court society, Elias described history as a process of civilization leading to the modern notion of a body that is disciplined and civilized.

3. "I can" (*Ich kann* in German) is the term used by Husserl in his unpublished writings (Merleau-Ponty 2002, 159n92).

4. For a feminist critique, see McNay (1991).

5. The later Foucault acknowledges that there is some degree of freedom and individual agency and thus resistance: "One must observe also that there cannot be relations of power unless the subjects are free. . . . That means that in the relations of power, there is necessarily the possibility of resistance, for if there were no possibility of resistance— [for instance,] of violent resistance, of escape, of ruse, of strategies that reverse the situation—there would be no relations of power" (Foucault 1984a, 123).

6. On the question whether Foucault understood that the body functions as the basis of critique and resistance, see Foucault (1984b, 87–88).

7. What is interesting for this book, however, is the fact that tentative evidence is emerging from the existing literature on trauma that other types of symptoms (than those defined for PTSD) may be rather prevalent among South African trauma survivors—that is, somatic symptoms (Kaminer and Eagle 2010, 58). When South African researchers explored the psychiatric effects of trauma more broadly, they researched reported somatic symptoms, i.e., bodily pains for which no physiological cause could be found. This led the authors to suggest that the impact of trauma in South Africa and other African countries may be broader than what emerges from a narrow focus on PTSD or depression (57, 150).

8. For an account of why the concept of PTSD is insufficient for the victims of human rights violations and other structural forms of violence, see Becker (1995) and Kaminer and Eagle (2010, 23–27).

9. For a critical reflection on the widespread separation of "common crime" and "political crime" in relation to the Guatemalan case, see Godoy (2005), but also Ross (2002).

10. See Jackman (2002) for a critique of the extent to which scholarly research focuses on physical or corporal injuries and how a legalistic view has resulted in an emphasis on interpersonal violence. Nordstrom (2004) highlights that we are always more likely to notice the physical aspect of violence, and political violence in particular, such as wounding, maiming, torture, and murder.

11. See, for instance, the joint work of Krog, Mpolweni, and Ratele (2009) in which the authors grapple with their initial inability to grasp indirect apartheid-era victimhood. It is a genuine account of how the TRC failed to decipher victims' testimonies and make them legible to the broader public.

Chapter 1

1. Cf. Bell and Ntsebeza (2003), Bonner and Nieftagodien (2003), Boraine and Levy (1995), Buur (2001), Chapman and Van der Merwe (2008), C. M. Cole (2009), Colvin (2004b), Derrida (2002), Doxader and Villa-Vicencio (2004), Du Bois-Pedain (2007), Dugard (1999), Gobodo-Madikizela and Van der Merwe (2007), Hayner (2001), Kaminer et al. (2001), Krog (1999), Mamdani (2002), Ndebele (1998), Norval (2001), Posel and Simpson (2003), Ross (2002), Simpson (1998), Terreblanche (2000), Villa-Vicencio and Verwoerd (2000), and Wilson (2000).

2. This is according to the founding Act of the Truth Commission, the Promotion of National Unity and Reconciliation Act of 1995, chap.1, sec.1.

3. With the assistance of the South African History Archive, Khulumani requested this information through a PAIA (Promotion of Access to Information Act of 2000) request to the TRC Unit, http://khulumani.net/khulumani/documents/file/52 -khulumani-news-may-2010.html (accessed September 2015).

4. The first high-profile prosecution of someone who had refused the amnesty option was of Dr. Wouter Basson, the head of the apartheid regime's chemical and biological weapons program. He was charged with committing multiple murders in 1998. In 2002, however, the High Court of Pretoria acquitted him on all sixty-seven charges related to Project Coast, a project under the clandestine units of the South African Defence Force, a decision the Supreme Court of Appeal confirmed. In 2005, the Constitutional Court overturned the decision. At this stage, the NPA must bring new charges against him, while Basson remains free and is practicing as a cardiologist in Cape Town. He was intermittently called before the Health Professions Council of South Africa for breaching medical ethics and also acquitted. The former minister of law and order, Adriaan Vlok, was prosecuted in August 2007. Former police general Johannes van der Merwe was also prosecuted for attempting to poison Reverend Frank Chikane. But both trials ended in a plea bargain, which meant that little was revealed in a trial about the

incidents. Eugene de Kock, commander of the notorious Vlakplaas, who received two life sentences and an additional sentence of 212 years of imprisonment (cf. Gobodo-Madikizela 2004), was granted presidential parole in January 2015. While the country was still under apartheid rule, Winnie Madikizela-Mandela was tried for her involvement in human rights abuses in relation to her Mandela United Football Club. She was convicted, but her jail sentence was reduced to a fine. The Amnesty Committee of the TRC heard her testimony as an alleged perpetrator in other allegations. She was responsible for committing gross human rights violations but had not sought amnesty (see also Sarkin-Hughes 2004, 84–85). The late general Magnus Malan, army chief and, later, defense minister, did apply for amnesty, which the Amnesty Committee refused (Sarkin-Hughes 2004, 80–81). It condemned his acts and passed on the findings to the NPA, which never took up the case. Before his testimony to the TRC, Malan was prosecuted for authorizing an assassination squad that was responsible for the death of women and children. However, he was acquitted in 1996, after a lengthy trial, on the grounds of lack of evidence.

5. In fact, the state subsequently made at least three attempts to either pardon convicted prisoners or to change the prosecution guidelines to further "decriminalize" abuses relating to the past.

6. The fifty exhumations were carried out by a special task team established by the TRC. This work came to a halt when the commission's mandate expired in 2003 (Truth and Reconciliation Commission South Africa 2003, vol. 6, p. 566). For a conclusion to its own work on exhumations, see the TRC final report (Truth and Reconciliation Commission South Africa 2003, vol. 6, p. 569).

7. The South African Coalition for Transitional Justice issued this statement.

8. See www.khulumani.net. Khulumani's work figures in several publications both by scholars and civil society organizations (Backer 2005, 2010; Bond 2008; Bond and Sharife 2009; Chapman and Van der Merwe 2008; Colvin 2004a, 2004b, 2006; Giannini et al. 2009; Gobodo-Madikizela and Van der Merwe 2007; Gunn 2007; Gunn and Krwala 2008; Hamber 2006, 2009; Kaminer and Eagle 2010; Madlingozi 2007a, 2007b, 2010; Makhalemele 2004; McLaughlin 2002, 2012; Saage-Maass and Golombek 2010; Stephens et al. 2008; Wilson 2000, 2001; Wilson and Hamber 2002).

9. The CSVR's Transitional Justice Programme runs the Truth Recovery Project in which it builds up the South African Disappearances Database. It is not a membership-based database like Khulumani but it addresses similar issues. In South Africa, there are also many military veteran and ex-combatant associations. Khulumani and these associations have different target groups, but there are surely overlaps in members. Government recently created a Department of Military Veterans, and, in 2011, Parliament passed the Military Veterans' Act, which empowers the department to assist military veterans. Most recently, government announced that benefits (based on a means test) would be paid to those most affected by their military service. Khulumani has criticized exclusiveness of the Act's mandate since it only provides for persons who received military training, which "ignore[s] the reality that within the country thousands of active citizens served as defenders of their communities in Self-Defence

Units and in other community-based operations to protect their communities from the daily violence perpetrated by the occupying SADF soldiers and members of the Security Police," from Khulumani's Submission to the President for his State of the Nation Address 2012, www.khulumani.net/khulumani/documents/category/7-engaging-state .html?download=89%3Akhulumani-submission-to-president-zuma-for-his-sona -7-february-2012 (accessed September 2015).

10. Marjorie Jobson, e-mail to author, September 3, 2015.

11. In its public statements, Khulumani remains vague about whether its categories of apartheid-era victimhood are the same as those defined by the TRC. Khulumani criticizes the narrow definitions applied by the TRC and emphasizes structural and systemic forms of violence. But its membership form nevertheless uses the same categories of injury. It is up to the statement taker (typically a Khulumani member) to broaden the definition of injury in a specific case. The applications are checked by the national office and hence presumably undergo some changes and recategorization.

12. The numbers are published in a newsletter from May 2010 (http://khulumani .net/khulumani/documents/file/52-khulumani-news-may-2010.html; accessed September 2015). It quotes membership statistics from October 2009; http://khulumani.net/ khulumani/documents/file/37-membership-statistics-2009.html; accessed September 2015). In 2010, Khulumani listed 48,619 members in its database. This figure is low, since there is always a time lag as the national office in Johannesburg counts up new members coming in from the provincial offices. When the figures were released in 2010, about 15,000 completed forms still needed to be processed, which brought the total number to over 60,000 members. In 2006, 18,995 members were registered, while an estimated 34,000 applications were still waiting to be processed. The membership in 2006 was thus closer to 54,000.

13. Three dependents, 12.1 percent; four dependents, 14.7 percent; five dependents, 13.7 percent; six dependents, 12 percent; seven dependents, 9.6 percent; eight dependents, 7.2 percent; nine dependents, 6.9 percent; ten dependents, 8.9 percent.

14. Presumably, many receive social grants, and many members who are over sixty years old receive an old-age pension. In 2015, the Old-Age Pension (for people above age sixty with an annual income lower than R64,680) and the Disability Grant each are R1,410 a month. The Child Support Grant is R330 a month (to receive this grant caregivers cannot earn more than R39,600 a year if they are single; a combined income cannot be above R79,200). Many members apply for a special pension, a process that often takes years; the decisions about who will receive the pension have not been made sufficiently transparent to the public.

15. Khulumani defines this as "killing with political motive" and includes instances of disappearances.

16. All the numbers, but specifically the comparatively low number of reported sexual assaults, should be read with caution.

17. This shift is particularly well documented for the Western Cape but is by no means exclusive to that province. Colvin (2004a, 2004b, 2006) traces how the Ex-Political Prisoners and Torture Survivor Group in the Western Cape separated from

the Trauma Centre and turned away from the psychotherapeutic approach to healing through individualized and case-based counseling. The group started to more aggressively and vocally engage ministries and the presidency over its demands. Soon, the issue of reparations for all the victims took center stage in the activities of the branch.

18. Richard Wilson, conversation with the author, August 26, 2011. Wilson used the term "charismatic leadership" to describe his experiences doing fieldwork in South Africa in the 1990s. See also Gebhardt (1994) and M. Weber (1968). One member of this "charismatic generation" was the late Duma Khumalo, best documented in Wilson's work (2000, 2001, 139).

19. Up to 1999, Khulumani was a subsidiary of the CSVR. The CSVR ran workshops to inform people about the TRC and had helped with statement taking in the communities.

20. Occasional funders of programs rolled out at the national level are the Foundation for Human Rights, Medico International, United Nations Office on Drugs and Crime, National Lottery Distribution Trust Fund, and the Rosa Luxemburg Foundation. The office manager of Khulumani Western Cape is funded by the Fund for Development and Partnership in Africa (FEPA). The provincial offices typically do their own fundraising but also occasionally profit from national projects that involve the provinces.

21. Marjorie Jobson is a former chairperson of the national board and the former acting director. Dr. Jobson has a background as a Black Sash activist and is a trained medical doctor.

22. The national board has seven members: Shirley Gunn, Brandon Hamber, Marjorie Jobson (ex officio), Kabelo Lengane, Tshepo Madlingozi, Musa Ndlovu, and Paul Verryn.

23. The South African History Archive, which curates an archive and offers information training; the ICTJ, which operates globally and has an office in Cape Town; the CSVR and its "healing from torture" program; the Trauma Centre for Torture Survivors, which offers seminars and psychological support; the Legal Resource Centre, which offers legal advice, support, and litigation services; military veteran organizations such as South African Military Veterans, Umkhonto we Sizwe Military Veterans Association, Azanian People's Liberation Army Military Veterans Association, and Azanian National Liberation Army Military Veterans Association; the South African Non-Torture Consortium (SANToC) of which Khulumani is a part; and the Institute for the Healing of Memories.

24. *Azanian People's Organization (AZAPO) and Others v. The President of the Republic of South Africa and Others*, 1996 (4) SA 671, Constitutional Court of South Africa. The amnesty provision of the Interim Constitution and the challenge to it have been the topics of a number of publications (Sarkin 2008; Sarkin-Hughes 2004; Van Marle 2007).

25. "Prosecuting Policy and Directives Relating to Prosecution of Offenses Emanating from Conflicts of the Past and Which Were Committed on or Before 11 May 1994," promulgated December 1, 2005, app. A.

26. Statement by President Mbeki to the National House of Parliament and the Nation, at the Tabling of the Report of the Truth and Reconciliation Commission, April 15,

2003. It is difficult to find exact numbers. In 2006, the NPA was said to be investigating about six cases and preparing them for trial, http://www.iol.co.za/news/south-africa/apartheid-massacres-go-to-court-1.275009 (accessed September 2015). Apparently, this happened in the framework of the amended prosecution guidelines. See Bell and Ntsebeza (2003, 344) on some of the persons "who have—often literally—got away with murder."

27. *Nkadimeng and Others v. National Director of Public Prosecutions and Others* (32709/07). The applicants were four widows (Nyameka Goniwe, Nombuyeselo Nolita Mhlauli, Sindiswa Elizabeth Mkhonto, and Nomonde Calata) and Thembi Phumelele-Nkadimeng. The widows are known as the "Cradock Four." Their late husbands were anti-apartheid activists who were abducted and killed by Security Branch policemen in 1985. The TRC had rejected six out of seven amnesty applications of these policemen. Only one, Eugene de Kock, was granted amnesty.

To my knowledge, no one was granted indemnity from prosecution under the new guidelines. It was merely the constitutionality of the amendments that was challenged in court. However, the applicants in the court challenge were victims whose stories suggest that the state has the evidence to pursue prosecutions, which the High Court decision confirmed was the NDPP's obligation.

28. *Nkadimeng and Others v. National Director of Public Prosecutions and Others* (32709/07) [2008] ZAGPHC 422.

29. Ibid., para. 15.4.3.1.

30. Ibid., para. 15.4.4.

31. Ibid., para. 15.5.3.

32. Mbeki announced the creation of the reference group in his 2003 speech. He confirmed it in his "Address of the President of South Africa, Thabo Mbeki, to the Joint Sitting of Parliament to report on the processing of some Presidential Pardons—Cape Town" of 2007.

33. The coalition includes victims' and civil society organizations: Khulumani Support Group, the CSVR, ICTJ, IJR, Human Rights Media Centre (HRMC), Freedom of Expression Institute, and South African History Archives.

34. *Centre for the Study of Violence and Reconciliation and Others v. President of the Republic of South Africa and Others* (15320/09) [2009], ZAGPPHC 35 (April 29), North Gauteng High Court, Pretoria, http://www.saflii.org/cgi-bin/disp.pl?file=za/cases/ZAGPPHC/2009/35.html&query=%20csvr (accessed September 2015).

35. Under section 84(2)(j) of the Constitution of the Republic of South Africa, 1996 (Act 108 of 1996).

36. *Centre for the Study of Violence and Reconciliation et al. v. President of the Republic of South Africa and Others* (15320/09) [2009] para.7.4.2, ZAGPPHC 35 (April 29), North Gauteng High Court, Pretoria, http://www.saflii.org/za/cases/ZAGPPHC/2009/35.html (accessed September 2015).

37. http://www.justice.gov.za/forms/form_polpardons.htm (accessed September 2015).

Up to forty-six pardon applications were from African National Congress members (ninety counts of murder, fifty-two counts of attempted murder), thirty-one from Pan African Congress (PAC; thirty-one counts of murder, eighteen counts of attempted murder), twenty-one from the IFP (seventy-eight counts of murder, twenty-eight counts of attempted murder), and eight from the AWB (seventeen counts of murder, thirteen counts of attempted murder). This is according to a count done by Khulumani Support Group. Document available under http://www.khulumani.net/khulumani/documents/file/54-analysis-of-pres-pardons-list-oct-2010.html (accessed September 2015).

38. Statement on the Report of the TRC Joint Sitting of the Houses of Parliament in Cape Town, February 25, 1999; my emphasis.

39. SANGOCO issued its "Statement by SANGOCO to Request Support and Solidarity on the Issue of Apartheid-Caused Debt and Reparations" on June 1, 1998, http://apartheid-reparations.ch/documents/suedafrika/e_1998-06-16_Sangoco.pdf (accessed September 2015). Ever since, this has been an important point of orientation for national campaigns, which formed part of the international campaign, such as those in Switzerland, Germany, and the UK against their own governments and companies with headquarters in respective countries. Most of these national campaigns grew from anti-apartheid movements pushing for sanctions and offering solidarity with liberation movements across Southern Africa.

40. For example, the Universal Declaration of Human Rights, art. 8; the International Covenant on Civil and Political Rights, arts. 2(3), 9(5), and 14(6); the International Convention on the Elimination of all Forms of Racial Discrimination, art. 6; the Convention of the Rights of the Child, art. 39, the Convention against Torture and other Cruel Inhuman and Degrading Treatment, art. 14; and the Rome Statute for an International Criminal Court, art. 75. See also McCarthy (2009). The state's obligation to provide reparations also figures in regional instruments such as the African Charter on Human and Peoples' Rights, art. 21(2). The South African state fulfilled part of this obligation—the guarantee of non-repetition—with legal measures, such as the new constitution. The National Unity and Reconciliation Act of 1995, which established the Truth and Reconciliation Commission, acknowledged this obligation in general; the Act foresees the creation of a fund to pay out financial reparations to victims.

41. Michael Hausfeld was a partner at the US law firm Cohen, Milstein, Hausfeld and Toll (today Cohen, Milstein, Sellers and Toll), and since late 2008 has been a partner at the international litigations firm Hausfeld (www.hausfeld.com).

42. The plaintiffs were six South Africans. One of them, Dorothy Molefi, is the mother of thirteen-year-old Hector Petersen, who was shot dead by the South African Police in the 1976 Soweto school riots. A picture in which Mbuyisa Makhubo is carrying his body, made him an icon of the Soweto uprising and of resistance to the apartheid regime.

43. Matter of Edward D. Fagan, M-2732, M-3148, M-3193; Supreme Court of the United States, Appellate Division, First Judicial Department.

44. In his "Statement to the National Houses of Parliament and the Nation," Mbeki also announced that the state would not impose a wealth tax on business (rejecting the committee's recommendation of a one-time tax).

45. This phone call is often cited without a source: "Initially, the South African government under former Minister of Justice Dullah Omar had vowed to remain neutral. That would change after Colin Powell, on behalf of the Bush administration, approached Omar's successor, Penuell Maduna, in 2003. Prodded by Washington, Pretoria ultimately invoked national sovereignty in opposing the lawsuits" (Sharife 2009); confirmed in Bond (2008).

46. Brief of Amici Curiae Former Commissioners and Committee Members of South Africa's Truth and Reconciliation Commission in Support of Appellants, August 30, 2005, p. 10, fn 10, http://kosa.org/documents/05-08_TRC_amicus.pdf (accessed September 2015).

47. Debate on the Truth and Reconciliation Commission Report: Speech by Minister of Trade and Industry, Alec Erwin, April 15, 2003.

48. Ibid.

49. Address by the Minister of Education, Professor Kader Asmal, MP, in the Debate on the Truth and Reconciliation Report, National Assembly, Cape Town, April 15, 2003. He would, seven years later, surprise human rights organizations, activists, and the plaintiffs with his amicus curiae brief to the Second Circuit Court of Appeals, in which he argued that corporations cannot be held liable under customary international law.

50. Terry Bell, interview by the author, Cape Town, January 13, 2006.

51. The Submission of Interest (October 27, 2003) is quoted on page 9 of Brief for the United States as Amicus Curiae Supporting Appellees filed to the US Second Circuit Court of Appeals on November 20, 2009, http://www.scribd.com/doc/23603048/U-S-Statement-of-Interest-in-Apartheid-Reparation-Claims-under-the-Alien-Tort-Statute (accessed September 2015).

52. For research into the relation between Switzerland and apartheid South Africa, see Kreis (2005). For a study on the relation between German companies and the apartheid regime, see Morgenrath and Wellmer (2003).

53. *Sosa v. Alvarez-Machain*, 542 U.S. at 729. Justice Souter, for the majority, referred to the pending apartheid litigations in footnote 21 at 733 and noted that "[i]n such cases, there is a strong argument that federal courts should give serious weight to the Executive Branch's view of the case's impact on foreign policy."

54. The Court further stated that the rulings of the international criminal tribunals such as the ICTY, the ICTR, and the Nuremberg Tribunal were not binding sources of international law. Furthermore, the Apartheid Convention had not been ratified by such major powers such as the United States, the UK, Germany, France, Canada, and Japan, and the Convention was not binding international law. The decision is available at www.apartheid-reparations.ch/documents/reparationen/e_200412_sprizzo.pdf (accessed September 2015).

55. *Khulumani v. Barclay National Bank*, 504 F.3d 254, 260 (2d Cir. 2007).

56. The named plaintiffs in the amended complaint are Sakwe Balintulo, Dennis Brutus, Mark Fransch, Elsie Gishi, Lesiba Kekana, Archington Madondo, Mpho Masemola, Michael Mbele, Catherine Mlangeni, Reuben Mphela, Thulani Nunu, Thandiwe Shezi, and Thobile Sikani.

57. http://hrp.law.harvard.edu/wp-content/uploads/2011/01/Scheindlin-MTD -decision-4.8.09.pdf (accessed May 2016).

58. Brief of Amici Curiae Commissioners and Committee Members of South Africa's Truth and Reconciliation Commission in Support of Appellants, August 30, 2005. The brief is accessible on http://kosa.org/documents/05-08_TRC_amicus.pdf (accessed September 2015).

59. For an in-depth study on how the Swiss banks supported the apartheid regime, see Madörin (2008).

60. Min. Justice Jeff Radebe, letter to J. Scheindlin, US Court (2009), Khulumani Documents, Khulumani Support Group website, http://www.khulumani.net/ khulumani/documents/file/12-min.justice-jeff-radebe-letter-to-us-court-2009.html (accessed September 2015).

61. Twelve plaintiffs allege that Royal Dutch Petroleum aided and abetted human rights violations committed against them and their murdered or executed relatives by the Abacha military dictatorship in the Niger Delta between 1992 and 1995. This case was preceded by the more widely known *Wiwa v. Shell* case, which was eventually settled out of court, in 2009.

62. The decision and the dissenting opinion are available on www.ccrjustice.org/ files/2010.09.17_Kiobel_Majority_Opinion_and_Dissent.pdf (accessed September 2015).

63. The question of the applicability of the ATS is generally seen as producing a "circuit split." The 11th Circuit Court has upheld corporate liability. Attorneys of both parties try to mobilize this split for their advantage.

64. For the decision, refer to http://www.supremecourt.gov/opinions/12pdf/ 10-1491_l6gn.pdf (accessed September 2015).

65. For the decision, refer to http://www.ca2.uscourts.gov/decisions/ isysquery/5648222e-efaf-47e1-933a-931392439995/1/doc/14-4104_opn.pdf#xml=http (accessed February 2016).

Chapter 2

1. These are questions I have explored previously in Kesselring (2015a).

2. In April 2013, her son passed away. Ms. Kotta was very shocked; she was not expecting it she told me.

3. See Josette Cole (1987) for a rare comprehensive account on the formal and informal townships and their internal fighting. She focuses on Crossroads in the 1970s and 1980s and documents the violence caused by gangs, witdoeke and the apartheid security forces and police.

4. In 2003, Beauty Kotta participated in a memory and healing project run by the Human Rights Media Centre and Khulumani Western Cape called "Breaking the

Silence: A Luta Continua." The project entailed the drawing of so-called body maps, which were then exhibited in South Africa (IZIKO Slave Lodge in Cape Town in 2006/7 and the Apartheid Museum in Johannesburg in 2004, Red Location Museum in Port Elizabeth) and abroad (Slough Museum in London, St. Martin-Le-Grand, University of York, University of Monrovia, Liberia).

5. I understand this "singling out" socially and do not refer to what psychologist and psychoanalysts see as a necessary process of estrangement in order for a person to assume maturity.

6. In the United States, where the apartheid litigations were filed, group litigations became a prominent means of litigation as late as in the 1960s. They evolved from Equity Rule 48, promulgated by the US Supreme Court in 1842, which allowed for representative suits in situations where there were too many individual parties. Equity Rule 48 did not, however, allow these suits to represent similarly situated absent parties. Through various revisions of the equity rules, the incorporation of what was now Rule 38 into the Federal Rules of Civil Procedures as Rule 23 in 1938 and a major revision of the Federal Rules in 1966, the so-called opt-out class action finally became a standard option (Backhaus, Cassone, and Ramello 2012). This was the beginning of the present-day class action. Today, a class action binds all members of the class except those who object and opt-out. Business, which is predominantly targeted by class actions, has tried to limit their scope, for instance, by lobbying or through contracts obliging consumers to waive their right to a class action. Also, decisions of the US Supreme Court have strongly encouraged arbitration as a means to settle (Sternlight 2000). Class actions are highly contested, not only in the United States, but also in other places where they are slowly taking root in varying forms. For instance, the Green Paper of the European Commission "Damages Actions for Breach of the EC Antitrust Rules" promotes the development of private enforcement of antitrust rules in the European Union. Victims of competition law should recover damages for losses they suffered. For an overview of the current discussions, see Backhaus et al. (2012).

7. Giorgio Agamben (1999) famously elaborated on this distinction (cf. Fassin 2008).

8. An "expert witness" is a third category, but is not of prime interest here. She is an expert who is called to provide testimony on a technical matter or a matter on which she possesses professional expertise (rather than direct observation of an event).

9. Apart from the (non-public) Khulumani database containing roughly 104,000 entries in 2015, which far surpasses the TRC report in the number of testimonies.

10. Ross (2002, 175n) points to the fact that victims who testify before the commission were "doubly positioned," because they experienced apartheid and the particular violation they testified about. With regard to these two dimensions of testifying, the name of the commission—Truth and Reconciliation Commission—can thus be applied literarily: *reconciliation* generated by the personhood of the victims; *truth* generated by factual events described in their testimonies.

11. This counts for the International Criminal Tribunal for Rwanda (ICTR) and the International Criminal Tribunal for the Former Yugoslavia (ICTY) but not for the International Criminal Court (ICC), where victims' legal representatives are parties to the trial.

12. In the Matter of: In re South African Apartheid Litigation, transcript of the hearing on February 26, 2009, Southern District Reporters, New York, original file 92qQsaaC.txt, pp.es 1–105. Quotations from the hearing are taken from the transcript (hereafter cited as "South African Apartheid Litigation").

13. Amended Complaint for Docket MDL No.02-md-1499 (JES); Jury Trial Demanded, Class Action.

14. Torture includes rape. Between 1960 and 1994 South African security forces allegedly were the perpetrators of all such violations.

15. South African Apartheid Litigation, p. 80, ll. 13, 17–18.

16. Ibid., ll. 18–25.

17. Ibid., p. 99, ll. 3–6.

18. Ibid., p. 86, ll. 5–6; p.100, ll. 22–23.

19. Ibid., p.88, ll. 21–24.

20. Ibid., p. 89, ll. 4–14.

21. Ibid., p. 89, l. 18; p. 93, l. 9–10.

22. Ibid., p. 93, l. 24—p. 94, l. 3.

23. Ibid., p. 101, ll. 4, 5–6, 16–17; p. 102, ll. 23–24; p.103, ll. 2–3, 6.

24. Following the hearing, Judge Scheindlin issued her order of April 8, 2009, which allowed the cases to go forward on the condition that changes requested in the order were made.

25. The Constitutional Court first provided a brief review of the Constitution's protection of socioeconomic rights, holding that "any claim based on socio-economic rights must necessarily engage the right to dignity. The lack of adequate food, housing, and health care is the unfortunate lot of too many people in this country and is a blight on their dignity. Each time an applicant approaches the courts claiming that his or her socio-economic rights have been infringed the right to dignity is invariably implicated." *Jaftha v. Schoeman*, 2005 (1) BCLR 78 (Constitutional Court) at 16.

26. Sec. 27.1b reads: "Everyone has the right to have access to (b) sufficient food and water." Sec. 28.1c reads: "Every child has the right (c) to basic nutrition, shelter, basic health care services and social services."

27. *Numerosity* is one of the four standards applicant representatives generally have to show in order to prove that they adequately represent the interests of all class members (the other three are commonality, adequacy, and typicality).

28. "Anyone listed in this section has the right to approach a competent court, alleging that a right in the Bill of Rights has been infringed or threatened, and the court may grant appropriate relief, including a declaration of rights. The persons who may approach a court are . . . (c) anyone acting as a member of, or in the interest of, a group or class of persons."

29. The court could hear rebuttal evidence to a sample of class members. This is a compromise between one class action and hundreds of thousands of individual suits.

30. Only once tried in a HR/ATS case: *Hilao v. Estate of Marcos*, 103 F.3d 767 (9th Cir. 1996): a human rights class action against the Philippine dictator Ferdinand Marcos. The 9th Circuit Court approved a sampling procedure, the findings of which were presented to the jury. Like the Apartheid Litigation, the case was brought under the Alien Tort Statute. It was an opt-in class action.

31. It wants to strike the balance between liberty and equality values: It partly challenges the company's insistence on the *individualization* approach (*liberty*) and it takes seriously the fact that pro rata amounts (through aggregate determinations of liability and damages) do not consider individually varying injury (*equality*) (Lahav 2010).

32. Maybe this gives us a clue about how to understand the civil plaintiff's role, as Laura Nader (2002, 211) notes in *The Life of the Law*: "[T]he civil plaintiff's role will be appreciated as something more than presenting a dispute to be managed."

33. The International Criminal Court has a Victims' Trust Fund through which to compensate the victims of crimes (Rome Statute, Article 79). It is independent from the Court and is mandated to implement Court-ordered reparations and to provide physical and psychosocial rehabilitation or material support to victims of crimes within the jurisdiction of the Court. This is an important international recognition of the need of reparations (generated by fines and forfeitures but also voluntary contributions by states and private donors). It advocates community redress rather than individual payouts.

34. Debate on the Truth and Reconciliation Commission Report: Speech by Minister of Trade and Industry, Alec Erwin, April 15, 2003.

Chapter 3

1. Jonathan Claasen (age 21), Shaun Magmoed (age 15), and Michael Miranda (age 11).

2. Goodman Mali (age 19) and Mabhuti Fatman (age 20).

3. The CBS archival footage of the Athlone shooting by Chris Everson is accessible on the HRMC website: http://www.hrmc.org.za/index.php?option=com_content&view =article&id=63&Itemid=65 (accessed September 2015).

4. Transcripts of the Trojan Horse hearings can be found on the official TRC website, http://www.justice.gov.za/trc/special/#thh. At the June 2 hearing, Ebrahim Rasool, then Western Cape's minister of health, said in his context statement that the Trojan Horse killings symbolized the growing desperation of the apartheid regime, which had responded with increased brutality to so-called popular unrest and protest in the Western Cape townships. Special Hearing, Trojan Horse Hearing, June 2, 1997, http://www .justice.gov.za/trc/special/trojan/rasool.htm (accessed February 2016).

5. My use of the words *deportation* and *deport* is not meant to suggest that I recognize the former homelands as independent states. Also, I could not find out what the precise connection between the drums and her recollection of her dead baby was.

6. One such incident I witnessed was the special screening of the South African movie *Zulu Love Letter* for Khulumani members at the V&A Cinema Nouveau in

2005 (directed by Ramadan Suleman and produced by JBA Production and Native at Large).

7. See also Colvin (2004a) for a detailed account of the process that resulted in the rejection of social-psychological support at Khulumani Western Cape.

8. It was also performed at the 6th Annual National Oral History Conference at the River Club in Observatory, Cape Town, in October 2009.

9. Scholars often interpret silent memories as silenced or forgotten by hegemonies, as a "politically or ideologically loaded absence" that needs to be overcome. As a result of scholars' political or moral ideas of (re-)empowerment and contestations or revisions of the past, "ethnography fails to seek phenomenological accounts of the silent presence of the past" (Kidron 2009, 8). More recently, and as part of an emerging anthropology of memory, anthropologists have emphasized grounded research of actual mnemonic and non-monumental practices. On embodied past, see for instance Werbner (1998) and White (2008). The ethnographies uphold the dialectical thinking between macro processes (hegemonic and colonial and postcolonial violence) and their subjects' embodied pasts.

10. Several medical anthropologists have argued that the reason there is no language for pain is that it is so personal and subjective and that it is impossible to quantify and measure suffering. See Das (1997), Frank (2002), and Kleinman and Kleinman (1994).

11. See Christopher Colvin's (2004a) work on Khulumani and the transformation from story-telling as a therapeutic tool to a means of political mobilization.

12. I knew many of the Khulumani members in the audience and also met them weeks and months later. I did not speak to them about the theater performance, though, and no one brought it up either. I only talked to one Khulumani member who herself could not attend the meeting (see below).

13. Pumla Gobodo-Madikizela, Special Hearing, Trojan Horse hearing, Ebrahim Rasool's testimony, June 2, 1997; my emphasis. For the transcript of the hearing, see http://www.justice.gov.za/trc/special/trojan/rasool.htm (accessed February 2016).

14. The commission on the whole never had a clear idea of what reconciliation entailed. Richard Wilson suggests that this may have been partly deliberate, owing to "a number of factors including the pragmatic realization on the part of commissioners that if they defined a key objective, then they could be held accountable for not achieving it, and it was obvious to commissioners that attempts at reconciling individuals would achieve only mixed results. In the context of a largely critical media, unleashing such a messy and unmanageable process would be leaving a hostage to fortune. In addition, reconciliation, like all central unifying metaphors, would function best as a kind of social glue when it was left indeterminate. Different groups with dissimilar agendas could then appeal to reconciliation to advance their own objectives" (Wilson 2001, 19).

15. I do not intend to give the full history but confine it to South Africa. See the introduction for a discussion of my approach to therapeutic notions of trauma and traumatization.

16. One could go further and argue that not only the therapeutic dimension of bearing witness was important notion in the TRC's work but also the confession and its supposedly therapeutic benefit was (not only for perpetrators but also for victims). Foucault (1987) writes on how psychotherapy replaced confession in church.

17. When I saw Ms. Mgweba again in April 2013, her son was married, and his new wife was working at the stall. He had also found a job as a security guard.

18. I later had a chance to talk to her sister, who portrayed their relationship as important and still very supportive. She did not, however, emphasize how much emotional weight her sister took on from her in those years.

19. The riotous assemblies act needed the presence of a policeman to proclaim the assembly illegal (see, for instance, the Riotous Assemblies and Suppression of Communism Amendment Act No. 15 of 1954 and its amendments of 1974 and 1978; or the Internal Security Amendment Act No. 5 of 1986 that granted further control over illegal gatherings. States of emergency were limited in time and place.

20. According to the South African Police Service's crime report of 2010–11, 132 per 100,000 persons have been experienced sexual offences. This does not include the majority of the cases, which go unreported.

21. Letter written by a counselor at the Trauma Centre in support of the renewal of Mr. Mphahlele's disability grant.

22. It is in perfect line with the poststructuralist concept of the self. The self is the location of multiple subjectivities, which are potentially contradictory. These subjectivities are established within discourses and discursive practices (Merry 2003).

23. Kidron argues that silence deviates from the Eurocentric psychosocial norm of voice. In this view, the absence of voice signals avoidance and repression, or even socially suspect personal secrecy or collective, political subjugation: "Whether the issue is personal, communal, or national silence, well-being is thought to be contingent on the liberation of voice" (Kidron 2009, 5ff.).

24. I thank Fiona Ross for pointing this out to me.

Chapter 4

1. Portions of this chapter are adapted from © 2014 "Experiences of Violence and the Formation of the Political: Embodied Memory and Victimhood in South Africa," in *The Politics of Governance: Actors and Articulations in Africa and Beyond*, edited by Till Förster and Lucy Koechlin, 151–79. Conceptualising Comparative Politics. New York: Routledge. Reproduced by permission of Taylor and Francis Group, LLC, a division of Informa PLC. Permission conveyed through Copyright Clearance Center, Inc.

2. See Madlingozi (2007a, 12) for a slightly different use of such victims' subject position: "Bad victims," according to him, are those who claim reparations and campaign for social justice and who, in doing so, "expose the poverty of this elite compromise, which involves maintaining the ill-gotten gains provided that a section of the new elite is placed in positions of economic power and privilege." "Good victims" are those who belong to the new elite, have been well connected as members of liberation movements, profit from the new access to the post-1994 wealth, and generally can afford not to

demand reparations. Madlingozi thus emphasizes the distinction between those "mostly ordinary and often poor township residents" (who, according to Madlingozi and Fullard and Rousseau [2004], made up the bulk of the 21,000 victims who testified to the TRC) who demand reparations and a new elite who hold high positions in government and in corporations because of their close ties to the former liberation movements and today's ruling party, the ANC. Madlingozi cites the Khulumani Support Group as an example of the former and treats it as a homogenous group.

3. Apart from the institutional formation of a dominant victims' subject position, I do not look at the practices that lead to the formation of a "majority opinion" on apartheid-era victimhood. There remains a gap between my portrayal of the broader society and the actual practices that shape such opinions. My work presents the majority opinion through victims' perspectives on the societal expectations they feel and express.

4. Chris Hani became involved in anti-apartheid protests; joined the military wing of the ANC, Umkhonto we Sizwe; went into exile 1962; and later became the leader of the South African Communist Party and the head of Umkhonto we Sizwe. He was assassinated in April 1993.

5. See also chapter 1. The meetings are a remnant and a continuation of meetings held at the Trauma Centre that offered counseling to ex-political prisoners and torture survivors in the post-TRC years. For a detailed analysis of what was Khulumani Western Cape then, see Colvin (2004a, 2004b).

6. South African attorney Charles Abrahams is partner in the small law firm Abrahams Kiewitz Attorneys in Bellville, Western Cape, just outside Cape Town, which specializes in public interest and human rights cases. He finished his master's degree in international law at the University of Cape Town and wrote his thesis on the question of the apartheid debt. Jubilee South Africa used his research for its campaign on the matter and he became Jubilee's legal adviser. Later, he was sanctioned by the Khulumani Support Group to be South Africa's attorney in any potential apartheid litigation, together with American attorney Michael Hausfeld, an expert on Alien Tort Statute, as his US counterpart. Abrahams Kiewitz worked on the South African cases against Anglo Platinum (regarding displacement), AngloGold Ashanti (regarding silicosis), Glencor (regarding asbestosis), and the bread companies testing the instrument of class actions in South Africa, among others. Most recently, in August 2012, Abrahams filed papers at a regional court in Johannesburg, inquiring whether the court recognized their case against AngloGold Ashanti, Gold Fields, and Harmony as a class action. The allegations are negligence that resulted in the workers contracting lung diseases, such as silicosis and tuberculosis, in recent decades.

7. More specifically, the majority decision ruled that the ATS cannot be used to sue corporations for violations of international law because customary international law only confers jurisdiction over natural persons; see chapter 1 for more details.

8. The plaintiffs filed a petition to rehear the case, but the Court of Appeals left intact the original ruling, in a 5–5 split decision on February 4, 2011. For subsequent developments, see chapter 1.

9. Sakwe Balintulo stands as personal representative for his late brother Sabe Balintulo, who was shot dead by the South African Police on March 15, 1973, along with fifteen others.

10. The Groote Schuur Minute refers to the conclusion of negotiations between the unbanned ANC and the National Party Government signed in Cape Town on May 4, 1990, three months after the release of Nelson Mandela. The negotiations were about the release of the hundreds of lower ranking political prisoners still held in South African prisons and immunity from prosecution for political exiles returning to South Africa. Together with the conclusion of negotiations in Pretoria, in August 1990 (the Pretoria Minute), they led to the passing of the Indemnity Act 1990, which empowered the President to grant indemnity from prosecution "either unconditionally or on the conditions he may deem fit." The issue of amnesty for the security forces of the National Party regime and the release of political prisoners was later a central point of disagreement during the CODESA (Convention for a Democratic South Africa) talks.

11. It is important to note that Abrahams obviously thought it a moment conducive to such actions. There were also times when he cautioned members against marching to Parliament, because he felt that giving too much visibility to the political and social grounding of the lawsuit could potentially harm its legal success.

12. It was also the first time that the lawyer so openly and unambiguously suggested an out-of-court settlement as the only way forward. The first out-of-court settlement overture from a defendant company was made by General Motors in March 2011 and was realized in 2012; see chapter 1.

Chapter 5

1. Ms. Mvenge was successfully operated on twice in 2012. When I visited her in August 2012, she had grown very thin and looked much older but was recovering.

2. The forcible removal of people and demolition of their homes, as was commonplace under apartheid rule (Platzky, Walker, and Surplus People Project 1985), is increasingly being seen in post-apartheid South Africa, too. In some incidents, the police used live ammunition, as in the tragedy at the Lonmin mine in Marikana in August 2012.

3. In a way, providing financial redress offers an opportunity to embark on something new. On the other hand, a policy of redress may lose its effectiveness when victimhood extends beyond the apartheid era. More structural changes are needed.

4. I am hesitant to use the verbs "to overcome" or "to transcend" because they imply that the past has been successfully left behind. "To emancipate," in contrast, contains the notion of allowing a space to past experiences without necessarily leaving them behind, which is more consistent with what I argue in terms of bodily memory in general.

5. On how theater and the law interplay, see C. M. Cole (2007, 2009); for a critique thereof, see Arendt (1992).

6. When I went back to the center in April 2013, they had recently gotten electricity.

7. The TRC held a special hearing, in June 1997, on the violence in Cape Flats in the 1980s; Johnson Ngxobongwana was invited to testify but failed to appear. He

had, however, appeared at an in camera hearing on May 29, 1997. http://mg.co.za/article/1997-06-10-top-cop-fingers-pw-botha-le-grange (accessed September 2015).

8. Ms. Nunu explained, "I was assumed to be a leader because I had books and wrote down things about the comrades. So I went to stay at Melford Yamile's place at Nyanga Bush with [my son] Luthando" (quoted in Gunn and Krwala 2008, 110).

9. This is not to say that reparations do not have an impact or are not desired. For a discussion of this point, see the conclusion to this book.

10. My use of the term *acting out* bears no connection to the (largely negative) psychoanalytical understanding of it. I use it simply to emphasize the dimension of practice and public performance.

Chapter 6

1. On friendship and shared activity during field research, see Ridler (1996). See Wacquant (2004) for a prime example of how social scientists try out methodologies to access other people's experiences by way of shared activities; in his case, he learned how to box while researching boxers in an American ghetto.

2. In Husserl's phenomenology, the term *pre-predicated* is usually used. I use *nonpredicated* because I do not want to suggest a chronological order, a point I will come back to at the end of the chapter.

3. I certainly believe that observational data can and should include a record of bodily interaction (and that anthropologist can learn a lot about how to describe body practice from body culture, theater, or sports studies). There is a danger, however, that this kind of data will be interpreted in a behavioristic manner only. Analyzing the bodily movements of people must be complemented with a phenomenological approach to yield an understanding what these kinds of bodily interaction may mean; otherwise one can easily slip into primatology and project it onto persons (e.g., Sugawara 2005).

4. I do not want to suggest a chronological or hierarchical order between *notification* and *noting*. How to write about the body and bodily experiences (in both field notes and publications) is at least as pertinent as the question of how to adopt a sensory and intersubjective approach in our research practices.

5. Kusenbach (2003) elaborates on what she calls the "go-along method," in which she, more or less systematically and in an informant-driven way, accompanies people on their daily errands and other practical everyday activities in urban settings. "Goalong" as method oscillates between interviewing and observation. It remains unclear to me how exactly the researcher can access the informants' spatial, social, and emotional experiences that emerge in these joint activities (cf. Gilbert 1990). One important advantage of "going along" is, of course, that it helps the researcher to better understand how knowledge relates to immediate action, more so than in interviews or by observing the informant.

6. Strictly analytically, one has to distinguish between the process of the formation of something shared and the product that results from it. The latter entails a shared intentionality and includes everything from an idea to an action. Here, I lump them together because my main interest is in how we establish a shared reference to a part of

the world. I am thus interested in intersubjectivity as the basis for recognizing the other, and not as the product itself. One could, of course, argue that intersubjectivity is already a product.

7. According to Emirbayer and Mische (1998), imagination is one element of agency. Förster understands imagination as a practice. I do not attempt to place my use of *imagination* into these theoretical discussions.

8. Borneman (2011) calls this something the "third intersubjective."

9. For Husserl (1929, 91), "nature is an intersubjective reality and a reality for me and my companions of the moment but [also] for us and for everyone who can come to a *mutual understanding* with us about things and about other people" (quoted in Duranti 2010, 22). This reminds us that while there is always the possibility that intersubjectivity leads to an understanding, it can easily fail.

10. In a similar vein, Throop (2012, 87–88) interprets a key moment in Malinowski's research on the Trobriand with his inability to fully understand casual talk. On intersubjectivity seen from a linguistically oriented anthropology, see Duranti (1993). Duranti (2010, 17) also provides a detailed analysis of Husserl's use of intersubjectivity, which, according to Duranti, includes acts that do not involve language.

11. Within the constraints of a chapter, I cannot adequately reflect on the relationship between the two registers, and I would be very reluctant to turn it into a methodological maxim. Jackson (1989, 135), in contrast, writing on rituals among the Kuranko in northeastern Sierra Leone, suggests an "ethical preference" for embodied communication over speech: "While words and concepts distinguish and divide, bodiliness unites and forms the grounds of an emphatic, even a universal, understanding."

12. Both Jackson and Stoller have explored the "power of the between," i.e., intersubjectivity, in their recent reflections on their earlier research experience, which dealt with human suffering, want, and creativity. For both, regarding storytelling as a path to exploring how we learn from one another helps them to come to theoretical insights.

13. Here, I refer to the colloquial understanding of what empathy is. Hollan (2008) corrects this use of empathy by arguing that it not only involves the experience of understanding the other (as it is typically explained) but also the experience of being understood; it is hence an intersubjective process. For cutting-edge research on empathy (not so much as methodology but as a human condition), see Hollan and Throop (2008). I agree with Hollan and Throop (2008) and Gieser (2008), who include a bodily dimension in their understanding of empathy (see also Halpern [2001], who writes on empathy in a clinical context; but it is, unfortunately, conceptually very vague). While my concern here is with *what* can possibly be shared, a focus on empathy maintains a "first person-like perspective" (Hollan and Throop 2008, 390) by asking *how* we can share it, though.

14. Zigon (2007) is critical of an anthropology of moralities, which diffuses the social and the moral, and suggests limiting it to what he calls a "moral breakdown."

15. Rosaldo (1993, 1–21) movingly shows what can be foreclosed to the researcher if she has not first experienced something similar to her informants' experiences in the

context of her own life. Consider, however, Throop (2010b) for an account of how similar experiences may in fact conceal aspects of another person's lived reality.

16. For more on ethics grounded in ethnographic sensibilities, see Jackson (2005) and Kleinman (1999).

Conclusion

1. As a result of the exclusivity of the possibility of change as performed by the economic and the political elite, the personal sacrifices people made and could tolerate in the name of liberation look different. Liberation in itself becomes bitter to victims if the sacrifice liberation had (supposedly) demanded does not find adequate acknowledgment.

2. Consider Thabo Mbeki in his presidential Statement on the Report of the TRC Joint Sitting of the Houses of Parliament (Cape Town, February 25, 1999), chap. 1.

Bibliography

Agamben, Giorgio. 1999. *Remnants of Auschwitz: The Witness and the Archive.* Brooklyn, NY: Zone Books.

Agar, Michael H. 1985. *Speaking of Ethnography.* Washington, DC: Sage.

Alexander, Peter. 2010. "Rebellion of the Poor: South Africa's Service Delivery Protests: A Preliminary Analysis." *Review of African Political Economy* 37 (123): 25–40.

Arendt, Hannah. 1958. *The Human Condition.* Chicago: University of Chicago Press.

———. 1992. *Eichmann in Jerusalem: A Report on the Banality of Evil.* London: Penguin.

Aronson, Jay D. 2011. "The Strengths and Limitations of South Africa's Search for Apartheid-Era Missing Persons." *International Journal of Transitional Justice* 5 (2): 262–81.

Ashforth, Adam. 1998. "Reflections on Spiritual Insecurity in a Modern African City (Soweto)." *African Studies Review* 41 (3): 39–67.

———. 2005. *Witchcraft, Violence, and Democracy in South Africa.* Chicago: University of Chicago Press.

Backer, David. 2005. "Evaluating Transitional Justice in South Africa from a Victim's Perspective." *Journal of the International Institute* 12 (2). http://hdl.handle.net/2027/spo.4750978.0012.207.

———. 2010. "Watching a Bargain Unravel? A Panel Study of Victims' Attitudes about Transitional Justice in Cape Town, South Africa." *International Journal of Transitional Justice* 4 (3): 443–56.

Backhaus, Jürgen G., Alberto Cassone, and Giovanni B. Ramello, eds. 2012. *Class Actions for Europe: Perspectives from Law and Economics: Lessons from America.* Northampton, MA: Edward Elgar.

Baxi, Upendra. 2000. "Postcolonial Legality." In *A Companion to Postcolonial Studies*, edited by Henry Schwarz and Sangeeta Ray, 540–55. Blackwell Companions in Cultural Studies. Oxford: Blackwell.

———. 2012. *The Future of Human Rights.* 3rd ed. New Delhi: Oxford India Paperbacks.

Becker, David. 1995. "The Deficiency of the Concept of Posttraumatic Stress Disorder When Dealing with Victims of Human Rights Violations." In *Beyond Trauma: Cultural and Societal Dynamics*, edited by Rolf J. Kleber, Charles R. Figley, and Berthold P. R. Gersons, 99–114. New York: Plenum.

Beinart, William, and Marcelle C. Dawson, eds. 2010. *Popular Politics and Resistance Movements in South Africa*. Johannesburg: Wits University Press.

Bell, Terry, and Dumisa B. Ntsebeza. 2003. *Unfinished Business: South Africa, Apartheid and Truth*. London: Verso.

Bergson, Henri. 1994. *Matter and Memory*. Translated by N. M. Paul and W. S. Palmer. New York: Zone Books.

Bevernage, Berber. 2012. *History, Memory and State-Sponsored Violence: Time and Justice*. Approaches to History 4. New York: Routledge.

Biehl, Joao. 2005. *Vita: Life in a Zone of Social Abandonment*. Berkeley: University of California Press.

Boddy, Janice. 1989. *Wombs and Alien Spirits: Women, Men, and the Zar Cult in Northern Sudan*. Madison: University of Wisconsin Press.

Bois-Pedain, Antje Du, ed. 2007. *Transitional Amnesty in South Africa*. Cambridge: Cambridge University Press.

Bond, Patrick. 2008. "Can Reparations for Apartheid Profits Be Won in US Courts?" *Africa Insight* 38 (2): 13–25.

Bond, Patrick, and Khadija Sharife. 2009. "Apartheid Reparations and the Contestation of Corporate Power in Africa." *Review of African Political Economy* 36 (119): 115–25.

Bonner, Philip, and Noor Nieftagodien. 2003. "The Truth and Reconciliation Commission and the Pursuit of 'Social Truth': The Case of Kathorus." In *Commissioning the Past: Understanding South Africa's Truth and Reconciliation Commission*, edited by Deborah Posel and Graeme Simpson, 173–203. Johannesburg: Wits University Press.

Boraine, Alex, and Janet Levy, eds. 1995. *The Healing of a Nation?* Cape Town: Justice in Transition.

Borer, Tristan Anne. 2003. "A Taxonomy of Victims and Perpetrators: Human Rights and Reconciliation in South Africa." *Human Rights Quarterly* 25 (4): 1088–116.

Borneman, John. 2011. "Daydreaming, Intimacy, and the Intersubjective Third in Fieldwork Encounters in Syria." *American Ethnologist* 38 (2): 234–48.

Bourdieu, Pierre. 1977. *Outline of a Theory of Practice*. Translated by Richard Nice. Cambridge: Cambridge University Press.

———. 1986. "The Force of Law: Toward a Sociology of the Juridical Field." *Hastings Law Journal* 38: 814–55.

Bower, Tom. 1997. *Blood Money: The Swiss, the Nazis and the Looted Billions*. London: Pan Books.

Brown, Wendy. 1995. *States of Injury: Power and Freedom in Late Modernity*. Princeton, NJ: Princeton University Press.

Buckley-Zistel, Susanne, and Ruth Stanley, eds. 2011. *Gender in Transitional Justice*. Governance and Limited Statehood Series. London: Palgrave Macmillan.

Butler, Judith. 1993. *Bodies That Matter: On the Discursive Limits of "Sex."* London: Routledge.

———. 1997. *Excitable Speech: A Politics of the Performative*. London: Routledge.

———. 2005. *Giving an Account of Oneself*. New York: Fordham University Press.

Buur, Lars. 2001. "The South African Truth and Reconciliation Commission: A Technique of Nation-State Formation." In *States of Imagination: Ethnographic Explorations of the Postcolonial State*, edited by Thomas Blom Hansen and Finn Steppuat, 149–81. Durham, NC: Duke University Press.

Casey, Edward S. 1996. "How to Get from Space to Place in a Fairly Short Space of Time." In *Senses of Place*, edited by Steven Feld and Keith H. Basso, 13–52. School of American Research Advanced Seminar Series. Santa Fe, NM: School for Advanced Research Press.

Chapman, Audrey R., and Hugo Van der Merwe, eds. 2008. *Truth and Reconciliation in South Africa: Did the TRC Deliver?* Philadelphia: University of Pennsylvania Press.

Clark, Phil. 2010. *The Gacaca Courts, Post-genocide Justice and Reconciliation in Rwanda: Justice without Lawyers*. Cambridge: Cambridge University Press.

Clifford, James, and George E. Marcus, eds. 1986. *Writing Culture: The Poetics and Politics of Ethnography*. Experiments in Contemporary Anthropology: A School of American Research Advanced Seminar. Berkeley: University of California Press.

Cockburn, Cynthia. 2004. "The Continuum of Violence: A Gender Perspective on War and Peace." In *Site of Violence: Gender and Conflict Zones*, edited by Wenon Giles and Jennifer Hyndman, 24–44. Berkeley: University of California Press.

Cohen, Lawrence. 1998. *No Aging in India: Alzheimer's, the Bad Family, and Other Modern Things*. Berkeley: University of California Press.

Cole, Catherine M. 2007. "Performance, Transitional Justice, and the Law: South Africa's Truth and Reconciliation Commission." *Theatre Journal* 59 (2): 167–87.

———. 2009. *Performing South Africa's Truth Commission: Stages of Transition*. Bloomington: Indiana University Press.

Cole, Josette. 1987. *Crossroads: The Politics of Reform and Repression 1976–1986*. Johannesburg: Ravan.

———. 2012. *Behind and beyond the Eiselen Line*. Cape Town: St. George's Cathedral Crypt Memory and Witness Centre.

Collins, Harry M. 2010. *Tacit and Explicit Knowledge*. Chicago: University of Chicago Press.

Colvin, Christopher. 2004a. "Ambivalent Narrations: Pursuing the Political through Traumatic Storytelling." *PoLAR: Political and Legal Anthropology Review* 27 (1): 72–89.

———. 2004b. "Performing the Signs of Injury: Critical Perspectives on Traumatic Storytelling after Apartheid." PhD diss., University of Virginia, Charlottesville.

———. 2006. "Shifting Geographies of Suffering and Recovery: Traumatic Storytelling after Apartheid." In *Borders and Healers: Brokering Therapeutic Resources in Southeast Africa*, edited by Tracy J. Luedke and Harry G. West. Bloomington: Indiana University Press.

Comaroff, Jean. 1985. *Body of Power, Spirit of Resistance: The Culture and History of a South African People*. Chicago: University of Chicago Press.

Comaroff, Jean, and John L. Comaroff. 1999. "Occult Economies and the Violence of Abstraction: Notes from the South African Postcolony." *American Ethnologist* 26 (2): 279–303.

———. 2003. "Reflections on Liberalism, Policulturalism, and ID-ology: Citizenship and Difference in South Africa." *Social Identities* 9 (4): 445–74.

———. 2006. "Law and Disorder in the Postcolony: An Introduction." In *Law and Disorder in the Postcolony*, 1–56. Chicago: University of Chicago Press.

———. 2007. "Law and Disorder in the Postcolony." *Social Anthropology* 15 (2): 133–52.

Conley, John M., and William M. O'Barr. 1990. *Rules versus Relationships: The Ethnography of Legal Discourse.* Chicago: University of Chicago Press.

Connerton, Paul. 1989. *How Societies Remember.* Cambridge: Cambridge University Press.

———. 2011. *The Spirit of Mourning: History, Memory and the Body.* Cambridge: Cambridge University Press.

Crawford-Pinnerup, Anna. 2000. "An Assessment of the Impact of Urgent Interim Reparations." In *From Rhetoric to Responsibility: Making Reparations to the Survivors of Past Political Violence in South Africa*, edited by Brandon Hamber and Tlhoki Mofokeng. Johannesburg: CSVR.

Cronin, Jeremy. 1999. "A Luta Dis-continua? The TRC Final Report and the Nation-Building Project." Paper presented at the TRC: Commissioning the Past? History Workshop at the University of the Witwatersrand, Johannesburg, June 11–14.

Csordas, Thomas. 1990. "Embodiment as a Paradigm for Anthropology." *Ethos* 18 (1): 5–47.

———. 1993. "Somatic Modes of Attention." *Cultural Anthropology* 8 (2): 135–56.

———. 1995. *Embodiment and Experience: The Existential Ground of Culture and Self.* Cambridge: Cambridge University Press.

Daniel, E. Valentine. 1996. *Charred Lullabies: Chapters in an Anthropography of Violence.* Princeton, NJ: Princeton University Press.

Das, Veena. 1995. *Critical Events: An Anthropological Perspective on Contemporary India.* Delhi: Oxford University Press.

———. 1996. "Language and Body: Transactions in the Construction of Pain." *Daedalus* 125 (1): 67–91.

———. 1997. "Language and Body: Transactions in the Construction of Pain." In *Social Suffering*, edited by Arthur Kleinman, Veena Das, and Margaret Lock, 67–91. Berkeley: University of California Press.

———. 2006. *Life and Words: Violence and the Descent into the Ordinary.* Berkeley: University of California Press.

Das, Veena, and Ranendra K. Das. 2007. "How the Body Speaks: Illness and the Lifeworld among the Urban Poor." In *Subjectivity: Ethnographic Investigations*, edited by Joao Biehl, Byron Good, and Arthur Kleinman, 66–97. Ethnographic Studies in Subjectivity 7. Berkeley: University of California Press.

Das, Veena, Arthur Kleinman, Margaret Lock, Mamphela Ramphele, and Pamela Reynolds, eds. 2001. *Remaking a World: Violence, Social Suffering, and Recovery.* Berkeley: University of California Press.

Derrida, Jacques. 2002. "Archive Fever in South Africa." In *Refiguring the Archive*, edited by Carolyn Hamilton, Verne Harries, Jane Taylor, Michele Pickover, Graeme Reid, and Razia Saleh, 38–80. Cape Town: David Philip.

Desjarlais, Robert R. 2003. *Sensory Biographies: Lives and Deaths among Nepal's Yolmo Buddhists.* Berkeley: University of California Press.

Desmond, Cosmas. 1970. *The Discarded People.* Braamfontein, Transvaal: Christian Institute of South Africa.

Douglas, Mary. 1973. *Natural Symbols Explorations in Cosmology.* Harmondsworth, UK: Penguin.

Doxader, Erik, and Charles Villa-Vicencio, eds. 2004. *To Repair the Irreparable: Reparation and Reconstruction in South Africa.* Cape Town: David Philip.

Dugard, John. 1999. "Dealing with Crimes of a Past Regime. Is Amnesty Still an Option?" *Leiden Journal of International Law* 12 (4): 1001–15.

Duranti, Alessandro. 1993. "Truth and Intentionality: An Ethnographic Critique." *Cultural Anthropology* 8 (2): 214–45.

———. 2010. "Husserl, Intersubjectivity and Anthropology." *Anthropological Theory* 10 (1–2): 16–35.

Elias, Norbert. 2000. *The Civilizing Process: Sociogenetic and Psychogenetic Investigations.* Oxford: Blackwell.

Emirbayer, Mustafa, and Ann Mische. 1998. "What Is Agency?" *American Journal of Sociology* 103 (4): 962–1023.

Fabian, Johannes. 1995. "Ethnographic Misunderstanding and the Perils of Context." *American Anthropologist* 97 (1): 41–50.

Fabricius, Peter. 2012. "Digging Up the Dirt." *Sunday Tribune* (Durban), February 9.

Farmer, Paul. 1997. "On Suffering and Structural Violence: A View from Below." In *Social Suffering*, edited by Arthur Kleinman, Veena Das, and Margaret Lock, 261–84. Berkeley: University of California Press.

———. 2004. "An Anthropology of Structural Violence." *Current Anthropology* 45 (3): 305–25.

Fassin, Didier. 2007. *When Bodies Remember: Experiences and Politics of AIDS in South Africa.* Berkeley: University of California Press.

———. 2008. "The Humanitarian Politics of Testimony: Subjectification through Trauma in the Israeli-Palestinian Conflict." *Cultural Anthropology* 23 (3): 531–58.

———. 2009. *The Empire of Trauma: An Inquiry into the Condition of Victimhood.* Princeton, NJ: Princeton University Press.

Fassin, Didier, and Estelle D'Halluin. 2005. "The Truth from the Body: Medical Certificates as Ultimate Evidence for Asylum Seekers." *American Anthropologist* 107 (4): 597–608.

———. 2007. "Critical Evidence: The Politics of Trauma in French Asylum Policies." *Ethos* 35 (3): 300–329.

Fassin, Didier, Frédéric Le Marcis, and Todd Lethata. 2008. "Life and Times of Magda A: Telling a Story of Violence in South Africa." *Current Anthropology* 49 (2): 225–46.

Featherstone, Mike, Mike Hepworth, and Bryan S. Turner, eds. 1991. *The Body: Social Process and Cultural Theory*. Theory, Culture and Society. London: Sage.

Feldman, Allen. 1991. *Formations of Violence: The Narrative of the Body and Political Terror in Northern Ireland*. Chicago: University of Chicago Press.

———. 2003. "Strange Fruit: The South African Truth Commission and the Demonic Economies of Violence." *Social Analysis* 46 (3): 234–65.

Felman, Shoshana, and Dori Laub. 1992. *Testimony: Crises of Witnessing in Literature, Psychoanalysis and History*. New York: Routledge.

Ferguson, James. 2015. *Give a Man a Fish: Reflections on the New Politics of Distribution*. Durham, NC: Duke University Press.

Förster, Till. 2001. "Sehen und Beobachten: Ethnographie nach der Postmoderne." *Sozialersinn* 3: 459–84.

———. 2011. "Emic Evaluation Approach: Some Remarks on Its Epistemological Background." In *The Emic Evaluation Approach: Epistemologies, Experience, and Ethnographic Practice*, edited by Till Förster and Lucy Koechlin, 3–14. Basel Papers on Political Transformations 3. Basel: University of Basel, Institute of Social Anthropology.

———. 2015. "The Formation of Governance: The Politics of Governance and Their Theoretical Dimensions." In *The Politics of Governance: Actors and Articulations in Africa and Beyond*, edited by Till Förster and Lucy Koechlin, 197–218. Conceptualising Comparative Politics 3. London: Routledge.

Foster, Don, Dennis Davis, and Diane Sandler. 1987. *Detention and Torture in South Africa: Psychological, Legal and Historical Studies*. Cape Town: David Philip.

Foucault, Michel. 1984a. "The Ethics of Care for the Self: An Interview with Michel Foucault on January 20, 1984." *Philosophy and Social Criticism* 12: 112–31.

———. 1984b. "Nietzsche, Genealogy, History." In *The Foucault Reader*, edited by Paul Rabinow, 76–100. New York: Pantheon.

———. 1987. *Sexualität und Wahrheit: Erster Band: Der Wille zum Wissen*. Frankfurt: Suhrkamp.

Frank, Arthur W. 2002. *At the Will of the Body: Reflections on Illness*. Boston: Mariner Books.

Freire, Paulo. 2007. *Pedagogy of the Oppressed*. New York: Continuum.

French, Jan H. 2009. *Legalizing Identities: Becoming Black or Indian in Brazil's Northeast*. Chapel Hill: University of North Carolina Press.

Friedman, John S. 2003. "Paying for Apartheid." *The Nation*, May 15.

Fullard, Madeleine, and Nicky Rousseau. 2004. "An Imperfect Past: The Truth and Reconciliation Commission in Transition." In *State of the Nation: South Africa, 2003–2004*, edited by John Daniel, Adam Habib, Roger Southall, and the Human Sciences Research Council, Democracy and Governance Research Programme, 78–104. Cape Town: HSRC.

Galtung, Johan. 1969. "Violence, Peace, and Peace Research." *Journal of Peace Research* 6 (3): 167–91.

Garfinkel, Harold. 1967. *Studies in Ethnomethodology*. Englewood Cliffs, NJ: Prentice Hall.

Gebhardt, Winifred. 1994. *Charisma Als Lebensform: Zur Soziologie Des Alternativen Lebens*. Schriften zur Kultursoziologie 14. Berlin: Reimer.

Geertz, Clifford. 1973. *The Interpretation of Culture*. New York: Basic Books.

———. 1986. "Epilogue: Making Experience, Authoring Selves." In *The Anthropology of Experience*, edited by Victor Turner and Edward Bruner, 373–80. Chicago: University of Illinois Press.

Gengenbach, Heidi. 2010. *Binding Memories: Women as Makers and Tellers of History in Magude, Mozambique*. New York: Columbia University Press. http://www.gutenberg -e.org/geh01/main.html.

Geschiere, Peter. 1997. *The Modernity of Witchcraft: Politics and the Occult in Postcolonial Africa*. Charlottesville: University of Virginia Press.

Gewald, Jan-Bart. 1999. *Herero Heroes: A Socio-political History of the Herero of Namibia, 1890–1923*. Athens: Ohio University Press.

Giannini, Tyler, Susan Farbstein, Samantha Bent, and Miles Jackson. 2009. *Prosecuting Apartheid-Era Crimes? A South African Dialogue on Justice*. Cambridge, MA: Human Rights Program, Harvard Law School.

Giddens, Anthony. 1986. *The Constitution of Society: Outline of the Theory of Structuration*. Berkeley: University of California Press.

Gieser, Thorsten. 2008. "Embodiment, Emotion and Empathy a Phenomenological Approach to Apprenticeship Learning." *Anthropological Theory* 8 (3): 299–318.

Gilbert, Margaret. 1990. "Walking Together: A Paradigmatic Social Phenomenon." *Midwest Studies in Philosophy* 15 (1): 1–14.

———. 1992. *On Social Facts*. Princeton, NJ: Princeton University Press.

———. 2009. "Shared Intention and Personal Intentions." *Philosophical Studies* 144 (1): 167–87.

Girtler, Roland. 2001. *Methoden der Feldforschung*. Vienna: UTB.

Givoni, Michal. 2011. "The Ethics of Witnessing and the Politics of the Governed." *SSRN eLibrary*. http://papers.ssrn.com/sol3/papers.cfm?abstract_id=1903479.

Gobodo-Madikizela, Pumla. 2004. *A Human Being Died That Night: A South African Woman Confronts the Legacy of Apartheid*. New York: Houghton Mifflin Harcourt.

Gobodo-Madikizela, Pumla, and Chris Van der Merwe. 2007. *Narrating Our Healing: Perspectives on Working through Trauma*. Cambridge: Cambridge Scholars Press.

Godoy, Angela Snodgrass. 2005. "La Muchacha Respondona: Reflections on the Razor's Edge between Crime and Human Rights." *Human Rights Quarterly* 27 (2): 597–624.

Gómez-Barris, Macarena. 2009. *Where Memory Dwells: Culture and State Violence in Chile*. Berkeley: University of California Press.

Good, Byron J. 1992. "A Body in Pain: The Making of a World of Chronic Pain." In *Pain as Human Experience: An Anthropological Perspective*, edited by Mary-Jo DelVecchio Good, Paul E. Brodwin, Arthur Kleinman, and Byron J. Good, 29–48. Berkeley: University of California Press.

Good, Mary-Jo DelVecchio, Paul E. Brodwin, Byron J. Good, and Arthur Kleinman, eds. 1992. *Pain as Human Experience: An Anthropological Perspective*. Berkeley: University of California Press.

Goodale, Mark. 2006. "Toward a Critical Anthropology of Human Rights." *Current Anthropology* 47 (3): 485–511.

Goodale, Mark, and Sally Engle Merry, eds. 2007. *The Practice of Human Rights: Tracking Law between the Global and the Local*. Cambridge: Cambridge University Press.

Govier, Trudy. 2015. *Victims and Victimhood*. Calgary: Broadview.

Griffiths, Anne, Keebet von Benda-Beckmann, and Franz von Benda-Beckmann, eds. 2005. *Mobile People, Mobile Law: Expanding Legal Relations in a Contracting World*. Burlington, VT: Ashgate.

Grosz, Elizabeth A. 2004. *The Nick of Time: Politics, Evolution, and the Untimely*. Durham, NC: Duke University Press.

Gunn, Shirley. 2007. *If Trees Could Speak: The Trojan Horse Story*. Cape Town: HRMC.

Gunn, Shirley, and Sinazo Krwala, eds. 2008. *Knocking On: . . . Mothers and Daughters in Struggle in South Africa*. Johannesburg: CSVR/HRMC.

Gupta, Akhil, and James Ferguson, eds. 1997. *Anthropological Locations: Boundaries and Grounds of a Field Science*. Berkeley: University of California Press.

Halpern, Jodi. 2001. *From Detached Concern to Empathy: Humanizing Medical Practice*. Oxford: Oxford University Press.

Hamber, Brandon. 2006. "Narrowing the Micro and Macro: A Psychological Perspective on Reparations in Societies in Transition." In *The Handbook of Reparations*, edited by Pablo De Greiff, 560–88. Oxford: Oxford University Press.

———. 2009. *Transforming Societies after Political Violence: Truth, Reconciliation, and Mental Health*. Dordrecht: Springer.

Hastrup, Kirsten. 1994. "Anthropological Knowledge Incorporated: Discussion." In *Social Experience and Anthropological Knowledge*, edited by Kirsten Hastrup and Peter Hervik, 168–80. London: Routledge.

———. 2003. "Representing the Common Good: The Limit of Legal Language." In *Human Rights in Global Perspective: Anthropological Studies of Rights, Claims and Entitlements*, edited by Richard A. Wilson and Jon P. Mitchell, 16–32. London: Routledge.

Hastrup, Kirsten, and Peter Hervik, eds. 1994. *Social Experience and Anthropological Knowledge*. London: Routledge.

Hayner, Priscilla B. 2001. *Unspeakable Truths: Confronting State Terror and Atrocity*. London: Routledge.

Heidegger, Martin. 1996. *Being and Time*. Albany: State University of New York Press.

Henderson, Patricia. 1999. "Living with Fragility." PhD diss., University of Cape Town.

Henner, Peter. 2009. *Human Rights and the Alien Tort Statute: Law, History, and Analysis*. Chicago: American Bar Association.

Hertz, Robert. 1960. *Death and the Right Hand*. Translated by Rodney and Claudia Needham. Aberdeen: Cohen and West.

Herzfeld, Michael. 2009. "The Cultural Politics of Gesture: Reflections on the Embodiment of Ethnographic Practice." *Ethnography* 10 (2): 131–52.

Hollan, Douglas. 2008. "Being There: On the Imaginative Aspects of Understanding Others and Being Understood." *Ethos* 36 (4): 475–89.

Hollan, Douglas, and C. Jason Throop. 2008. "Whatever Happened to Empathy? Introduction." *Ethos* 36 (4): 385–401.

Honneth, Axel. 2003. *Unsichtbarkeit: Stationen einer Theorie der Intersubjektivität*. Frankfurt: Suhrkamp.

Howes, David, ed. 2005. *The Empire of Senses: The Sensory Culture Reader*. Oxford: Berg.

Humphrey, Michael. 2005. "Reconciliation and the Therapeutic State." *Journal of Intercultural Studies* 26 (3): 203–20.

Husserl, Edmund. 1929. *Cartesianische Meditationen: Eine Einleitung in die Phänomenologie*. Hamburg: Meiner.

Ingold, Tim. 2007. "Earth, Sky, Wind, and Weather." *Journal of the Royal Anthropological Institute* 13: S19–38.

Jackman, Mary R. 2002. "Violence in Social Life." *Annual Review of Sociology* 28 (1): 387–415.

Jackson, Michael. 1989. *Paths toward a Clearing: Radical Empiricism and Ethnographic Inquiry*. Bloomington: Indiana University Press.

———, ed. 1996. *Things as They Are: New Directions in Phenomenological Anthropology*. Bloomington: Indiana University Press.

———. 1998. *Minima Ethnographica*. Chicago: University of Chicago Press.

———. 2002. *Politics of Storytelling: Violence, Transgression and Intersubjectivity*. Copenhagen: Museum Tusculanum Press.

———. 2004. *In Sierra Leone*. Durham, NC: Duke University Press.

———. 2005. *Existential Anthropology: Events, Exigencies and Effects*. New York: Berghahn.

———. 2011. *Life within Limits: Well-Being in a World of Want*. Durham, NC: Duke University Press.

Kagee, Ashraf. 2006. "The Relationship between Statement-Giving at the South African Truth and Reconciliation Commission and Psychological Distress among Former Political Detainees." *South African Journal of Psychology* 36: 880–94.

Kaminer, Debra, and Gillian Eagle. 2010. *Traumatic Stress in South Africa*. Johannesburg: Wits University Press.

Kaminer, Debra, Dan J. Stein, Irene Mbanga, and Nompumeielo Zungu-Dirwayi. 2001. "The Truth and Reconciliation Commission in South Africa: Relation to Psychiatric Status and Forgiveness among Survivors of Human Rights Abuses." *British Journal of Psychiatry* 178 (4): 373–77.

Kapp, Jean-Pierre. 2003. "Südafrika lehnt Sammelklagen ab: Gespräch mit dem südafrikanischen Präsidenten." *Neue Zürcher Zeitung*, June 11.

Keck, Margaret E., and Kathryn Sikkink. 1998. *Activists beyond Borders: Advocacy Networks in International Politics*. Ithaca, NY: Cornell University Press.

Kesselring, Rita. 2012. "Corporate Apartheid-Era Human Rights Violations before U.S. Courts: Political and Legal Controversies around Victimhood in Today's South Africa." *Stichproben: Vienna Journal of African Studies* 23: 77–105.

———. 2014. "Experiences of Violence and the Formation of the Political: Embodied Memory and Victimhood in South Africa." In *The Politics of Governance: Actors and Articulations in Africa and Beyond*, edited by Till Förster and Lucy Koechlin, 151–79. Conceptualising Comparative Politics. London: Routledge.

———. 2015a. "Case Pending: Practices of Inclusion and Exclusion in a Class of Plaintiffs." *Journal Anthropology Southern Africa* 38 (1–2): 16–28.

———. 2015b. "Cultural Reproduction and Memory: Past, Present and Future." In *Explorations in African History: Reading Patrick Harries*, edited by Veit Arlt, Stephanie Bishop, and Pascal Schmid, 23–28. Basel: Basler Afrika Bibliographien.

———. 2015c. "Moments of Dislocation: Why the Body Matters in Ethnographic Research." Basel Papers on Political Transformations 8. Basel: University of Basel, Institute of Social Anthropology.

Kidron, Carol A. 2009. "Towards an Ethnography of Silence: The Lived Presence of the Past in the Everyday Life of Holocaust Trauma Survivors and Their Descendants in Israel." *Current Anthropology* 50 (1): 5–27.

Klaaren, Jonathan, and Howard Varney. 2000. "A Second Bite at the Amnesty Cherry? Constitutional and Policy Issues around Legislation for a Second Amnesty." *South African Law Journal* 117: 572–93.

Kleinman, Arthur. 1999. "Experience and Its Moral Modes: Culture, Human Conditions, and Disorder." In *The Tanner Lectures on Human Values*, edited by Grethe Peterson, 357–420. Salt Lake City: University of Utah Press.

Kleinman, Arthur, and Joan Kleinman. 1991. "Suffering and Its Professional Transformation: Toward an Ethnography of Interpersonal Experience." *Culture, Medicine and Psychiatry* 15 (3): 275–301.

———. 1994. "How Bodies Remember: Social Memory and Bodily Experience of Criticism, Resistance, and Delegitimation Following China's Cultural Revolution." *New Literary History* 25 (3): 707–23.

Kreis, Georg. 2005. *Die Schweiz und Südafrika 1948–1994*. Bern: Haupt.

Krog, Antjie. 1999. *Country of My Skull*. London: Vintage.

Krog, Antjie, Nosisi Mpolweni, and Kopano Ratele. 2009. *There Was This Goat: Investigating the Truth Commission Testimony of Notrose Nobomvu Konile*. Pietermaritzburg: University of KwaZulu-Natal Press.

Krüger, Gesine. 1999. *Kriegsbewältigung und Geschichtsbewusstrein: Realität, Deutung und Verarbeitung des deutschen Kolonialkriegs in Namibia 1904 bis 1907*. Kritische Studien zur Geschichtswissenschaft 133. Göttingen: Vandenhoeck und Ruprecht.

Kusenbach, Margarethe. 2003. "Street Phenomenology: The Go-Along as Ethnographic Research Tool." *Ethnography* 4 (3): 455–85.

Lahav, Alexandra D. 2010. "The Curse of Bigness and the Optimal Size of Class Actions." *Vanderbilt Law Review En Banc* 63: 117–31.

Lambek, Michael. 1993. *Knowledge and Practice in Mayotte: Local Discourses of Islam, Sorcery and Spirit Possession.* Toronto: University of Toronto Press.

———. 1998. "Body and Mind in Mind, Body and Mind in Body: Some Anthropological Interventions in a Long Conversation." In *Bodies and Persons: Comparative Perspectives from Africa and Melanesia,* edited by Michael Lambek and Andrew Strathern, 103–26. Cambridge: Cambridge University Press.

Lambek, Michael, and Andrew Strathern, eds. 1998. *Bodies and Persons: Comparative Perspectives from Africa and Melanesia.* Cambridge: Cambridge University Press.

Langer, Lawrence L. 1991. *Holocaust Testimonies: The Ruins of Memory.* New Haven, CT: Yale University Press.

Leder, Drew. 1990. *The Absent Body.* Chicago: University of Chicago Press.

Lévinas, Emmanuel. 2003. *Die Zeit und der Andere.* Philosophische Bibliothek 546. Hamburg: Meiner.

Lock, Margaret. 2001. "Alienation of Body Parts and the Biopolitics of Immortalized Cell Lines." *Body and Society* 7 (2): 63–91.

Lock, Margaret, and Judith Farquhar. 2007. *Beyond the Body Proper: Reading the Anthropology of Material Life.* Durham, NC: Duke University Press.

Madlingozi, Tshepo. 2007a. "Good Victim, Bad Victim: Apartheid's Beneficiaries, Victims, and the Struggle for Social Justice." In *Law, Memory, and the Legacy of Apartheid: Ten Years after AZAPO v. President of South Africa,* edited by Karin Van Marle, 107–26. Pretoria: Pretoria University Law Press.

———. 2007b. "Post-apartheid Social Movements and the Quest for the Elusive "New" South Africa." *Journal of Law and Society* 34 (1): 77–98.

———. 2010. "On Transitional Justice Entrepreneurs and the Production of Victims." *Journal of Human Rights Practice* 2 (2): 208–28.

Makhalemele, Oupa. 2004. "Southern Africa Reconciliation Project: Khulumani Case Study." Southern Africa Reconciliation Project 2004. Johannesburg: CSVR.

Mamdani, Mahmood. 2002. "Amnesty or Impunity? A Preliminary Critique of the Report of the Truth and Reconciliation Commission of South Africa." *Diacritics* 32 (3–4): 33–59.

Marchand, Trevor. 2008. "Muscles, Morals and Mind: Craft Apprenticeship and the Formation of Person." *British Journal of Educational Studies* 56 (3): 245–71.

Marschall, Sabine. 2010. "Commemorating the "Trojan Horse" Massacre in Cape Town: The Tension between Vernacular and Official Expressions of Memory." *Visual Studies* 25 (2): 135–48.

Mascia-Lees, Frances, ed. 2011. *A Companion to the Anthropology of the Body and Embodiment.* Malden, MA: Wiley-Blackwell.

Mattei, Ugo. 2003. "A Theory of Imperial Law: A Study on U.S. Hegemony and the Latin Resistance." *Indiana Journal of Global Legal Studies* 10 (1): 383–448.

Mauss, Marcel. 1934. "Les Techniques du Corps." *Journal de Psychologie* 32 (3–4): 1–23.

———. 1973. "Techniques of the Body." *Economy and Society* 2: 70–88.

McLaughlin, Cahal. 2002. *We Never Give Up.* Cape Town: HRMC.

———. 2012. *We Never Give Up II.* Cape Town: HRMC.

McNay, Lois. 1991. "The Foucauldian Body and the Exclusion of Experience." *Hypatia* 6 (3).

Mda, Zakes. 2002. *Ways of Dying.* New York: Picador USA.

Meckled-García, Saladin, and Basak Çali, eds. 2005. *The Legalization of Human Rights: Multidisciplinary Approaches.* London: Routledge.

Meierhenrich, Jens. 2008. *The Legacies of Law: Long-Run Consequences of Legal Development in South Africa, 1652–2000.* New York: Cambridge University Press.

Meintjes, Sheila, Anu Pillay, and Meredeth Turshen, eds. 2001. *The Aftermath: Women in Post-conflict Transformation.* London: Zed Books.

Menjívar, Cecilia. 2011. *Enduring Violence: Ladina Women's Lives in Guatemala.* Berkeley: University of California Press.

Merleau-Ponty, Maurice. 1962. *Phenomenology of Perception.* Translated by C. Smith. London: Routledge.

——. 1969. *The Visible and the Invisible.* Evanston, IL: Northwestern University Press.

——. 2002. *Phenomenology of Perception.* New York: Humanities Press.

Merry, Sally Engle. 1990. *Getting Justice and Getting Even: Legal Consciousness among Working-Class Americans.* Language and Legal Discourse Series. Chicago: University of Chicago Press.

——. 2003. "Rights Talk and the Experience of Law: Implementing Women's Human Rights to Protection from Violence." *Human Rights Quarterly* 25 (2): 343–81.

——. 2008. "Transnational Human Rights and Local Activism: Mapping the Middle." *American Anthropologist* 108 (1): 38–51.

Mertz, Elizabeth, ed. 2008. *The Role of Social Science in Law.* International Library of Essays in Law and Society. Burlington, VT: Ashgate.

Moore, Henrietta. 1994. "The Problem of Explaining Violence in the Social Sciences." In *Sex and Violence: Issues in Representation and Experience,* edited by Penelope Harvey and Peter Gow, 138–55. New York: Routledge.

Moore, Sally Falk. 2001. "Certainties Undone: Fifty Turbulent Years of Legal Anthropology, 1949–1999." *Journal of the Royal Anthropological Institute* 7 (1): 95–116.

Morgenrath, Birgit, and Gottfried Wellmer. 2003. *Deutsches Kapital am Kap: Kollaboration mit dem Apartheidregime.* Hamburg: Nautilus.

Nader, Laura. 2002. *The Life of the Law: Anthropological Projects.* Berkeley: University of California Press.

Napier, David. 2014. *Making Things Better: A Workbook on Ritual, Cultural Values, and Environmental Behavior.* Oxford: Oxford University Press.

Ndebele, Njabulo. 1998. "Memory, Metaphor, and the Triumph of Narrative." In *Negotiating the Past: The Making of Memory in South Africa,* edited by Sarah Nuttall and Carli Coetzee, 19–28. Oxford: Oxford University Press.

Niehaus, Isak. 2005. "Witches and Zombies of the South African Lowveld: Discourse, Accusations and Subjective Reality." *Journal of the Royal Anthropological Institute* 11 (2): 191–210.

Niezen, Ronald. 2010. *Public Justice and the Anthropology of Law.* Cambridge: Cambridge University Press.

Nordstrom, Carolyn. 2004. *Shadows of War: Violence, Power, and International Profiteering in the Twenty-First Century.* Berkeley: University of California Press.

Norval, Aletta. 2001. "Reconstructing National Identity and Renegotiating Memory: The Work of the TRC." In *States of Imagination: Ethnographic Explorations of the Postcolonial State,* edited by Thomas Blom Hansen and Finn Stepputat, 182–202. Durham, NC: Duke University Press.

Okely, Judith. 1994. "Vicarious and Sensory Knowledge of Chronology and Change: Ageing in Rural France." In *Social Experience and Anthropological Knowledge,* edited by Kirsten Hastrup and Peter Hervik, 45–64. London: Routledge.

———. 2005. "Gypsy Justice versus Gorgio Law: Interrelations of Difference." *Sociological Review* 53 (4): 691–709.

———. 2012. *Anthropological Practice: Fieldwork and the Ethnographic Method.* London: Berg.

Ostrow, James M. 1990. *Social Sensitivity: A Study of Habit and Experience.* Albany: State University of New York Press.

Ottenberg, Simon. 1990. "Thirty Years of Fieldnotes: Changing Relationship to the Text." In *Fieldnotes: The Makings of Anthropology,* edited by Roger Sanjek, 139–60. Ithaca, NY: Cornell University Press.

Pambazuka News. 2003. "South Africa: A Right to Reparations through Legal Action." September 4. http://www.pambazuka.org/en/category/rights/16896.

Pink, Sarah. 2008. "An Urban Tour: The Sensory Sociality of Ethnographic Place-Making." *Ethnography* 9 (2): 175–96.

———. 2009. *Doing Sensory Ethnography.* London: Sage.

Platzky, Laurine, Cherryl Walker, and Surplus People Project. 1985. *The Surplus People: Forced Removals in South Africa.* Johannesburg: Ravan.

Polanyi, Michael. 1967. *The Tacit Dimension.* Garden City, NY: Anchor.

Popitz, Heinrich. 2006. *Soziale Normen.* Frankfurt: Suhrkamp.

Posel, Deborah, and Graeme Simpson, eds. 2003. *Commissioning the Past: Understanding South Africa's Truth and Reconciliation Commission.* Johannesburg: Wits University Press.

Pouligny, Béatrice. 2007. "'Breaking the Silence: A Luta Continua': An Art Project about Memory and Healing in Post-apartheid South Africa." In collaboration with Shirley Gunn and Zukiswa Khalipha. CERI-Sciences Po/CNRS, Paris, France, and Georgetown University, School of Foreign Service, Washington, DC.

Ramphele, Mamphela. 1995. "The Challenge Facing South Africa." In *The Healing of a Nation?,* edited by Alex Boraine and Janet Levy, 33–36. Cape Town: Justice in Transition.

———. 1997. "Political Widowhood in South Africa: The Embodiment of Ambiguity." In *Social Suffering,* edited by Arthur Kleinman, Veena Das, and Margaret Lock, 99–118. Berkeley: University of California Press.

Randeria, Shalini. 2003. "Footless Experts vs. Rooted Cosmopolitans: Biodiversity Conversation, Transnationalisation of Law and Conflict among Civil Society Actors in India." *Tsantsa* 8: 74–85.

Reynolds, Pamela. 1989. *Childhood in Crossroads: Cognition and Society in South Africa.* Johannesburg: New Africa Books.

———. 1995. *The Ground of All Making: State Violence, the Family and Political Activists.* Pretoria: Human Sciences Research Council Press.

Ridler, Keith. 1996. "If Not the Words: Shared Practical Activity and Friendship in Fieldwork." In *Things as They Are: New Directions in Phenomenological Anthropology*, edited by Michael Jackson, 238–58. Bloomington: Indiana University Press.

Robins, Steven L., ed. 2005. *Limits to Liberation after Apartheid: Citizenship, Governance and Culture.* Athens: Ohio University Press.

———. 2009. *From Revolution to Rights in South Africa: Social Movements, NGOs and Popular Politics after Apartheid.* Pietermaritzburg: University of KwaZulu-Natal Press.

Rosaldo, Renato. 1993. "Grief and a Headhunter's Rage." In *Culture and Truth: The Remaking of Social Analysis*, 1–21. Boston: Beacon.

Ross, Fiona C. 2002. *Bearing Witness: Women and the Truth and Reconciliation Commission.* London: Pluto.

———. 2003. "Using Rights to Measure Wrongs: A Case Study of Method and Moral in the Work of the South African Truth and Reconciliation Commission." In *Human Rights in Global Perspective: Anthropological Studies of Rights, Claims and Entitlements*, edited by Richard A. Wilson and Jon P. Mitchell, 163–82. London: Routledge.

Roux, Wessel Le, and Karin Van Marle, eds. 2008. *Post-apartheid Fragments: Law, Politics and Critique.* Pretoria: University of South Africa Press.

Rubio-Marín, Ruth, ed. 2006. *What Happened to the Women? Gender and Reparations for Human Rights Violations.* New York: Social Science Research Council.

Saage-Maass, Miriam, and Wiebke Golombek. 2010. "Transnationality in Court: In Re South African Apartheid Litigation, 02-MDL-1499, U.S. District Court, Southern District of New York (Manhattan), April 8, 2009." *European Journal of Transitional Studies* 2 (2): 5–25.

Sanders, Mark. 2007. *Ambiguities of Witnessing: Law and Literature in the Time of a Truth Commission.* Johannesburg: Wits University Press.

Sanjek, Roger, ed. 1990. *Fieldnotes: The Makings of Anthropology.* Ithaca, NY: Cornell University Press.

———. 1991. "The Ethnographic Present." *Man* 26 (4): 609–28.

Sarkin, Jeremy. 2008. "An Evaluation of the South African Amnesty Process." In *Truth and Reconciliation in South Africa: Did the TRC Deliver?*, edited by Audrey R. Chapman and Hugo Van der Merwe, 93–115. Philadelphia: University of Pennsylvania Press.

Sarkin-Hughes, Jeremy. 2004. *Carrots and Sticks: The TRC and the South African Amnesty Process.* Antwerp: Intersentia.

Scarry, Elaine. 1985. *The Body in Pain: The Making and Unmaking of the World.* Oxford: Oxford University Press.

Scheper-Hughes, Nancy. 1997. "Specificities: Peace-Time Crimes." *Social Identities* 3 (3): 471–98.

Scheper-Hughes, Nancy, and Philippe Bourgois, eds. 2004. "Introduction: Making Sense of Violence." *Violence in War and Peace: An Anthology*, 1–31. Malden, MA: Blackwell.

Scheper-Hughes, Nancy, and Margaret M. Lock. 1987. "The Mindful Body: A Prolegomenon to Future Work in Medical Anthropology." *Medical Anthropology Quarterly* 1 (1): 6–41.

Schütz, Alfred, and Thomas Luckmann. 1974. *The Structures of the Life-World*. London: Heinemann.

———. 2003. *Strukturen der Lebenswelt*. Konstanz: UVK Verlagsgesellschaft.

Sennett, Richard. 2008. *The Craftsman*. New Haven, CT: Yale University Press.

Sharife, Khadija. 2009. "Fixing the Legacy of Apartheid." *Foreign Policy in Focus*, April 29. http://fpif.org/fixing_the_legacy_of_apartheid/.

Shaw, Rosalind. 2012. "Displacing Violence: Making Pentecostal Memory in Postwar Sierra Leone." *Cultural Anthropology* 22 (1): 66–93.

Simpson, Graeme. 1998. "A Brief Evaluation of South Africa's Truth and Reconciliation Commission: Some Lessons for Societies in Transition." Cape Town: CSVR.

Sooka, Yasmin. 2003. "Apartheid's Victims in the Midst of Amnesty's Promise." In *The Provocations of Amnesty: Memory, Justice and Impunity*, edited by Charles Villa-Vicencio and Erik Doxtader, 309–14. Claremont, South Africa: David Philip.

Spittler, Gerd. 2001. "Teilnehmende Beobachtung als dichte Teilnahme." *Zeitschrift für Ethnologie* 126: 1–25.

Stephens, Beth, Judith Chomsky, Jennifer Green, Paul Hoffman, and Michael Ratner, eds. 2008. *International Human Rights Litigation in U.S. Courts*. Leiden: Brill.

Sternlight, Jean R. 2000. "As Mandatory Binding Arbitration Meets the Class Action, Will the Class Action Survive?" *William and Mary Law Review* 42 (1). http://scholarship.law.wm.edu/wmlr/vol42/iss1/3.

Stoller, Paul. 1989. *The Taste of Ethnographic Things: The Senses in Anthropology*. Contemporary Ethnography Series. Philadelphia: University of Pennsylvania Press.

———. 1995. *Embodying Colonial Memories: Spirit Possession, Power and the Hauka in West Africa*. New York: Routledge.

———. 1997. *Sensuous Scholarship*. Philadelphia: University of Pennsylvania Press.

———. 2008. *The Power of the Between: An Anthropological Odyssey*. Chicago: University of Chicago Press.

Straker, G., and Sanctuaries Counselling Team. 1987. "The Continuous Traumatic Stress Syndrome: The Single Therapeutic Interview." *Psychology in Society* 8: 48–78.

Strathern, Andrew, and Pamela J. Stewart. 1998. "Embodiment and Communications: Two Frameworks for the Analysis of Ritual." *Social Anthropology* 6: 237–51.

Sudnow, David. 1993. *Ways of the Hand*. Cambridge, MA: MIT Press.

Sugawara, Kazuyoshi. 2005. "Possession, Equality and Gender Relations in IGui Discourse." In *Property and Equality*. Vol. 1, *Ritualisation, Sharing, Egalitarianism*, edited by Thomas Widlok and Wolde Gossa Tadesse, 105–29. New York: Berghahn.

Summerfield, Derek. 1995. "Addressing Human Response to War and Atrocity: Major Challenges in Research and Practices and the Limitations of Western Psychiatric

Models." In *Beyond Trauma: Cultural and Societal Dynamics*, edited by Rolf J. Kleber, Charles R. Figley, and Berthold P. R. Gersons, 17–30. New York: Plenum.

———. 1999. "A Critique of Seven Assumptions Behind Psychological Trauma Programmes in War-Affected Areas." *Social Science and Medicine* 48 (10): 1449–62.

———. 2001. "The Invention of Post-traumatic Stress Disorder and the Social Usefulness of a Psychiatric Category." *British Medical Journal* 322 (7278): 95–98.

Taussig, Michael. 1992. *The Nervous System*. London: Taylor and Francis.

Terreblanche, Sampie. 2000. "Dealing with Systematic Economic Injustice." In *Looking Back, Reaching Forward: Reflections on the Truth and Reconciliation Commission of South Africa*, edited by Charles Villa-Vicencio and Wilhelm Verwoerd, 265–76. Cape Town: University of Cape Town Press.

Throop, C. Jason. 2010a. *Suffering and Sentiment: Exploring the Vicissitudes of Experience and Pain in Yap*. Berkeley: University of California Press.

———. 2010b. "Latitudes of Loss: On the Vicissitudes of Empathy." *American Ethnologist* 37 (4): 771–82.

———. 2012. "On Inaccessibility and Vulnerability: Some Horizons of Compatibility between Phenomenology and Psychoanalysis." *Ethos* 40 (1): 75–96.

Torpey, John C. 2003. *Politics and the Past: On Repairing Historical Injustices*. Lanham, MD: Rowman and Littlefield.

Truth and Reconciliation Commission South Africa. 2003. *Truth and Reconciliation Commission Final Report*. Vols. 6 and 7. Cape Town: Juta and Co.

Turner, Victor. 1969. *The Ritual Process: Structure and Anti-structure*. Ithaca, NY: Cornell University Press.

———. 1974. *Dramas, Fields and Metaphors: Symbolic Action in Human Society*. Ithaca, NY: Cornell University Press.

Turner, Victor, and Edward Bruner, eds. 1986. *The Anthropology of Experience*. Urbana: University of Illinois Press.

Van Gennep, Arnold. 2010. *The Rites of Passage*. London: Routledge.

Van Marle, Karin, ed. 2007. *Law, Memory, and the Legacy of Apartheid: Ten Years after AZAPO v. President of South Africa*. Pretoria: Pretoria University Law Press.

———. 2008. "Lives of Action, Thinking and Revolt: A Feminist Call for Politics and Becoming in Post-apartheid South Africa." In *Post-apartheid Fragments: Law, Politics and Critique*, edited by Wessel Le Roux and Karin Van Marle, 34–58. Pretoria: University of South Africa Press.

Villa-Vicencio, Charles, and Wilhelm Verwoerd, eds. 2000. *Looking Back, Reaching Forward: Reflections on the Truth and Reconciliation Commission of South Africa*. Cape Town: University of Cape Town Press.

Wacquant, Loïc. 2004. *Body and Soul: Notebooks of an Apprentice Boxer*. New York: Oxford University Press.

Wafer, Jim. 1991. *The Taste of Blood: Spirit Possession in Brazilian Candomble*. Philadelphia: University of Pennsylvania Press.

Weber, Bruce. 2008. "John E. Sprizzo, 73, U.S. Judge, Dies." *New York Times*, December 18.

Weber, Max. 1968. *On Charisma and Institution Building*. Chicago: University of Chicago Press.

Weiss, Peter. 2012. "Should Corporations Have More Leeway to Kill Than People Do?" *New York Times*, February 24.

Wells, Julia C. 1983. "Why Women Rebel: A Comparative Study of South African Women's Resistance in Bloemfontein (1913) and Johannesburg (1958)." *Journal of Southern African Studies* 10 (1): 55–70.

———. 1993. *We Now Demand! The History of Women's Resistance to Pass Laws in South Africa*. Johannesburg: Wits University Press.

Werbner, Richard, ed. 1998. *Memory and the Postcolony: African Anthropology and the Critique of Power*. London: Zed Books.

White, Geoffrey M. 2008. "Emotional Remembering: The Pragmatics of National Memory." *Ethos* 27 (4): 505–29.

Widlok, Thomas. 2009. "Van Veraf Naar Dichtbij: The Standing of the Antipodes in a Flat World." Radboud Repository, Inaugural Address RU, March 6. http://repository.ubn.ru.nl/handle/2066/77162.

Wikan, Unni. 1991. "Toward an Experience-Near Anthropology." *Cultural Anthropology* 6 (3): 285–305.

Wilson, Monica, and Archie Mafeje. 1963. *Langa: A Study of Social Groups in an African Township*. Oxford: Oxford University Press.

Wilson, Richard A. 2000. "Reconciliation and Revenge in Post-apartheid South Africa: Rethinking Legal Pluralism and Human Rights." *Current Anthropology* 41 (1): 75–98.

———. 2001. *The Politics of Truth and Reconciliation in South Africa: Legitimizing the Post-apartheid State*. Cambridge: Cambridge University Press.

Wilson, Richard A., and Brandon Hamber. 2002. "Symbolic Closure through Memory, Reparation and Revenge in Post-conflict Societies." *Journal of Human Rights* 1 (1): 35–53.

Wilson, Richard A., and Jon P. Mitchell, eds. 2003. *Human Rights in Global Perspective: Anthropological Studies of Rights, Claims and Entitlements*. London: Routledge.

Winter, Jay. 1998. *Sites of Memory, Sites of Mourning: The Great War in European Cultural History*. Cambridge: Cambridge University Press.

Zigon, Jarrett. 2007. "Moral Breakdown and the Ethical Demand: A Theoretical Framework for an Anthropology of Moralities." *Anthropological Theory* 7 (2): 131–50.

Index

Page numbers followed by the letter *f* indicate material in figures.

Abalimi (Philippi-based association), 152
Abrahams, Charles, 40, 51f, 66, 123–27, 223n6, 224n11
Abrahams Kiewitz Attorneys, 66, 223n6
acknowledgment of injustice, 98–99, 105–6
acting out past experiences, 153, 225n10
action as resistance to structure, 204
African National Congress (ANC), 120–22, 126, 194, 215n37, 223n2, 224n10
"afterlife" versus "aftermath," 14
Agamben, Giorgio, 218n7
Agar, Michael H., 176
agency of the body, 9
AIDS, 135
Albertus, Farreed, 66
Albutt, Ryan, 37
Alien Tort Statute (US), 38, 41–46, 217n63, 220n30, 223n7
amnesty, 25, 34–35, 196–97, 214n27
ANC (African National Congress), 120–22, 126, 194, 215n37, 223n2, 224n10
Anglo American Corporation, 40
anthropological methodology: bodily dimension of, 7–11, 169, 205; and habituation, 172; role of participation in, 168; and shared experience, 177
Anthropology of Experience, The (Turner and Bruner), 178
apartheid: deportations under, 138; established ending date of, 63–64; litigations on, 32, 38–43; as routinized suffering, 144–45; victim subjectivity, 181
Apartheid Debt and Reparations Campaign, 40

Apartheid Debt and Reparations Task Team, 39
Apartheid Reparation Database, 28, 32, 128, 212n12, 218n9
Arendt, Hannah, 169, 188, 190–91, 195
articulation of injury, pain, 104–6, 189, 191
Asmal, Kader, 42, 216n49
Athlone (township), 78–79
attention and the body, 171–77, 183
Australia, 43
Azanian People's Organization (AZAPO) and Others v. The President of the Republic of South Africa and Others, 34

Balintulo, Sabe, 224n9
Balintulo, Sakwe, 125, 224n9
Balintulo et al. v. Daimler AG et al., 125, 197
Banque Indo Suez, 40
Barclays National Bank, 40, 44
Barron, Francis P., 62–63
Bassier, Tasneem, 66
Basson, Wouter, 210n4
Bell, Terry, 43
Bellville (township), 16
Benjamin, Trevor, 66
Biko, Stephen, 103
Bill Clinton Foundation, 136
bill of rights, South Africa, 67
Blood Money (Bower), 102
bodily dimension of ethnography, 169–70, 175, 187, 225n3
body: anthropology of, 7–11, 205; and argument for victim subjectivity, 108; bodily care to children, 153; and bodily hexis,

body (*continued*)
    9; bodily memory of harm, 189; body-
    bound evidence, 121; as both product
    and source, 9, 152; deployment of in lib-
    eration struggle, 108; detachment from
    experiences, 191; emancipation and, 11;
    factualness of, 107; habitual memory of,
    158–65; and illness narratives, 204–5;
    mind-body dualism, 205–6; and possi-
    bility of change, 11; and power, 9
Body and Soul (Wacquant), 9
Body in Pain, The (Scarry), 77, 83
body maps, 87, 218n4
Borneman, John, 226n8
Bourdieu, Pierre, 2, 7–9, 57, 175, 202, 204
Bower, Tom, 102
bread cartel cases, 66–70
"Breaking the Silence" memory project, 87,
    146, 217–18n4
Brown, Wendy, 6
Brown's Farm, 139, 151, 160
Bruner, Edward, 178
Bush, G. W., administration, 43
Butler, Judith, 16, 130, 187

Cabranes, José, 124
Calata, Nomonde, 214n27
Cape Flats, 79–80, 148, 150–52, 224n7
casspirs (mine-resistant ambush protected
    vehicles), 150
categories, fitting into, 103
Centre for the Study of Violence and Rec-
    onciliation (CSVR), 35, 39, 155, 211n9,
    213n19
ceremony versus ritual, 81–82
charismatic leadership/generation, 213n18
Chikane, Frank, 37, 210n4
*Children's Resource Centre Trust and Others
    v. Pioneer Foods Ltd and Others*, 66–67
Child Support Grant, 92–93, 139, 212n14
chronic illness, 137; diabetes, 135–37, 168;
    habit memories based on injuries, 142–
    43; from untreated wounds, deprivation,
    137–38, 139, 168. *See also* pain
chronologies: arbitrariness of, 104, 105–6;
    of pain, 141
Ciskei, 136, 138
*Citizens United v. Federal Election Commis-
    sion*, 46–47

civil society organizations, 33, 36, 47, 66,
    128, 197–98
class actions, 57–58; bread cartel cases,
    66–70; composition of class in, 62; "for-
    eignness" of, 68; opt-out, 218n6; proving
    variations of harm, 69, 72; relying on
    solidarity and similarity, 70; resulting
    in individuation, differentiation, 71–72,
    203; United States, 218n6. *See also* South
    African Apartheid Litigation
Clifford, James, 170
Cole, Josette, 54, 56, 87, 136, 149–50, 217n3
collective action, political, 5–6, 11, 117, 124,
    127–28, 131, 204
collectivist identity, 24, 42, 74, 98, 104
Colvin, Christopher, 212–13n17, 221n7,
    221n11
Comaroff, Jean, 5, 6, 9, 131
Comaroff, John, 5, 6, 131
commemorations, conundrum of, 81
Commerzbank, 40
confession, 196, 222n16
conflict of interest questions, 67
Congress of African Trade Unions
    (COSATU), 39
Connerton, Paul: on commemorations, 81;
    on habitual knowledge, 175; on habitual
    versus personal memory, 141; on incor-
    porated injury, 108; on inscribing prac-
    tices, 10, 108; on "routinized" violence
    and suffering, 3, 143–44, 158; *The Spirit
    of Mourning*, 143–44
Constitution: section 28 of, 69; section 38c
    of, 68; socioeconomic rights in, 67
*Consumers Case (Children's Resource Centre
    Trust and Others v. Pioneer Foods Ltd
    and Others)*, 66–67, 69–70
continuity of inequalities, 73
corporate accountability for human rights
    breaches, 39–40, 65–66, 124
COSATU (Congress of African Trade
    Unions), 39
Cradock Four, 214n27
crèche (Nontsebenziswano Educare Cen-
    tre), 148–53
Crédit Lyonnais, 40
Credit Suisse Group, 40
Crossroads (township), 16, 54, 217n3;
    apartheid-era raids, killings in, 54,

86–87, 90, 149–50; "clean-up" of, 55–56; feuds with squatter camps, 160; strongman Yamile, 149; Trojan Horse Massacre, 78–81
Csordas, Thomas, 10, 171, 205
CSVR (Centre for the Study of Violence and Reconciliation), 35, 39, 155, 211n9, 213n19
"culture of legality," 5

Daimler Chrysler, 40, 45
Das, Veena, 83
de Beers, 40
debt release/relief lobbying, 38
decriminalization of apartheid-era crimes, 196–200, 211n5
de-inscribing experiences, 157
de Kock, Eugene, 211n4, 214n27
Department of Justice, TRC Unit, 26
deportations under apartheid, 80, 90–91, 136, 138, 220n5
Derrida, Jacques, 8
Descartes, René, 8, 205
Deutsche Bank, 40
diabetes, 135–37, 168. *See also* chronic illness
dignity, right to, 35, 119, 152, 162, 219n25
disability grants, 138–39, 212n14
disappearances, investigation of, 26, 211n9
dominant forms of victimhood, 57–58, 121, 130, 189–93, 195, 198, 200
doubly positioned victims, 218n10
Dresdner Bank, 40
Du Bois-Pedain, Antje, 25
Duranti, Alessandro, 179, 226n10
Dyaluvane, Sixolile, 135

Eagle, Gillian, 88
"eating money" (undue enrichment), 70
elderly victims, 146, 155, 168, 177–80
Elias, Norbert, 209n2
emancipation: detachment and, 191; habituation and, 141–43; legal recourse as path toward, 196–200; processes of, 141–42, 162–65; from sedimented bodily victimhood, 11, 127–28, 153
embodiment: of knowledge/discourse, 2–3, 131, 201; of memory, 204; of pain and

suffering, 172, 187–88, 191; paradigm, 10–11, 187
Emirbayer, Mustafa, 226n7
empathy, 95, 178, 182, 184, 226n13
"emplacement," 175
environment as a source of recognition, 175
episodic suffering, 143–44
Equity Rule 48 (US Supreme Court), 218n6
Erwin, Alec, 42, 74
ethnographic epoché, 184
ethnographic method, 167–72, 183, 206
"ethnography of experience," 10
Evans, Donald, 43
evidence: individual experiences as, 61; part of legal claim-making, 56–57, 60
exhumations, 26, 95, 211n6
experience memories, 128–29, 131, 142, 162
"experience-near anthropology," 10
expert witnesses, 59, 218n8
Ex-Political Prisoners and Torture Survivors, 85, 100, 212–13n17
"extra-judicial killings" category, 28

Fabian, Johannes, 176
Fagan, Ed, 40, 43
Fassin, Didier, 204
"fetishism of the law," 5
field research as experience, 172–74
"fires of 1986" raid, 54–56, 86–87, 90, 136, 150
Fluor, 40
"force of the law," 7, 20, 57, 72, 202
Ford Motor Company, 44
Förster, Till, 172, 180
Foucault, Michel, 8–11; bodily dimension of social action, 204–5; on freedom and relations of power, 209n5; on the law, 201; on psychotherapy replacing confession, 222n16; on subject positions, 130
France, 40
Freudian psychotherapy, 88
Fujitsu, 44–45
Fullard, Madeleine, 26
funeral rites, 95–96, 139

Garfinkel, Harold, 142
Geertz, Clifford, 177–78, 181–82
General Motors Corporation, 44–45, 203
Germany, 26, 40, 43, 102

Gieser, Thorsten, 226n13
Gishi, Elsie, 116f, 217n56
Givoni, Michal, 60
"go-along method," 225n5
Gobodo-Madikizela, Pumla, 87
Gómez-Barris, Macarena, 14
Goniwe, Nyameka, 214n27
Good, Mary-Jo DelVecchio, 93, 105
"good victim" status, 119, 130, 222–23n2
governance, forms of, 129–30
Greenwald, David, 63–64
Grootboom case, 67
Groote Schuur Minute, 125, 224n10
Grosz, Elizabeth, 10–11
guarantee of non-repetition, 215n40
Guatemala, 210n9
Guevara, Che, 101
Gugulethu (township), 16
Gunn, Shirley, 78, 80, 213n22

habit/habitual memories, 128–29, 131,
    141–42, 158–65
habitual knowledge, 174–75, 177, 181
habituation, 172–73, 204
habitus, 8–9, 122, 188, 204–5, 209n2
Hani, Chris, 122, 223n4
Hastrup, Kirsten, 83, 170–71, 188
Hausfeld, Michael, 40, 64–65, 215n41, 223n6
healed personhood role, 192–93
healing by proxy, 24, 194, 203
Heidegger, Martin, 174
heroism as road to healing, 193
Hertz, Robert, 209n1
high blood pressure, 91–92, 97, 135, 137, 146
Hilao v. Estate of Marcos, 220n30
historical catastrophe or trauma, 144
Hlaise, Lungile (pseud.), 96–100, 106, 109
Hoffman, Paul, 40, 43, 63
Hollan, Douglas, 226n13
Honneth, Axel, 106
horizons and attention, 171, 173, 175, 181
Human Rights Media Centre (HRMC),
    78–80
Husserl, Edmund, 12, 177, 179, 183, 209n3,
    225n2, 226nn9–10

IBM, 40, 44–45
ICC (International Criminal Court),
    219n11, 220n33

ICTJ (International Centre for Transitional
    Justice), 35, 213n23, 214n33
ICTR (International Criminal Tribunal for
    Rwanda), 216n54, 219n11
ICTY (International Criminal Tribunal for
    the Former Yugoslavia), 219n11
If Trees Could Speak (Gunn), 78–82
ignorance to cognitive knowledge, 174
IJR (Institute for Justice and Reconcilia-
    tions), 39
imagination and shared experience, 177–
    80, 226n7
incorporated injury, 108
Indemnity Act (1990), 224n10
"indiscriminate shootings" category, 28
individualization approach, 220n31
Individual Reparation Grants, 25
individuals: and class actions, 71–73; versus
    collective, 6, 19–20, 200–201; individu-
    ation, 57–58, 60, 65, 71–73, 203; and
    Khulumani, 31, 40, 48; and TRC, 23–27,
    39; in US courts, 46
"informational bellwether hearings," 71–72
inscribed signs of injury, 108
Institute for Justice and Reconciliations
    (IJR), 39, 214n33
inter-generationally transmitted PTSD, 104
International Apartheid Debt and Repara-
    tions Campaign, 38
International Centre for Transitional Justice
    (ICTJ), 35, 213n23, 214n33
International Criminal Court (ICC),
    219n11, 220n33
International Criminal Tribunal for
    Rwanda (ICTR), 216n54, 219n11
International Criminal Tribunal for the
    Former Yugoslavia (ICTY), 219n11
International Jubilee 2000 Coalition, 38–39
international law, 216n54; policy amend-
    ments challenge based on, 35; repara-
    tions obligations under, 39; and US Alien
    Tort Statute, 41–46, 217n63, 220n30,
    223n7. *See also* United States
intersubjectivity, 179, 180–84, 189,
    226n12
interventionism, 129–30

Jackman, Mary R., 210n10
Jackson, Michael, 10, 180–81, 226nn11–12

Jaftha v. Schoeman (Constitutional Court), 219n25
Jali, Nomatoza Irena, 148–50, 152–54, 160, 163
Jama, Engelina Nomarashiya, 113f, 148–50, 152–54, 160, 163
Jobson, Marjorie, 30, 213n21

Kaminer, Debra, 88
Khali, Ethel Nosipo, 52f, 111f, 134–35, 138
Khayelitsha (township), 16, 55, 151
Khulumani et al. v. Barclays National Bank et al., 40, 61
Khulumani Support Group, 49f, 51f; in class action lawsuits, 65; and conception of victimhood, 33, 104, 140, 212n11; and debt release campaign, 39; DOJ refusing to use list of, 128; and dominant discourse, 202; initiating civil actions, 3–4; launch of, 27, 29; Maureen Mazibuko's position in, 146–47; membership of, 27–28, 104, 199; needs of members, 29; as "one-stop shop" for advice, 120; oral communication within, 124; professional and international support for, 123; professionalization of, 47; relationship with NGOs, civil society organizations, 32–33; relationship with state, 32–33, 125–27; storytelling at meetings, 85; structure and leadership of, 30–32, 47; treatment of lawyers in meetings, 125–27; turn to the state by, 30; Victim Empowerment Program, 156; violations reported by members, 28–29; *Zulu Love Letter* screening, 220–21n6
Khumalo, Duma, 213n18
Kidron, Carol A., 212n9, 222n23
Kiobel and Others v. Royal Dutch Petroleum Company and Others, 45, 46, 124–25
Kleinman, Arthur, 10, 83
Kleinman, Joan, 10, 83
Komga, 54, 138
Kotta, Beauty Notle, 53–54, 57–60, 86–87, 217n4
Krog, Antjie, 210n11
KTC (township), 16, 55, 87, 108, 136–37, 150
Kuranko, 10, 226n11
Kusenbach, Margarethe, 225n5

Lahav, Alexandra D., 71–72
Lambek, Michael, 10
Langa (township), 16, 102, 136, 149
Leder, Drew, 83, 188
legal anthropology, 5, 7, 22, 206
legal remedies: analysis of law and of body, 4; individualizing nature of law, 203–4; law and lived experience, 7, 201–2; law as broker, 123–28; as nonemancipatory, 2, 4, 74, 163–64, 195, 224n3; procedure and responsibility, 198–99; refusals to conform to legal discourse, 57; relationship of to politics, 4–6, 126–28, 196–200; theories of legalization, 200–204
LegalWise, 119
"Les Techniques du Corps" (Mauss), 8
Lévinas, Emmanuel, 181
Lévi-Strauss, Claude, 8
liberation struggle/movement, 135–37; as a collective, 74; disappointment in results of, 3; dogma against silence in, 189; funerals as political forums for, 95–96; "good victims" from, 222–23n2; and individual suffering, 73–74; international supporters of, 215n39; members requesting pardons, 37; not for personal gain, 38; recognition from, 127; sacrifice still not acknowledged, 99, 227n1; unpatriotic to question sacrifices for, 106; women in, 108, 136–37, 139, 160
Life of the Law, The (Nader), 220n32
lifeworld, sharing a, 105
"limits to liberation," 29, 139
list of victims, 25, 27, 33, 128–29, 195
lived victimhood, 4, 14, 130, 192, 195
Lock, Margaret, 205
Luckmann, Thomas, 10, 105–6, 174–75, 184
Lungisile Ntsebeza et al. v. Daimler Chrysler Corporation et al., 40, 61

Mabandla, Brigitte, 44
Mabilisa, Amanda, 121–23, 128, 131
Madikizela-Mandela, Winnie, 211n4
Madlingozi, Tshepo, 28, 213n22, 222–23n2
Maduna, Penuell, 42, 216n45
Mafeje, Archie, 136
"magic" of sensory knowledge, 177–79
Magnet Theatre, *If Trees Could Speak* production, 78–82

Makhubo, Mbuyisa, 215n42
Malan, Magnus, 211n4
Malinowski, Bronislaw, 226n10
malnutrition, 138
Mamdani, Mahmood, 25
"mandated breakdowns," 176
Mandela, Nelson, 40, 47, 58, 64, 125–26, 192–93
marching during World War I, 173–74, 176
Marcos, Ferdinand, 220n30
Marcus, George E., 170
marginality, 141
Mastafa v. Chevron Corp., 46
Mauss, Marcel, 8, 172–73, 175–76
Mazibuko, Maureen, 134–37, 145–48
Mbeki, Thabo, administration of: against adjudication in foreign courts, 41; amnesty views of, 34–35; blocking TRC, 32; creating pardon reference group, 197, 214n32; as defendant in *Daimler Chrysler* case, 40; rejecting wealth tax, 216n44; response to TRC recommendations, 25, 30; seeking redress seen as selfish, unpatriotic, 74; support for pardons, 36; supporting corporations over victims, 47; victim anger toward, 125; views on apartheid-era victimhood, 38
Mdunyelwa, Ntombentsha, 116f, 136, 138
medicalization of one's self, 100–104
Meierhenrich, Jens, 73
Merleau-Ponty, Maurice, 8, 11, 171
Mfuleni (township), 16, 146–47
Mgweba, Happiness Bongeka, 90, 92, 94, 109
Mgweba, Nontsasa Eunice, 89–95, 109, 222n17
Mhlauli, Nombuyeselo Nolita, 214n27
military gait incompatibilities, 173–74, 176
military veterans, 211n9
mind-body dualism, 84, 205–6
Mische, Ann, 226n7
Missing Persons Task Team, 26
mistakes as source of insight, 176
Mkhonto, Sindiswa Elizabeth, 214n27
Molefi, Dorothy, 215n42
moments of dislocation, 176, 183–85
Moore, Henrietta, 14
"moral breakdown" as knowledge source, 176, 183, 226n14

Mothlanthe, Kgalema, 36
"motivated thematic relevance," 174
mourning: articulating through performance, 154–58; as a bodily practice, 145–48; denial of, 95–100, 106; memorials as sites of, 143–44; tacit practices of, 133–41; through retributive justice, 144
Mphahlele, Brian, 52f, 66, 70, 100–103, 109
Mpolweni, Nosisi, 210n11
Mukaddam v. Pioneer Foods Ltd. and Others, 66
mutual recognition, 93
Mvana, Nomthandazo, 66
Mvenge, Alice, 111f, 135, 137, 224n1
Mvenge, Lulama Lucia, 111f

Nader, Laura, 5, 220n32
narrative of the new South Africa, 106
"narrative therapy," 88
National Directorate of Public Prosecutions (NDPP), 35, 214n27
National Prosecution Authority (NPA), 25, 197
National Steering Committee, Khulumani, 30, 96–99
Nazi victims' unclaimed assets, 40
Ndeya, Janet, 111f, 135
NDPP (National Directorate of Public Prosecutions), 35, 214n27
Needs Assessment Form, 28
negative obligations, 67
neoliberalism, 47
Netherlands, 26, 40
New Crossroads (township), 16
"newness," search for, 110
News of Salvation, 134
"new theme," 174
Ngcebetsha, John, 40
NGOs: NGO-ization, 31; standing regarding pardons, 36
Ngxobongwana, Johnson, 149–50, 224–25n7
Nigeria, 124
Nongwe, 149
nonpathology, 104
nonphysical violence, 16
nonpredicated injuries, 152
nonpredicated knowledge, 172, 174–77, 182
nonpredicated solidarity, 189

"nonpredicated" versus "pre-predicated,"
183, 225n2
nonstate actors, international law on, 39
Nontsebenziswano Educare Centre, 148–53
nonverbal communication, 168, 170–71
Nordstrom, Carolyn, 210n10
normalization of suffering, 145
notification versus noting, 225n4
Novartis, 40
NPA (National Prosecution Authority), 25,
197
Ntsebeza, Dumisa, 40, 214n26
Ntsebeza et al. v. Daimler Chrysler Corporation et al., 197
numerosity standard, 219n27
Nunu, Sindiswa, 52f, 151, 225n8
Nuremberg trials, 3, 144, 216n54
Nyanga (township), 16, 56, 90, 137
Nyanga Bush, 54–55, 87, 136, 225n8
Nyanga Extension, 54, 87, 136

obligations, positive and negative, 67
Okely, Judith, 177–79
old-age pensions, 93, 139, 212n14
Omar, Dullah, 216n45
opt-out class action, 218n6
overwriting/acting out past experiences, 153

pain: benefits, dangers of sharing, 78; and
Cartesian dualism, 84; certainty only of
one's own, 103; chronic, 93–94; chronologies of, 141; coping mechanisms for,
104–5; destroying capacity to communicate, 188; as isolating, private experience,
188; and lack of closure, 98; and meaning, 90, 94–95; medicalizing of, 101; no
language for, 77, 83, 107, 221n10; physical sharing of, 92–93; preventing forgiveness, 98; privacy of, 97; rationalizing, 94;
scholarship on, 84; sharing of, 99, 100;
sociability of, 82, 89–90, 94–95; unmaking the world, 105; voices of experts over
victims, 83
Pain as Human Experience (Good), 93
pardons, 36–37, 215n37
pass laws, 135–36, 138, 150–51
past, 1, 104
Paul, Elizabeth, 134
paying attention, 171–77

personalization of injury, 57–58
personal versus habitual memory, 141–42
personhood, legalization of, 2
Petersen, Hector, 215n42
pharmaceutical industry, 102–3
Phelane, Mr. (pseud.), 117–21, 128, 131
Philippi (township), 16; crèche (Nontsebenziswano Educare Centre), 148–53;
mourning practices in, 133–41, 145–48;
shared victimhood in, 159–60
Phumelele-Nkadimeng, Thembi, 214n27
Pink, Sarah, 175
Pioneer Foods, 66
place, theories of, 175
plaintiffs: attempting to relate to law, 73;
includes attorneys, 62; as legal entities or
as persons, 61–65
politics/the political: courts as alternative
to, 200–201; emerging from social recognition, 131; habit memories as basis for,
128–29; versus legal path to justice, 196–
200; politically articulated victimhood,
189; political versus common crime,
210n9; will in government, 125–27
positive obligations of the state, 67
poststructuralism, 60, 222n22
post-traumatic stress disorder (PTSD), 15,
83, 100, 104, 209n7, 210n8
Powell, Colin, 42, 216n45
power and the body, 9–10
power of speaking about suffered harm,
82–83
"power of the between," 226n12. *See also*
intersubjectivity
predicative knowledge, 176
Premier Foods, 66
premises of this book, 11
"pre-predicated," 12, 183, 225n2
President's Fund, 26, 128
Pretoria Minute, 224n10
progressive realization standard, 67–68
Project Coast, 210n4
"prolonged arbitrary detention" category, 28
Promotion of National Unity and Reconciliation Act, 26
prosecution of perpetrators, 24–25, 27,
34–35, 79, 98, 194, 197, 210n4
Prosecution Policy, 34–35, 197
proxy by person, 194

psychiatric treatment, 100
PTSD (post-traumatic stress disorder), 15,
    83, 100, 104, 209n7, 210n8
public realm, 169, 190–91
Puwana, Zukiswa, 125, 180

Radebe, Jeff, 45
Ramphele, Mamphela, 48, 94, 95–96, 105
rape/sexual assault, 29, 96–97, 99, 106, 155
Rasool, Ebrahim, 220n4
Ratele, Kopano, 210n11
RDP (Reconstruction and Development
    Programme), 54, 90, 134–36, 151
recognition: versus acknowledgment, 106;
    as goal, 191; of habitual knowledge, 175;
    legal recourse as path toward, 196–200;
    as process, 174, 181; relating experiences
    for, 201; from shared experience, 178–82,
    185; through sensory/bodily informa-
    tion, 175
reconciliation, 24, 35, 88, 120, 192, 218n10,
    221n14
reparations, 24–25, 27, 39, 194–96, 198,
    215n40
researchers and the researched, 175, 185,
    205–6
research protocol, 16–18
retraumatization, 85
retributive justice, mourning through, 144
Rheinmetall Group AG, 44–45
Right2Know campaign, 50f
right to dignity, 35, 119, 152, 162, 219n25
right to sufficient nutrition, 67
ritual, 81–82, 95, 143–45, 158, 226n11
Rosaldo, Renato, 226–27n15
Ross, Fiona C., 58, 210n9, 218n10, 222n24
routinized violence and suffering, 143–45,
    158, 188
Royal Dutch Petroleum, 45–46, 217n61
rule of law, 35, 198
rural people in urban environment, 139
Rwandan genocide, 3

Salt River Community House, 49f, 79, 82,
    84–86, 123
sample hearings to manage class actions,
    71–72
Sanders, Mark, 95

SANGOCO (South African National NGO
    Coalition), 39, 215n39
Sanjek, Roger, 183
Sasol, 40
Scarry, Elaine, 77, 83, 103, 107, 188
Scheindlin, Shira, 45–46, 62, 64, 124,
    219n24
Scheper-Hughes, Nancy, 205
Schütz, Alfred, 10, 105–6, 174–75, 184
second socialization, 172
sedimented perceptions/experiences, 11,
    129–30, 141, 187–88, 195, 202
"seeing" versus "observing," 172
Selota, Ms. (pseud.), 155–57, 161, 164
shared perception and recognition, 22,
    180–84
shared references, 180, 182, 184, 225–26n6
sharing experience and imagining, 178–82,
    185
Shell Oil Company, 124–25, 217n61
silence, 60, 67, 98–100, 103–4, 189, 222n23.
    See also "Breaking the Silence" memory
    project
silent memories, 221n9
"singling out," 24, 73–74, 218n5
social acknowledgment, lack of, 99, 109
social individuation, 65, 71–73, 204
socialization, second, 172
socialized pain, 82, 89–90
"socially informed body," 9
social movements, 200–201
social organizing, forms of, 31
social status and violence, 158–59
socioeconomic rights, 65–67, 158, 219n25
solidarity, experiences of, 203–4
Solomon, Marcus, 69
"somatic modes of attention," 171
somatic symptoms, 209n7
Songhay, 10, 170
Sosa v. Alvarez-Machain, 43, 46, 216n53
Souter, David, 216n53
South African Apartheid Litigation, 61–62,
    219n12
South African Coalition Against Apartheid
    Debt, 38
South African Coalition of Transitional
    Justice, 36
South African Council of Churches, 39

South African National NGO Coalition (SANGOCO), 39, 215n39
Special Dispensation for Presidential Pardons, 36–37
special pensions, 103, 117, 120, 139, 212n14
Sprizzo, John E., 42–43, 45
squatter camps, 54, 87, 109, 149–50, 160
statement takers, 24, 118–19, 212n11
Stiglitz, Joseph, 42
Stoller, Paul, 10, 170, 226n12
stress, 92–94
structural violence/victimhood, 14, 24, 53, 57–58, 65–70, 74
structures, society's, 8–9, 201, 204–5
suffered harm, 39, 57, 82–83
suffering, responses to, 143–45
Sulzer, 40
superstes, 58–61, 71, 84
suspicious subject positions, 71, 74, 109–10, 192, 203
Swiss Apartheid Debt and Reparations Campaign, 42
Switzerland, 26, 40, 43, 102
symbolic redress, 194–95

Taste of Ethnographic Things, The (Stoller), 170
teargas, 86, 90–91, 136–37, 150
techniques of the body, 8, 173
"testimony approach" to trauma, 88
testimony to TRC, 211n4; ambivalence of witnesses, 87; asking for funeral rites, 95; by Beauty Notle Kotta, 56, 58–59; evidentiary-based, 60; on exhumations, 26; to make victimhood legible, 57; by Ms. Selota, 161; by Nontsasa Eunice Mgweba, 92; numbers of victims, 24; as political and legal act, 58–59; and post-structuralism, 60; psychological impact of, 88; reliance on, 61; and victim subjectivity, 30. See also witnessing/witnesses before court
testis, 58–59, 71, 84
"theme change," 174
"thick knowledge," 179
Throop, C. Jason, 184, 226n10, 226n13, 227n15

Tiger Consumer Brands, 66
torture: children witnesses of, 156; "forcibly imprisoned and tortured" category, 103; lingering effects in elderly, 156, 168, 178; organizations aiding victims of, 213n23; PTSD in survivors of, 100; Shell Oil complicity in, 124; testimony on, 24; "torture and inhumane treatment" category, 28–29; and victim relation to medical profession, 100, 103–4; of women in resistance, 137–38, 147, 156; younger generation not understanding, 102. See also Khulumani Support Group
"trading places" in research, 179
trained versus habituated skills, 173–74
"transitional justice" processes, 1–2, 22, 68 193–94, 196, 198
Transkei: as ancestral homeland, 54, 160; associations with, 138, 180; deportations to, 80, 91, 136, 138, 149, 160
TRC. See Truth and Reconciliation Commission
Treatment Action Campaign case, 67
Trojan Horse Massacre, 78–81
Truth and Reconciliation Commission (TRC), vii, 218n10; activities of, 24; archive closed to public, 26; and "closed list policy," 128; as collective act of mourning, 144; comparisons to Nuremberg, 3; Connerton on, 144; court rejection of "copy cat" provisions, 35; and definition of victimhood, 192; facilitating formalization of victimhood, 47; and family of Maureen Mazibuko, 147; final actions and report by, 25–26, 59; final report (2003), 196; goal of public acknowledgment, 191–92; as governing institution, 117; as institution for addressing past, 23; legal challenges to, 34; most victims not involved in, 1; official recognition as victims, 28; paid staff of, 30; providing amnesty to perpetrators, 3, 196; as "proxy" for perpetrators, 95; questions remaining regarding, 26; reparations payments, 24, 195; studying structural violence, 73; therapeutic impact of, 87; Trojan Horse hearings, 79
Truth Recovery Project, 211n9

Turner, Victor, 81–82, 89, 178, 193
Tutu, Desmond, 36, 42, 43, 45
Twala, Nolasti, 112f, 167–69, 180–82

UBS, 40, 44
United Democratic Front (UDF), 79
United Kingdom, 40, 43
United States, 40; Alien Tort Statute, 41;
    discovery phase of trial, 62; *Khulumani
    et al. v. Barclays National Bank et al.*,
    40–45, 61; Second Circuit Court of Ap-
    peals, 43–46, 124, 216n49; Supreme
    Court, 43–46, 218n6; victims' person-
    hood in, 61–65
universal human rights, appeal to, 5

van der Merwe, Johannes, 37, 210n4
Van Gennep, Arnold, 209n1
"vicariousness," 178–80
Victim Empowerment Program, 156
victimhood, 2, 9, 12; alternate identities to,
    153; anchored in embodied knowledge,
    131, 182; ceremonial separation from,
    158; dominant notion of versus indi-
    vidual dissent, 121–23; given to women,
    claimed by men, 15; interpretation and
    codification of, 156–57; lived, 4, 14, 130,
    192, 195; making it legible, 58–61; mu-
    tual support of shared, 131, 189; as polit-
    icized, legalized, bureaucratic, 117, 128;
    shared, 133, 140, 159, 190; tacit knowl-
    edge of, 140; transformation through the
    performance of, 154–58
victims: "bad" versus "good," 222–23n2; de-
    fining, 2; direct versus indirect, 117–18;
    families of, 147–48; "general" victims
    versus military veterans, 33; and limits
    of amnesty, 34; from nonpredicated to
    articulated, 12; and reparations list, 128–
    29; silence as option for, 189; subject
    positions of, 11–14; TRC conception

of, 24, 33; as witnesses or as plaintiffs,
    61–62
violence: child witnesses of, 109, 156, 159;
    experience of as social, 158–59; legal em-
    phasis on, 210n10; state versus criminal,
    97–98. *See also* torture
Vlok, Adriaan, 37, 210n4

Wacquant, Loïc, 9, 225n1
war veterans, 145
Washington, George, 41
wealth as path toward healing, 193
"we-relations," 184
Whitman, Pamela, 156
Wikan, Unni, 10
Williams, Renata, 67, 69
Wilson, Richard, 6, 213n18, 221n14
Winter, Jay, 143
witchcraft, 70–71, 97–99, 109
witdoeke, 54–56, 86, 90, 150, 217n3
witnessing violence in childhood, 109, 156,
    159
witnessing/witnesses before court: audience
    for, 157–58; Beauty Notle Kotta, 56; ex-
    pert witness, 59, 218n8; versus plaintiffs,
    61; as process, 60; role of, 58–59; thera-
    peutic dimension of, 88, 222n16; TRC
    difficulty in finding, 87. *See also* super-
    stes; testimony to TRC; testis
Wiwa v. Shell, 217n61
World Trauma Day commemoration,
    154–55
World War I (Great War), 143, 159
Writing Culture (Clifford and Marcus), 170,
    185

Yamile, 149

Zigon, Jarrett, 176, 183, 226n14
Zimbabwe, 33
Zuma, Jacob, 32, 37

Rights After Wrongs: Local Knowledge and Human Rights in Zimbabwe
Shannon Morreira
2016

If God Were a Human Rights Activist
Boaventura de Sousa Santos
2015

Digging for the Disappeared: Forensic Science after Atrocity
Adam Rosenblatt
2015

The Rise and Fall of Human Rights: Cynicism and Politics in Occupied Palestine
Lori Allen
2013

Campaigning for Justice: Human Rights Advocacy in Practice
Jo Becker
2012

In the Wake of Neoliberalism: Citizenship and Human Rights in Argentina
Karen Ann Faulk
2012

Values in Translation: Human Rights and the Culture of the World Bank
Galit A. Sarfaty
2012

Disquieting Gifts: Humanitarianism in New Delhi
Erica Bornstein
2012

Stones of Hope: How African Activists Reclaim Human Rights to Challenge Global Poverty
Edited by Lucie E. White and Jeremy Perelman
2011

Judging War, Judging History: Behind Truth and Reconciliation
Pierre Hazan
2010

Localizing Transitional Justice: Interventions and Priorities after Mass Violence
Edited by Rosalind Shaw and Lars Waldorf, with Pierre Hazan
2010

Surrendering to Utopia: An Anthropology of Human Rights
Mark Goodale
2009

Human Rights for the 21st Century: Sovereignty, Civil Society, Culture
Helen M. Stacy
2009

Human Rights Matters: Local Politics and National Human Rights Institutions
Julie A. Mertus
2009